Praise for *Lunchtime Learr*

'Lunchtimes will never be the same again! I love this kind of book – clear, sparkling, full of leadership insights, evidence and practicalities and written in an incisive, no-nonsense style. Lucy Ryan has a gift for cutting through the complex and landing serious leadership points in a digestible format. Recommended reading for anyone looking to increase their bandwidth and personal growth as a positive leader.' FIONA PARASHAR, CEO, LEADERSHIP COACHING LTD

'This book is an excellent leadership guide to enhancing resilience in an ever-changing world of work. The book contains many useful tips for managers and leaders to develop their own resilience, and ultimately create a more resilient team for the inevitable challenges organizations will face in the years ahead.' PROFESSOR SIR CARY COOPER CBE, 50TH ANNIVERSARY PROFESSOR OF ORGANIZATIONAL PSYCHOLOGY AND HEALTH, ALLIANCE MANCHESTER BUSINESS SCHOOL, UNIVERSITY OF MANCHESTER

'Never before have we needed to find and grow great leaders to support us in this new world. And those leaders need our support. And here it is. Lucy Ryan offers practical, wise and profound guidance in this book. I wish that every existing and aspiring leader reads this and more importantly lives the guidance offered here.' SUE KNIGHT, NLP MASTER TRAINER AND AUTHOR OF *NLP AT WORK*

'With thousands of leadership books out there, is there anything left to say? Well, very much so, if one is prepared to leave the endless theory and pop stories aside and get down to being really practical (while still evidence-driven). If you are a leader or walking towards leadership, this is a rare book that is likely to be useful! I love the ten top tips sections, clear diagrams, practical ideas, the lightness of the writing style and the feeling of the real "know-how" behind the narrative. This book is simply incredible, so enjoy!' PROFESSOR ILONA BONIWELL, EXECUTIVE DIRECTOR, POSITRAN AND MAPP PROGRAMME LEADER, ANGLIA RUSKIN UNIVERSITY

'An absolute gem. Full of practical, pragmatic and easy-to-grasp advice for everyone who has a passion for leading and developing people. I love how she uses memorable frameworks to help you structure and practice new techniques. Lucy Ryan has managed to cram so much inspirational advice into this book, which will be invaluable for leaders in this time of rapid change.' VICTORIA FOX, CEO, AAR GROUP

'Having participated in lots of Lucy Ryan's brilliant workshops, I jumped at the early chance to read this book. Lucy has managed to capture the magic of her workshops and coaching in page-form (I even read the pages in her voice!), leaving you armed and empowered to implement the strategies, tips and tricks that the pages are filled with, all after only a 30-minute cuppa. For anybody that's looking for guidance that lifts you up, course corrects and encourages healthy self-reflection then I could not recommend this book more.' JOANNA TRIPPETT, MANAGING DIRECTOR, BYTE LONDON

'Leadership isn't what it used to be. Thriving as a leader in rapidly evolving world requires an "agility toolkit" — which this resourceful volume provides!' PROFESSOR DAVID CLUTTERBUCK, SPECIAL AMBASSADOR, EUROPEAN MENTORING AND COACHING COUNCIL

'Lucy Ryan has huge credibility as a leadership coach, and it shows! This is an essential read focusing on the everyday inevitabilities you're expected to resolve in your leadership role. What impresses immediately is the accessibility of the content that is engagingly written, pragmatic and brimming with ideas, concepts, models, realistic case studies and reflective activities. Every chapter offers a multitude of applications that answer the questions common to leaders. The content has you wanting more right from the first page, is easy to digest and exceptionally well referenced. So, grab your lunch and a drink and be prepared to set a timer as this is a page turner.' DR LISE LEWIS, OWNER, BLUE SKY INTERNATIONAL AND EMCC GLOBAL SPECIAL AMBASSADOR

'Lucy Ryan's pragmatic and insightful style shines through, in this "go-to" leadership guide. Approach your reading with an open mind and let it hold you to account as a leader – it provides practical reference tools for newbies and reminds the more experienced of what's *really* important versus your inbox. An inspiration for all leaders and my personal kick-ass from time to time!' BECKY HEWITT, DIRECTOR OF PEOPLE, LEEDS BUILDING SOCIETY

'I have been so lucky to have Lucy Ryan as an executive coach for a number of years. This must-read book brings together all the models, experiences and guidance that I have had the benefit of learning from over the years in a way that is so typical of her straightforward, practical but powerful approach. It'll equip you to navigate challenges, maximize impact and build confidence and capability in your organization, making it an invaluable read for leaders at all stages of their career journey.' JULIE-ANN HAINES, CEO, PRINCIPALITY BUILDING SOCIETY

'*Lunchtime Learning for Leaders* is a book I wish had been written earlier in my career. The 16 chapters each leave the reader with practical examples for them to try on their leadership journey. I have been very lucky to work with Lucy Ryan over many years and reading this book takes me back to personal challenges that her guidance helped me to overcome. Feed your brain over lunch with the content of this book, it's one of the best reads out there.' DAMIAN THOMPSON, GROUP MANAGING DIRECTOR RETAIL FINANCE, ALDERMORE BANK PLC

'Lucy Ryan's insights in this wonderful book will help you serve others in your business by learning about leadership in a practical, accessible way with all the knowledge and tools you need, whatever stage you're at on your leadership journey. I know my team has been lucky to work with Lucy and transform their leadership with her support and I feel delighted to see her expertise in print and know you will benefit from the wisdom contained in these pages.' DEE FORD CBE, GROUP MANAGING DIRECTOR RADIO, BAUER MEDIA GROUP

'Lucy Ryan's extensive experience and wisdom shines through in this insightful book. Easy to read, super practical and very relevant to the real challenges faced by many leaders and managers. This is all about helping you find the best version of you as a leader and feels just like you have a coach in the room with you as an everyday guiding hand.' AILSA FIRTH, DIRECTOR OF HUMAN RESOURCES, ARVAL BNP PARIBAS

'Inspiration and practical support in equal measure. Like having Lucy Ryan on speed-dial… almost!' CLAIRE SADLER, EXECUTIVE DIRECTOR OF MARKETING, FUNDRAISING AND ENGAGEMENT, BRITISH HEART FOUNDATION

'Read AND learn while trying to be a leader through, and in the aftermath of a global pandemic, do I have the space for this? This is addressed right from the introduction, and it reminds you that learning is essential in leading. This isn't a book you pick up for just one lunchtime, but one you'll pick up over a career of leadership lunchtimes. It questions, challenges and provokes you to reflect, evaluate and ultimately develop as a leader, all the time giving you that clear and simple advice as to how to apply it tomorrow.' SIMON WELCH, PRINCIPAL, NATIONAL STAR COLLEGE

'At last! A practical guide for leaders to help us navigate the daily challenges of leading and managing teams. In this book

'Lucy Ryan offers a series of refreshing bite-size insights into how we can become both happier and more effective in our pursuit of developing motivated, high-performing teams. *Lunchtime Learning for Leaders* will change the way you think about yourself and will make you a more influential and resilient leader that your teams and customers will appreciate!' MATTHEW HILL, GROUP TALENT DIRECTOR, HOMESERVE PLC

'Should you buy this book? Only if you want bite-size practical advice that will help you lead, grow and thrive... in your lunch hour! Quite simply the only leadership book you need.' JON GHAZI, CEO, ANNELECT EMEA

'I wish I'd had this alongside me as I started my leadership journey – a guiding hand on your shoulder ready to help as you navigate most leadership challenges in a constructive, pragmatic and real-life manner. The chapters all resonate and provide good reminders to new and experienced leaders alike, while the chapter structure makes the whole book feel familiar. From the beginning, I felt as though I had my coach by my side – both gently challenging me to pause, think, reflect and then encouraging me forward to continue. I'm already thinking of who I'll recommend the book to and know I'll return to it time and again.' RHIAN LANGHAM, HEAD OF PEOPLE SERVICES, ADMIRAL GROUP PLC

Lunchtime Learning for Leaders

16 ways to grow your resilience and influence

Lucy Ryan

KoganPage

Publisher's note
Every possible effort has been made to ensure that the information contained in this book is accurate at the time of going to press, and the publishers and author cannot accept responsibility for any errors or omissions, however caused. No responsibility for loss or damage occasioned to any person acting, or refraining from action, as a result of the material in this publication can be accepted by the editor, the publisher or the author.

First published in Great Britain and the United States in 2021 by Kogan Page Limited

Apart from any fair dealing for the purposes of research or private study, or criticism or review, as permitted under the Copyright, Designs and Patents Act 1988, this publication may only be reproduced, stored or transmitted, in any form or by any means, with the prior permission in writing of the publishers, or in the case of reprographic reproduction in accordance with the terms and licences issued by the CLA. Enquiries concerning reproduction outside these terms should be sent to the publishers at the undermentioned addresses:

2nd Floor, 45 Gee Street	122 W 27th St, 10th Floor	4737/23 Ansari Road
London	New York, NY 10001	Daryaganj
EC1V 3RS	USA	New Delhi 110002
United Kingdom		India
www.koganpage.com		

Kogan Page books are printed on paper from sustainable forests.

© Lucy Ryan, 2021

The right of Lucy Ryan to be identified as the author of this work has been asserted by her in accordance with the Copyright, Designs and Patents Act 1988.

ISBNs
Hardback   978 1 3986 0256 4
Paperback   978 1 3986 0254 0
Ebook   978 1 3986 0255 7

British Library Cataloguing-in-Publication Data
A CIP record for this book is available from the British Library.

Library of Congress Cataloging-in-Publication Data
Names: Ryan, Lucy, author.
Title: Lunchtime learning for leaders : 16 ways to grow your resilience and influence / Lucy Ryan.
Description: London, United Kingdom ; New York, NY : Kogan Page, 2021. | Includes bibliographical references and index.
Identifiers: LCCN 2021032443 (print) | LCCN 2021032444 (ebook) | ISBN 9781398602540 (paperback) | ISBN 9781398602564 (hardback) | ISBN 9781398602557 (ebook)
Subjects: LCSH: Leadership. | Resilience (Personality trait) | Influence (Psychology)
Classification: LCC HD57.7 .R93 2021 (print) | LCC HD57.7 (ebook) | DDC 658.4/092—dc23
LC record available at https://lccn.loc.gov/2021032443
LC ebook record available at https://lccn.loc.gov/2021032444

Typeset by Hong Kong FIVE Workshop, Hong Kong
Print production managed by Jellyfish
Printed and bound by 4edge Limited, UK

CONTENTS

About the author xi
Foreword xii
Acknowledgments xiv

Introduction 1

PART ONE
Leading with insight 9

01 Practical strategies for maintaining your leadership balance 11

02 Managing your energy is the key to leadership resilience 25

03 Enhancing performance through the science of positive leadership 43

04 Increase your confidence to accelerate your leadership growth 56

PART TWO
Leading your team 73

05 Motivate me! How to empower your team with a 12-step process 75

06 Strengths-based coaching: Leverage the strengths of your team through every conversation 92

07 Less talk, more walk! How to lead a diverse team and drive a culture of belonging 107

08 Become a customer-focused leader, really! 121

PART THREE
Hitting roadbumps 139

09   Be a brilliant change leader 141

10   How to master difficult conversations with compassion and confidence 159

11   From survive to thrive: How to embed a resilient culture 174

PART FOUR
Leading with influence 193

12   Build your leadership brand (And be remembered, for the right reasons!) 195

13   From inform to inspire: How to deliver a successful presentation and get the action you want 209

14   How to extend your leadership influence, with integrity 223

PART FIVE
What next? 241

15   Enable your succession through progression planning 243

16   Time out: Reflections on happiness and leadership 259

References 275
Index 285

About the author

Dr Lucy Ryan has a well-earned reputation as a wise, vibrant leadership coach and a voice that leaders take seriously. With a masters in Positive Psychology and a PhD in Management and Leadership, she has developed over 10,000 global leaders blending psychology with practical, accessible guidance. In this book she draws on her extensive experience of training and coaching leaders to provide clear guidance, illuminating models and self-reflection to help leaders navigate the modern world of leadership.

Foreword

I get up to come to work every single day in the most exciting, innovative, digitally minded, and highly trusted creative medium – commercial radio. I love it – the challenge, the possibilities, the responsibility to inspire our listeners. With a team of 1,300 people and almost 20 million listeners every week, I'm so aware of the importance of leadership and the impact it will have on all of us. In fact, for me, the quality of our leadership is the greatest determining factor of our business success.

Radio has considerable influence over its audience. That ability – and responsibility – to influence is, I believe, the secret to leadership. Nothing more, nothing less. People have to want to follow you. No one makes progress without help and collaboration from others and no one person has all the answers.

For me, leaders who demonstrate a willingness to learn are the ones most likely to create followers and there's so much to learn about becoming a leader that people want to follow. So, when it comes to strengthening leadership capability in our organization, Lucy Ryan has always been the only coach I turn to and that's because I absolutely trust her with our top-level resource.

With Lucy's coaching, I have watched many of our leaders grow, as individuals as much as strategic leaders – developing the ability to lead their teams and our business into the next decade. They now recognize that being a leader means *more* responsibility and *more* service, not less service and more authority over others. Lucy listens, questions and guides, but also challenges them to step up and stand out, helping them forge transformational relationships in our complex, matrix business. Her coaching is exceptional, and this book of Lucy's learning is a great insight into how she has moved us all forward... and how that learning and expertise can help you.

Lucy's insights in this wonderful book will help you serve others in your business by learning about leadership in a practical, accessible way with all the knowledge and tools you need, whatever stage you're at on your leadership journey. I know my team has been lucky to work with Lucy and transform their leadership with her support and I feel delighted to see her expertise in print and know you will benefit from the wisdom contained in these pages.

Dee Ford CBE
Group Managing Director Radio
Bauer Media Group

Acknowledgements

They say it takes a village to raise a child, and I feel the same about 'birthing' a book! For such a solitary activity as writing, I've had the comfort blanket of friends and colleagues who have provided me with a guiding hand and gentle encouragement over the last 18 months.

Without Alison Jones' proposal writing challenge, this idea would have remained on the 'wish list' of things to do, rather than a published product, and her unsurpassed creativity and support for fledgling business book authors is inspiring. And such steady reassurance was regularly offered by Géraldine Collard, Commissioning Editor at Kogan Page, who had confidence in this book from the start and ensured this was a collaborative, fun endeavour. My appreciation extends to the whole team at Kogan Page, who manage to make you feel a special part of the publishing family. And my thanks to Matt Lloyd, who's a steadfast member of our team and who I rely on for creative guidance.

This is book is the product of 20 years spent in the company of inspiring leaders. My clients are passionate and purposeful, and I always appreciative for their company and collaboration. I'm particularly grateful to the following colleagues whose help with early reading of the book, contributions and positive feedback was invaluable: Julie Ann Haines, Jon Ghazi, Rhian Langham, Damian Thompson, Matt Hill, Becky Hewitt, Ailsa Firth, David Clutterbuck, Cary Cooper, Sue Knight, Victoria Fox, Simon Welch, Joanna Trippett, Claire Sadler, Sue Unerman and Kathryn Jacob. Special thanks to Dee Ford who took such an interest in this project and wrote the preface for me.

I'm blessed with tolerant, patient friends who listened to the 'imposter' diatribes and whose encouragement along the way has been outstanding! My dearest thanks to Fiona Parashar, Lise

Lewis, Rachel Dymond, Claire Schimmer, Janie Van Hool and my lovely sister, Sarah McNeill. And special thanks to Jo Hale, who is the positive anchor every friend and author needs!

My daughters, Amy and Livvy, buoy me up, make me laugh and keep me going. My mum, Elizabeth, lived with us through lockdown, listened to the progress every day and assisted with sound advice and always wine!

And Steve, you found the time to fulfil all the roles above, editor-in-chief, brilliant motivator, daily encouragement, and coffee on tap. You're my rock, my love, and my lifelong buddy. Thank you.

Introduction

When the world went quiet and stepped inside during 2020 this book was conceived and written. With space and time, I reflected on the rich 20-year experience I have of coaching leaders and what kind of a book would make a difference to you. And I realized that, far from writing a deep philosophical treatise on leadership (I did that for my PhD!), most leaders actually want a pithy, practical and positive read. A book that can be read, returned to and enjoyed at different stages of your career, accompanying the modern leader's complex journey of constant challenge and continuous learning.

Fundamentally, I believe that all great leaders are learners. And certainly, the leaders I coach have a deep desire to learn and develop but face two challenges in achieving this: time and application. The relentless pace of most organizations inhibits the luxury of taking extensive time out for courses and your own self-development. Coupled with this is the question asked by most leaders following training – *'yes, but how?'* How do I apply the learning to my environment? What exercises will make a significant difference to my team? What coaching questions should I ask?

To shape the content, I wrote down the most common questions that arrive at my coaching door. Here's a snapshot:

How do I know if I'm managing or leading?
I'm stepping up to a leadership position, what do I need to do differently?
How do I influence my manager more effectively?
Given the pressure I'm under, how do I remain resilient?
How do I prepare for a difficult conversation (so that we both walk away from it feeling OK)?
How do I balance my life?
How do I write a progression plan and realize everyone's ambitions?
How do I cut through the noise of so much change and get important stuff done?
I'd achieve so much more with increased confidence. Help me?
How do I build a diverse team where everyone feels a sense of belonging?
How do I develop a brand that still feels authentic to me at my best?
What does it mean to build strengths into my coaching (and how do I do it)?
Is it selfish to consider my own happiness as a leader?

The breadth of these questions goes to show just how much is expected of you as a leader and you could be forgiven for thinking that you have to be superhuman to be a great leader. At once you're a positive influencer, a patient teacher, an enabling coach, a change agent, an inspiring role model and a humble servant. Oh yes, and please get the day job done, quickly! Not only this but you have to consistently check your balance, that is, be vulnerable yet strong; confident but not arrogant; humble while decisive.

The truth about leadership is that you don't have to be superhuman, neither do you need all the answers. The shift that often has to happen is away from you doing all the 'knowing' and the 'showing how', to enabling the team to find their own answers and creating the environment where this is possible. At times what is needed from you is counter-intuitive to what you want to do. You want to fix but need to empower.

And let me clarify what I mean by a leader. To me, *it's anyone who holds themselves accountable for developing the potential in others* and can hold true to this practice alongside the many demands placed on you in today's changing world. Particularly the pressure to perform, the pace of change, the demands of your stakeholders and maintaining the energy to lead. In my experience, the best leaders have the courage to lead *through* continual learning.

Resilience and influence

This book is structured in five parts, with two themes of Resilience and Influence permeating through the chapters. I know you'll want to infuse your organization with resilience (and how to do this is explored in Chapter 11), but the airlines get it right when they urge you to 'put your own oxygen mask on first'. If you burn out, the dominoes start to fall. I consistently argue that the most critical skill of leadership is about preserving your energy to lead, particularly as the more exposure you have, the greater the expectations of you. It's about achieving balance between managing and leading others (Chapter 1), being able to thrive more than just survive in your leadership role (Chapter 2) and feeling confident enough to show your vulnerability (Chapter 4). And achieving this is both an art and a science, so Chapter 3 lays out the scientific basis for positive leadership.

As a leader you cannot help but influence others. To lead is to influence, nothing more, nothing less. You're a role model and by your actions, behaviour, language and mindset people will judge you, decide whether or not to follow or trust you. Your team is a map of you and your shadow casts itself upon those under your authority. And that's why it's important to use your power with wisdom, perspective and compassion.

Part Two of this book delves into ways to lead others in a positive, respectful way through tailored motivation tactics (Chapter 5), using positive strengths in your leadership coaching (Chapter 6) and how to ensure the diverse team you're building has a sense of inclusion and belonging (Chapter 7). It's common that leadership books ignore the customer, the very people who keep you in business! As an influencer, I want to ensure that the customer remains in your landscape of influence, central to your team discussions and decisions (Chapter 8).

Most leaders I encounter earnestly want to be a positive influencer, visible for the right reasons, and to earn the trust of their followers. This is your brand and worthy of your consideration. As I say later in this book, be remembered for the right reasons (Chapter 12). For example, your very presence at a meeting may influence people positively or negatively (Chapter 14), while the style and nature of your presence, what you say or how you say it and the attitude you project speak volumes (Chapter 13). The smarter you get at knowing what you do, or what it is about you that impacts on others, the more personally effective you can become.

Hitting roadbumps

Roadbumps are an inevitable part of leadership and from adversity comes your future learning. As change is now an everyday occurrence, the modern leader needs considerable flexibility in their change leadership skills (Chapter 9). And with this pace of change comes the need to set appropriate expectations and have the difficult conversations you've been putting off (Chapter 10). The Covid-19 pandemic of 2020/21 was probably the biggest leadership crisis any reader of this book has faced in their career to date and it would be remiss not to explore ways in which you can embed future cultural resilience in your organization (Chapter 11). Perhaps it's only now that the criticality of these skills is being realized? What I've noticed in leaders who survive and thrive in the midst of challenge and change is they share five leadership behaviours (which can be learned and are encouraged through the book):

They show *courage* through vulnerability.
They have a *growth mindset*, seeing everything as an opportunity to learn.
They ask powerful and inspiring *questions*, instead of the habitual 'tug of tell'.
They take *action* rather than procrastinate; small steps forwards, day by day.
They consciously *reflect*, using their time and space wisely to gain insight.

What next?

What next, indeed? It's remarkable how few leaders have a succession plan and then wonder how they're going to make the leap forwards without anyone to take their place. Succession starts from day one in your new role. That is, the moment you take a leadership position, your job is to develop a progression plan for everyone in your team, to enable your own – and your team's – future succession (Chapter 15). Once you get this underway, it's incredibly liberating for everyone.

And as a pragmatic, positive psychologist, I couldn't leave this book without a brief reflection on happiness! Happiness and leadership are two concepts that rarely share the same page, as if it's your job to enable others at the exclusion of your own future happiness. But leaders who thrive build teams in the same vein, so take a powerful lunchtime break to reflect on the small steps you can take to lastingly increase your happiness.

How do I use the book?

Exactly as you want to. Not all of the topics will be relevant to you today. But all of them will be significant to you at some point in your career. So, dip in and out as you need to. There are 16 chapters and 16 relevant, critical leadership topics delivered in a way you can absorb in a short amount of time. And as I spend my time with leaders urging them to take a break and recharge their batteries, what better time to read this book than lunchtime!

Each chapter follows the same structure. After highlighting the problem, I'll introduce the latest thinking on the chosen topic and the evidence base, plus offer questions for self-reflection and ideas for action, through exercises and coaching questions. Unashamedly, each chapter has at least one model for you to use, try out and share with others. Anyone who has worked with me knows that I'm a great fan of simple models to explain complex topics. They act as a critical catalyst to a great conversation, with yourself, your colleagues or with your team.

For those of you who are *seriously* short of time, each chapter will close with a 'Ten Top Tips'!

So, let's begin

I understand you want to find space in your life to receive inspiration – as long as that time is used well – with brief, relevant and practical guidance. Ask yourself this tough question, '*what am I willing to change now?*' and consider this book as your personal coaching companion on your leadership journey.

My hope is that you feel encouraged and supported by me to take action around leadership topics that matter to you, in the way you want to do it, and find here a book to use often, and with passion.

PART ONE

Leading with insight

CHAPTER ONE

Practical strategies for maintaining your leadership balance

In a nutshell

What are the differences between managing, leading and coaching? How do you know what behaviours are needed for each state? Once you appreciate how to 'shape shift' depending on the demands of the organization, the team and the individual, you will be able to move from being a functional expert to a strategic leader.

What's the problem?

Finally, you've got Leader in your job title. And you won't be alone if you're now asking yourself, 'Am I a leader?' and, if so, 'What do I do more of to improve?' – two questions that are frequently brought to my coaching door, yet asked with a certain apprehension, as if you should know the answer. Let me help you here.

Most leaders rise up to a leadership via a number of management and functional roles, until you become a Head of…, a Director of…, a bona fide leader. The difficulty is that letting go of the functional role and growing into that of the leader is much harder than it seems at first sight. There are three reasons for this:

1 You don't know any better; no one has ever shown you the difference.
2 You are REALLY good at being a functional expert and that's what you've been paid to deliver for some time.
3 Great management is like an adrenaline spike: short term, fast, goal oriented. You know what everyone in your team is doing and you're directing the action. Your tentacles reach across the detail, the individuals, the jobs-to-be-done, the never-ending meetings, the ACTION! Leadership, in contrast, can seem, well, quite frankly, slow. So, back you go to the immediate action centre.

The big idea: Building balance and awareness

Leadership is complex and dynamic with many environments operating in a matrix arrangement. What this means is that building *balance* and *awareness* into your leadership toolkit is critical. You are looking to balance the roles of leading, managing and coaching, while increasing your awareness of your behaviour. If it sounds strange to suggest that managing should still be part of your leader toolkit, I'm just being realistic here. Only in the very biggest conglomerates do leaders solely 'think and do' strategy. For most leaders, there will be times you still have to get down to the job of managing, and 'doing the do'.

One useful way to start thinking about the differences between leadership, managing and coaching is with this simple diagram in Figure 1.1, with the three circles representing the three functions of your leadership role: leading, managing and coaching other people. To the left-hand side lies the dominant behaviour of 'telling' (with authority). You know what you want achieved, when, why and who to involve. To the right-hand side lies the central behaviour of 'asking' (enabling autonomy). Allowing someone else to decide how they want to complete something, when, why and who to involve. The interdependence of the three circles is a recognition that within this continuum of authority to autonomy lie 'grey areas' or, as I explain below, a dance between the circles.

FIGURE 1.1   The leadership balance

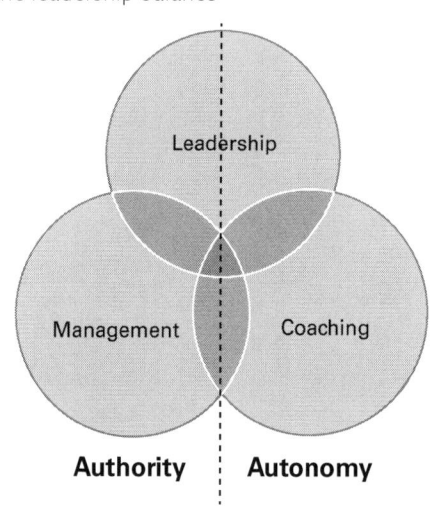

Dancing through leadership

As you can see from the diagram, there is an interdependence between the roles of being a manager, a leader and a coach. It is not either one or the other. You will need to have the capability to be both manager and leader, as well as to blend coaching into these roles. The art here is to understand how to choose the right role, at the right time with the right people!

To understand the difference between management and leadership, I'm going to borrow the metaphor of dancing from Ron Heifetz et al's book *The Practice of Adaptive Leadership (2009)*. It's a useful and contemporary way to understand the realistic flow from leadership to management and through to coaching.

Imagine a ballroom, with a sizeable dance floor and a balcony. In your role as a leader there will be continual movement stepping *onto* the dance floor and into the action and stepping *back* to the balcony.

Once you are on the dance floor in the midst of pacey management action, you'll be guiding the action, stepping *in* and telling people what to do – you have the authority. *Look at me, I'll show you how.*

But on the balcony, you'll be stepping back from the action. Observing, listening, noticing what is working and what is not, and strategizing the next set of moves. *Look at this, there could be a better way to do it.*

And this continual motion is complemented by your role as a leadership coach, where you step away, let go of telling and of authority. You offer autonomy with a guiding hand. *Look at yourself, you already have the resources to do this.*

Naturally, you are going to dance between all three of these roles. Sometimes your leadership skills come to the fore. You're strategic. You step back to see the big picture, inspire people to follow your vision and act as a change agent. You network broadly, building dynamic, connective relationships.

At other times, this is just a pipe dream, as you find yourself in the thick of it, managing short-term situations, assigning tasks, solving problems and guiding others. Basically, getting the very busy job of today done, with authority. And what about coaching in this very demanding working world? Among the maelstrom of day-to-day working life, you will consistently carve out time to coach your team, asking more than telling, guiding not directing. And all the time knowing that by giving autonomy in decision making, you equip your team to thrive in the future.

What I want to do in this chapter is to help you decide what 'shape' your diagram is in today, and where you want it to be to thrive as a leader in the future.

Try this out

Take a blank sheet of paper and draw three circles that reflect your leadership balance at the moment, with the size of the circles reflecting your current situation.

For example, in times of change and crisis, it is very common that your diagram might look like Figure 1.2. That is, significant time spent managing others, with less time on strategy or coaching. When there is an immediate need to focus on the short term this is a predictable diagram as you get change implemented, decisively, by the right people, in a timely way!

FIGURE 1.2   A management imbalance

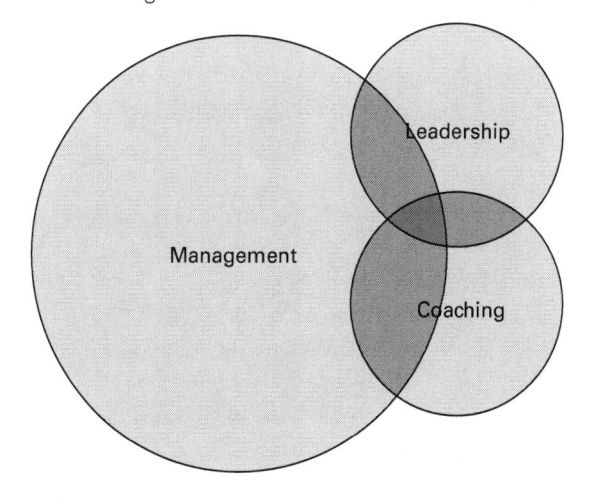

Perhaps it is less easy to recognize when your leadership circle has become too dominant, as in Figure 1.3. If over time you find your circles unbalanced in this direction, it's likely you have removed yourself from the action, from the dance floor, spending too much time on the balcony. If you recognize this, you'll have a sense that you have lost sight of what is happening on the ground, what your people or customers are feeling and where the real issues lie. You'll probably have a deep desire to reconnect at ground level.

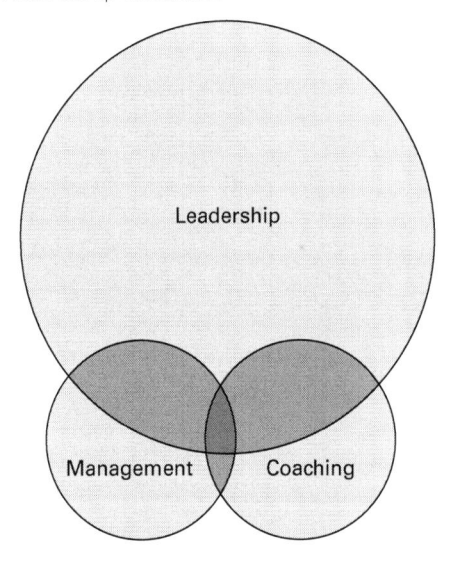

FIGURE 1.3 A leadership imbalance

And what if your coaching circle is larger than your other two circles as in Figure 1.4? Essentially, this means you'll be stepping back from managing and leading with the behaviours of delegation and trust coming forwards. While you're doing great work by giving your team autonomy, you'll still have to be careful that you grab the reins when necessary, have the essential difficult conversations and take decisive action when required. Balance is hard!

FIGURE 1.4   A coaching imbalance

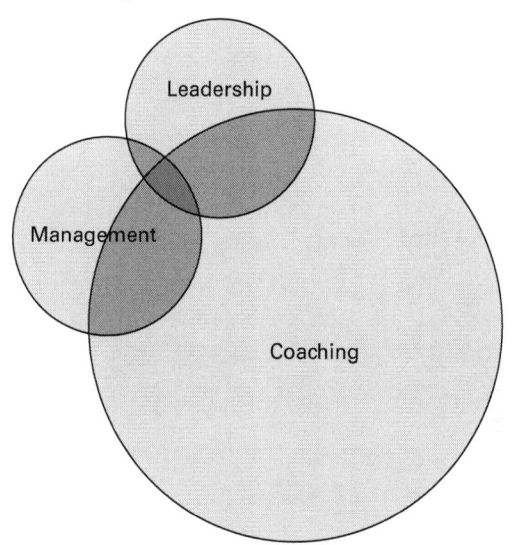

Time to reflect

1 What does your diagram tell you about your situation right now? (e.g., have you been in crisis mode recently and your management circle has dramatically increased?)
2 How long have the circles been in this shape? (e.g., are you leading from a habitual place, or is this a recent shift to a different shape of your diagram?)
3 What (or who) triggers you to move from one shape to another? (e.g., is there a meeting you regularly attend where you need to step up, but you remain silent or just commenting on task and process? Are there people you are more comfortable to coach, or teams you have led where coaching is a more natural part of your leadership role?)
4 What needs to change or flex? (as you look at your diagram, how do you want it to be different?)

Take a second sheet of paper and draw three circles that reflect your leadership balance in the future, with the size of the circles reflecting your desired situation.

Practical inspiration

Use this section if you are someone who wants some practical inspiration for re-aligning your leadership practice, so that you are able to flex more efficiently from being a functional expert to a strategic leader. Here are five practices to explore:

a Letting go
b From today to tomorrow: craft a new vision
c Networking for the future
d Create space to reflect
e Remaining agile

Letting go

Aha! Letting go. Perhaps the hardest shift of all to do. If you are a great manager, or functional expert, your identity will be wrapped up in your current job role. You are the 'go-to' person for perhaps IT, HR or Facilities. You know who to ask, how to get it done FASTER and BETTER than anyone else in the organization. You recruit in, delegate to, and trust other people in your team but ultimately, all decisions lead back to you. Not only this, but you are celebrated and rewarded for your expertise in this area.

Managing transitions guru William Bridges (2017) calls the time between endings and new beginnings the 'neutral zone', a 'neither here nor there' psychological space where identities are in flux and people feel they have lost the ground beneath their feet. But try thinking about your shift from Expert Manager to People Leader as an experiment. Test with small probes and projects to try out a new leadership role on a limited but tangible scale without committing to a particular direction.

For example:

- Attend a different committee meeting than usual and start to comment on broader issues than your functional area.
- Identify a leader within or without your organization with the skills and behaviour you want to emulate. Contact them and ask them for a mentor session.
- This month spend some time within a function that you have had limited contact with. Find out what their dominant issues are; how they communicate with the customer; how your function could help their function operate more effectively.
- Look at Chapter 14 and craft your 'influencing map' for extending your network.

From today to tomorrow: craft a new vision

By learning from the past, moving through the present and anticipating the future, you can consciously craft a new and interesting vision for your team. By using the 10 questions below (I've reworked a SWOT analysis for you), you're helping your team become more resourceful and resilient as they recognize their development, as individuals and as a team:

1 What new strengths have materialized in the team over the last six months?
2 What new ways of working (accelerated digital agenda? Work/life agenda?) have become evident that you can recognize and retain?
3 What positive, attitudinal shifts and beliefs have become apparent?
4 How can you capitalize and build on those strengths?
5 What weaknesses have become obvious?
6 What/who/which functions held you back?

7 What new opportunities and needs have emerged in your marketplace or in your culture?
8 What feels exciting? What's worth getting out of bed for today?
9 Who is not capitalizing on these emergent marketplaces/products/services (and you can fill this gap)?
10 What new threats are evident and where do they come from? (Locally? Globally? Health and wellbeing? Turnover and cultural change?)

Networking for the future

In her book, *Act Like a Leader, Think Like a Leader*, Herminia Ibarra (2015) explores the 'competency trap'. That is, the state that great functional managers achieve by just getting better at what they already do well. It's pretty clear that the better you are at something, the higher the opportunity cost of doing something else (and the higher the cost to the organization of losing you in that role).

So, to refresh your leadership perspective and start to network for the future, focus on what Ibarra calls 'Outsight' (rather than Insight), by building a new strategic network. As she says: 'Outsight is about the external perspective. It's about seeing things differently because you have expanded the activities you are involved in and the people you interact with. It gives you fresh stuff, instead of rehashing the old.' Over the next month:

- speak to three new people who offer you a different perspective on leadership;
- read/listen to/watch three new articles/podcasts/TED talks that shift your mindset;
- connect your team to the outside world. Everything is connected – your customers, competitors, peers and your suppliers. If you're just in your silo, you miss out.

Create space to reflect

When she became Principality Building Society's first female CEO in 2020, I was struck by Julie Ann Haines' advice to the senior leadership team to invest one day a week in self-development, growth and learning. The idea was met with incredulity. Eight hours! Many felt lucky to find one hour. Not only does Julie Ann practise what she preaches, but she has a sound point backed up by research. According to Ines Wichert's (2018) research on how to turn top talent into leaders, the leader who reflects:

- questions their assumptions and makes better decisions;
- learns faster and gets up to speed in new situations more quickly;
- doesn't make the same mistake twice;
- is ready to deal with unfamiliar circumstances by recognizing connections between seemingly unrelated situations.

You'll know if you are *Head Down*, rather than *Head Up* when you're on back-to-back calls or meetings, whether virtually or face to face and, as a modern leader, you are more 'on' and more accessible than ever before.

When I've asked leaders their reasons for not reflecting, three answers are apparent:

I don't see results quickly enough.
I don't enjoy the process.
I don't know how to do it (or, what do I reflect on?).

With a bias towards action for many leaders, the first point is unsurprising. Rewarded throughout your career for fast, decisive action, the art of slowing down can feel incompatible with leadership. For many it can feel like a forced waste of time. Give up expecting a 'return on investment'. This is unstructured thinking, not an efficiency exercise.

The most useful reflection involves the conscious consideration of your assumptions and actions. You can untangle knots of emotions and ideas. Reflection gives the brain an opportunity to rest amidst the chaos of doing, experiencing and talking. By pressing pause you allow the brain to consider multiple interpretations, different mindsets and alternative actions. All of which is critical to your future development.

If you're not sure what to reflect on, below are some questions to get you started. You will eventually find your own way that's useful just for you. Either schedule time in your calendar or use your downtime for reflection. I reflect when I'm swimming and the lengths go by without me noticing (except when it's very cold water!).

Start small and make progress in a non-judgemental way. Maybe just 15 minutes a day, or once a week.

Self:

- What am I proud of this week?
- What am I not proud of this week?
- When did I feel most and least engaged this week?
- What did I learn about myself this week that I didn't know before?
- How can I use this learning next week?
- What kind of a leader have I been this week?
- What kind of a follower have I been?
- How have I role-modelled my values?
- What am I avoiding?
- Is there an issue I'm still wrestling with? What can I do to create better solutions?
- What deserves my highest-quality attention in my leadership?
- What is the most novel, fun or outrageous idea I've heard this week? How can I nurture its growth?
- How can I bring more joy to work?

Others:

- How am I helping my team reach their goals?
- How am I getting in the way of my team making progress?
- What relationship has improved?
- What beliefs have I shifted that have allowed this?
- Which relationship still needs development?
- How am I contributing to my least enjoyable relationship?
- How did I bring joy to my team this week?

Remaining agile

Whether you are on the dance floor or the balcony, whether you're the coach or the leader – know that you'll need to swap between roles and remain agile. When you've skyrocketed into the detail, practise moving out again. Be conscious about this. When you're faced with a new role or situation that's very different from anything you've done before, experiment, test, try and act your way through it. Reflect afterwards and make changes for the next time. Remember how quickly you have made change happen before and don't get stuck in long-winded decision-making traps. You are now in the new age of agile leadership that has been tried, tested and accomplished.

Learn to accept unpredictability. Know that you have taken action in the face of unprecedented circumstances before, so don't let further change shake your mental resilience. Take heart in your own responsiveness and remain courageous and compassionate in the way you communicate and the actions you take.

Ten top tips for maintaining your leadership balance

1. Be intentional about your behaviour and know whether you are leading, managing or coaching.
2. If you're leading, step back. If you're managing, step in. If you're coaching, step away.

3. Be adaptive and responsive. In just one conversation, you might move between all three roles, which will require your resources of mental agility and behavioural flexibility.
4. Know your triggers. Who or what activates movement between the three circles? Is it time or seniority? Is it a certain person or something else?
5. Let go of your identity that is wrapped up in being an expert manager. Spread your leadership wings and broaden your wingspan across the organization.
6. Help your team become learners. All great leaders learn and encourage their team to do the same. Use the vision questions to encourage this learning.
7. Find ways to slow things down. You will make more mistakes the faster the pace, so use reflection time to steady your responses.
8. You are what you do. To make change happen, change your behaviour.
9. Ask more, tell less. Delegate more, direct less. Be a leadership coach and let go of your desire to hold onto control.
10. Be realistic. Achieving a perfect balance is improbable so develop self-insight and know when you have to stay in one role. Be kind to your flaws as much as your strengths!

CHAPTER TWO

Managing your energy is the key to leadership resilience

In a nutshell

Many leaders are too exhausted to lead well, and even more are not operating at their best. This chapter will explore what it really takes to have the physical, mental and emotional energy to lead successfully. Together with a 25-point Resilience Audit, this chapter is packed with practical strategies for paying attention to your personal wellness and leading with vitality.

What's the problem?

In these uniquely challenging times, the demand for resilient leadership has never been greater. The challenges you face are complex and interconnected, with problems that can only be solved by leaders who see the bigger picture and can adapt to an ever-changing context. The higher you rise as a leader, so will your workload. Challenges and potential stressors increase concomitantly, and you'll want the capacity to cope with, and work through, such situations.

This isn't about getting rid of all your stress. As Stephen Southwick (2018), Professor Emeritus of Psychiatry at Yale University, suggests, 'If you can cope today with all that's happening in the world around you, then when you're on the other side of it, you'll be stronger'. However, you will need to sustain your energy level under pressure. Put another way, resilience takes energy. There is no such thing as a resilient person, born with a silver spoon of natural 'bounce back-ability', nor is it a fixed trait. Instead, resilience is the result of a combination of inner strengths and outer resources, which enable you to adapt and flex in the face of challenging situations, so that you're able to recover well from setbacks, function almost normally – and in many circumstances, grow as a result of the situation (Reivich and Shattè, 2002).

Resilience takes energy.

As well as this, you also carry the responsibility of helping to protect the energy of the people within your team, as leadership is only sustainable if individuals and teams are able to consistently recover from setbacks. Indeed, it's more common for me to talk with leaders who look after their team's energy far more effectively than they protect their own.

So, while cultivating your energy in order to advance and thrive is the solution for building the capacity for resilience, the reality for many leaders is that of exhaustion and burnout (Loehr and Schwartz, 2003). When I ask leaders at resilience events, 'Who has observed too much toxic conflict in the workplace? Increased sickness and absence? Who has experienced burnout themselves?', invariably multiple hands shoot up. The sensation of being 'always on', at an intolerable pace, is prevalent.

And workplace statistics bear this out. Prior to the 2020 pandemic, the largest known UK stress study for the workplace (Mental Health Foundation, 2018) reported 74 per cent of respondents feeling so stressed in the previous year they had been overwhelmed or unable to cope. Writing in *Forbes* magazine, Thomas (2020) declared 'global burnout is rampant', noting that the World Health Organization has now added 'burnout' to its handout of medical diagnoses.

While leadership scholars contend that leadership resilience must be tackled at an organizational, systemic level (Moss, 2021), I argue for taking both an individual and a systemic approach (see Chapter 11 for the latter). It's often forgotten that a leader must learn to lead themselves first before they lead others, with self-leadership being the foundation stone for effective leadership, so that's where I'll start:

> Resilience is not a trampoline, where you're down one moment and up the next. It's more like climbing a mountain without a trail map. It takes time, strength, and help from people around you, and you'll likely experience setbacks along the way. But eventually you reach the top and look back at how far you've come (Hurley, 2020).

The big idea: Recharge your five batteries!

The skills and strategies we'll explore here are not a 'nice to have'. They're central to your survival as a leader and your ability to manage a flourishing team. This is about practising healthy resilience habits at home and at work, with the learning an integral part of your personal development plan.

In order to maintain your energy levels and thrive as a leader, imagine you have five connected batteries that require consistent attention and recharging:

Body
Mind
Heart
Connect
Purpose

	Physical resilience	How you manage your sleep, your diet and your exercise habits.
	Mental resilience	Your ability to focus and think flexibly, with a realistically optimistic lens.
	Emotional resilience	How you recognize your emotional state and regulate your emotional responses.
	Connective resilience	How you maintain and develop your significant social relationships with those you love and trust.
	Purposeful resilience	How you align your life with meaning, purpose and happiness.

This is personal. Only you will know if your sleep is disturbed, you're relying on alcohol, have stopped seeing your friends or are snapping at your kids in a disproportionate way. But your first step is to assess where life and work are draining and energizing you, so you can make some purposeful choices for change.

In this chapter, we'll start with the Resilience Healthcheck questions so you can assess your levels of energy. Then with the help of brief leader case studies, we'll explore some practical strategies for replenishing your energy and increasing your leadership resilience for the first four 'batteries'. In Chapter 16, we'll revisit the role of happiness and purpose in your life – this battery needs a whole chapter to itself!

Try this out

Resilience Healthcheck

Read the 25 statements of the Resilience Healthcheck. Give yourself a score out of 5 for each question, 0 = hardly ever, 3 = sometimes, 5 = consistently effective. Be honest and realistic. You don't have to show this to anyone.

Recharge your body

1. Every day I wake up feeling refreshed from my night's sleep.
2. My diet predominantly consists of freshly cooked, unprocessed food.
3. I eat regular meals throughout the day, replenishing my energy in a healthy way.
4. I minimize the time I sit, regularly stretching and moving my body.
5. I exercise five times a week, including two strength-training sessions.

Recharge your mind

1. I am proactive, more than I am reactive, in where I spend my time.
2. I can minimize distractions, focusing on one thing at a time.
3. I avoid ruminating or catastrophizing on potentially difficult situations and focus on what I can control.
4. I prioritize enough time for important activities with long-term value.
5. I leave space in my working day for reflection and quiet time.

Recharge your heart

1. I'm aware of my emotional state at any time throughout the day.
2. I know what triggers me into an unhelpful emotional state.

3 I restrain my feelings of frustration, impatience or anxiety, especially when times are demanding.
4 I can move myself out of a bad mood quickly.
5 I deliberately cultivate my positive emotions.

Recharge your connections

1 I nurture the significant relationships in my life with focused, loving attention.
2 I have close friends, in and out of work, who I trust.
3 I have effective work/life boundaries and work is not a feature of holiday time.
4 I prioritize time to have fun and regular 'downtime' with friends.
5 I savour my interactions with others, being present and showing genuine interest.

Recharge your purpose

1 I understand my strengths, and have time at work to be the best leader I can be.
2 I know where I'm heading and am passionate about my direction.
3 I can articulate my values and what is important to me.
4 My values are aligned with how I live my life in actuality.
5 Every day, I take time to reflect on what is important to the way I lead others.

Time to reflect

Your scores will be a reflection of what is going on in your life right now and it is unlikely that all five batteries will be fully charged at any one time. That is, your score is likely to be in the range of 70–80 points, midway on resilience. Higher than this, you've got some great habits already. Lower than this, there might be a current context that is skewing some of your scores, or you might be experiencing some long-term unhelpful habits. Reflecting on your scores, ask yourself the following questions:

a What are you most pleased about and that you'd like to strengthen?
b What shocks you the most and you'd like to improve?
c Which area of the Resilience Healthcheck needs most attention?
d What habits are you prepared to change, for consistent improvement?

In the next section, we'll explore some strategies for recharging the first four areas – recharging the body, mind, emotions and social connections – all of which will help you increase your above score. I've outlined some brief leader vignettes and as you read them in turn, just underline sentences that resonate for you and try the relevant exercises.

Practical inspiration

Recharging the body

'Burned out but still burning!' is Ned's shout. In a high-pressure role, Ned feels in control through constant activity. Four mornings a week, Ned is on the treadmill from 5–6 am. His meetings start at 7 am and can run through to 8 pm or later. He eats on the go and survives on adrenaline and coffee. He tries to sit down with his partner every evening for a meal, which he usually achieves, if work doesn't interrupt. He keeps weekends relatively free for his family (he has three young children under 14), although the last four Sundays have involved about four hours of work. He catches up on email – reading and sending – between 8 and 10 pm.

While Ned feels in control, he isn't. His sleep is disrupted and his blood pressure rising. He's having arguments with his partner about workload and he knows his children are missing time with him.

Recharging the body and making physical changes for the better is hard! I don't need to restate the prolific advice available (drink more water, eat more vegetables, don't work so late!) but it's a whole other matter to make personal decisions that are suitable for you, for your work and for your family. It's also a question of changing some ingrained habits so that you have 'reserves in the tank' for when the going gets tough.

What is worth reiterating is that other than eating and breathing, sleep is the most important factor for your levels of resilience. Most of my clients are seriously sleep deprived, so getting a quality 7–8 hours a night is critical. I admire Matthew Walker's (2017) book, *Why We Sleep*, and he's pretty insistent that the longer, and later, you work at night, the less efficient you become.

Exercise #1: Drains and energizers

The purpose of this exercise is to commit in writing what drains you and what energizes you, and to use the list to start recharging your physical energy. You can use this list to incorporate all activities at work and home that drain or energize (e.g. meetings or toxic relationships), but Figure 2.1 shows Ned's initial physical list.

When you look at his list, it's far too easy to say do less of the left-hand side and more from the right, as you have to work out what's realistic for you. For example, when I worked with Ned on his list, it was important to recognize that a full night's sleep might not be realistic right now but stopping meetings at lunchtime could be. It's all a question of balance. Here were some other practical decisions that Ned and I worked on in coaching – this is what he knew he could (and did) sustain:

- Keep three lunchtimes each week free. Agree with team.
- Use those lunchtimes for reflection, writing or reading.

FIGURE 2.1   Drains and energizers

Drains	Energizers
Disrupted sleep (baby crying)	8 hours blissful sleep!
Missing breakfast or snatched breakfast in the car	Breakfast time with kids
Skipping lunch	Some fuel, even at desk
Meetings through lunchtime	Recharge at lunchtime, whether walk, reading, writing
Not going outside	Some fresh air each day
Constant coffee	Balance of water and coffee
Not enough time to exercise	Any form of exercise!
Email in evening (although it's quiet) but content fires me up	Email managed during working day, Evenings off!

↓ Burnout

↓ Recharge

- Start a leadership journal for this time (suggested questions in Chapter 1).
- Fresh air every day, no matter how short.
- Change two treadmill sessions for two strength-training sessions.
- Exercise at weekends with the children (not by self), start new hobby together.
- Finish emails by 6 pm twice a week.

Try this out

Write out your own list of physical drains and energizers. Make it as broad and honest as you can. To achieve a better balance, what can you stop that drains you and increase that energizes you? Make your decisions realistic for your lifestyle, rather than what you feel you 'should do'.

Recharging the mind

Ava ruminates. A senior leader in the charity sector, Ava finds that when she's facing a potentially difficult situation, it goes round and round her head, nagging at her mind through the day and waking her up at night. It causes her anxiety, depletes her confidence and disrupts her ability to focus on work. Ava has a difficult conversation coming up with one of her team, who is underperforming. She's run the conversation through her mind multiple times and has convinced herself that it is going to go wrong!

Resilient individuals have the ability to positively adjust and adapt to a challenging situation, like a super material that can absorb strain and maintain its shape. This requires a mental and emotional flexibility that is a fundamental building block for resilience (Seligman, 2011). In 2012 Professor Ilona Boniwell and I co-wrote the UK's first resilience curriculum, SPARK, and coined the phrase the 'Sticky Path' to describe the sensation when our emotions and feelings collide. You'll know this yourself when you 'ruminate' about a situation; it goes round and round in your head, or perhaps you 'catastrophize'. This is particularly prevalent when there is uncertainty, rumours and an abundance of media information. Try not to let the Sticky Path gain traction in your head by asking yourself four great self-coaching questions, and then walk back down the Sticky Path.

Exercise #2: The Sticky Path

1. What do you have control of here?
2. What's the most positive, yet realistic, story you can tell yourself in this situation?
3. What small goals can you focus on today that will distract your thinking?

4 Who can you talk to (who will give you a different perspective and not advance your negative thinking)?

Underpinning these four questions lies the scientific foundations for mental resilience:

- **Control** only what you can control. Let go of things you cannot control. Importantly, put yourself in a position of mental and emotional control, which increases your personal agency.
- **Realistic optimism** is at the heart of mental resilience. Create a virtuous self-fulfilling prophecy and calm your mind with a story that is pragmatic, yet positive.
- **Focus** your brain through distraction.
- Seek out alternative narratives and broaden your **perspective**.

For example, looking back at Ava's habit of ruminating over potentially difficult situations, here are Ava's answers:

What do you have control of here?

I can prepare the conversation.
I can write out questions to ask.
I can ensure I'm in a calm state when holding the conversation.

What's the most positive, yet realistic, story you can tell yourself in this situation?

My colleague knows she is underperforming.
This won't be a surprise.
If I stick to the facts and remain empathic, we can achieve an OK solution.
I can handle myself in this situation.

What small goals can you focus on today that will distract your thinking?

First go for a walk.
Design presentation for next week's meeting.
Lunch with 2 x team.

Who can you talk to (who will give you a different perspective and not advance your negative thinking)?

Sarah – calm and reflective.
Reuben – always comes at things from a very different angle. Trust him.

Recharging the heart

Noah works in the digital sector, heading up the IT team. He leads a sizeable team and in his recent 360 reports received feedback about his lack of emotional control. Members of his team noted that he was quick to be triggered, difficult to get out of a mood, and the impact of his bad moods was contagious for the team. By 10 am everyone could be in a bad mood! Junior members of the team were avoiding him, and senior managers were feeling the need to protect others from him. After a difficult conversation with his boss, Noah confessed he had been ignoring his personal 'alarm bells' and needed to take this area of emotional intelligence seriously.

Your emotions are your personal alarm bells. It's easier to notice when you're feeling distracted, impatient or annoyed (and for others to see) than it is to track your thinking habits. But it's vital to hear these alarm bells. If you find yourself in perpetual stress, the body becomes overexposed to the release of adrenaline and cortisol, hormones that increase during stressful periods (Quinn et al, 2021). Both hormones have a precious role to play in our so-called 'fight or flight' response, but can also place you at risk of infection and an impaired immune system (Sapolsky, 2004).

Try this out

Exercise #3: From name to neutralize

This is a four-part exercise to learn to manage your emotional response. I think of each of these four stages as 'hot buttons', with the aim to neutralize their heat as you work through the stages.

FIGURE 2.2   Neutralizing your 'hot buttons'

1 NAME
- Learn to label your emotions. What are you feeling? Build a broad vocabulary of your emotional responses.
- Look at the list in the box and accurately label your emotions.

2 NOTICE
- What triggered this/these emotions? Write out a trigger journal and learn what your personal triggers are.
- Where do you feel the emotions in your body? Can you shift your state by moving differently?

3 NURTURE
- Understanding and accepting your negative emotions as a call to action. What do you want to be different?
- Build a positive emotional resource library, to use as a positive counterbalance.

4 NEUTRALIZE
- Deliberately build calming strategies into your life, through breathing, meditation, journalling.
- 'Stop for 60' before responding. Breathe deeply for 60 seconds; walk for 60 steps; wait 60 minutes before responding to the email.

> **WHAT ARE YOU FEELING?**
>
> | | |
> |---|---|
> | ☐ Defensive | ☐ Carefree |
> | ☐ Challenged | ☐ Incensed |
> | ☐ Optimistic | ☐ Proud |
> | ☐ Confident | ☐ Calm |
> | ☐ Exhausted | ☐ Impatient |
> | ☐ Angry | ☐ Tired |
> | ☐ Mellow | ☐ Stimulated |
> | ☐ Happy | ☐ Receptive |
> | ☐ Frustrated | ☐ Envious |
> | ☐ Anxious | ☐ Sad |
> | ☐ Empty | ☐ Peaceful |
> | ☐ Passive | ☐ Serene |
> | ☐ Eager | ☐ At ease |
> | ☐ Worried | ☐ Enthusiastic |
> | ☐ Irritable | ☐ Defiant |
> | ☐ Serene | ☐ Astonished |
> | ☐ Reflective | ☐ Depressed |
> | ☐ Fearful | ☐ Annoyed |
> | ☐ Excited | ☐ Engaged |
> | ☐ Hopeless | |

On reflection, Noah recognized that he was in a highly triggered state most of the day, reacting with annoyance and frustration to any distraction. These emotions registered in his body too as he scrunched up his face and hunched his body. He learned that simple movement could shift an emotional state. And while these two negative emotions were ringing loudly, his positive emotions were barely registering. He started a journal, naming and noticing his emotions, paying particular attention to his positive emotions.

Two positive emotions were particularly prevalent, gratitude and hope, and Noah decided to build on these emotions by writing about them every evening:

What am I grateful for today?
What has given me hope?
Who can I appreciate tomorrow?

'Stop for 60' was his lifeline for him and his team (with the playful suggestion from his team that he should talk to 60 people before responding!).

Recharging your connections

Ines is Head of Communications at an accountancy firm. She is extraordinarily busy and had decided to make some coping decisions. As a result, Ines made the decision to stop seeing her friends. She used to belong to a cycling team where they went out on a Saturday and saw her two best friends at least twice a month. It was with these friends she could kick back and laugh, whereas in the stress of her busy role, Ines feels she can only cope with balancing work and family demands. Maintaining friendships has been the area she feels she has to compromise on.

A high capacity to form attachments and bond with others is one of the pillars of resilience, as well as a core psychological need (Lieberman, 2013). Strong personal bonds are vital in supporting us as we recover from setbacks, and relationships based on trust are your secure foundations. Too often, resilience is seen as individual 'toughness', with western ideals focusing on the need to tap into the self for overcoming hardships, and as such ignoring the power of social support (Hartling, 2008).

You want, and need, a small network of people you know you can count on, both in your personal life and at work.

Tough times in business can be stressful, and in tough times it's tempting to retreat and close down your social connections. Shawn Achor's (2011) research suggests we should do the opposite: 'The people who survive stress the best are the ones who actually increase their social investments in the middle of stress.'

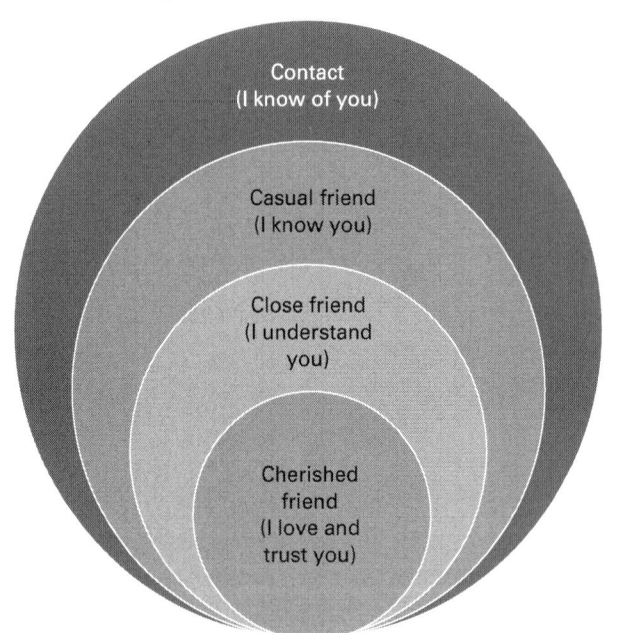

FIGURE 2.3   Friendship circles

- Contact (I know of you)
- Casual friend (I know you)
- Close friend (I understand you)
- Cherished friend (I love and trust you)

Time to reflect

Exercise #4: Reflecting on the friendship circles

There isn't a 'neat' exercise that will immediately shift Ines' friendship world, or yours. Like so much in life, this is an area that needs reflection, and this friendship circle is a good place to start. Ask yourself the following questions:

a If you reflect on the last week and allocate percentage figures across the friendship circle, who gets your time?
b How can you strengthen your ties with close friends?
c Are those you cherish getting enough significant, quality time with you?
d In what simple ways can you let the friends you understand, love and trust, know you are there for them?

What did Ines do?

During our coaching session, Ines was surprised by the Friendship Circle diagram. On reflection she recognized that, as the new Head of Communications at her firm, most of her time was spent online building contacts with strangers or acquaintances – some 80 per cent of her time. While much of this is necessary for her role, her 'spare' 20 per cent of available friendship time was dedicated to her family – with close and cherished friends squeezed out. She knew, for the moment, she couldn't give large amounts of time to hobbies, like cycling, but she could let her close friends know she cared and let her two cherished best friends back into her life. Ines made just two simple changes:

- Sent appreciation cards to her close friends – 'I'm here for you and I'll be back in your life soon!'
- Diarized time with her best friends for the next three months and agreed with her partner. Boundaried and prioritized.

As this chapter comes to a close, what you'll understand now is that resilience is a learned skill, with some behavioural habits that are in your power to choose. Fundamentally, it is your capacity to learn from the past, cope in the present and use this knowledge to build an optimistic future. As such, it is like building up muscles in the gym. If you don't use them, they become weak. If you use them and exercise them well – daily – they become strong and useful. Daily practice is important so that when you need strong muscles they are exercised and ready to be put into practice.

Top ten ways to recharge your energy and resilience

1. Learn from the past and use this knowledge to boost your capacity to cope in the future.
2. Hold the belief that you can manage your feelings and your ability to cope in stressful situations.
3. Demonstrate self-regulation, controlling your emotional impulses, feelings and reactions.
4. Practise self-care as much as you practise the care of others.
5. Build your positive emotional resource library. Notice and nurture your positive emotions!
6. Invest time in your significant relationships. Show appreciation to those you love and trust.
7. Think flexibly and accurately about the causes and implications of adversities.
8. Broaden your perspective and talk to people who have a different story to yours.
9. Develop comfort with asking for help and showing vulnerability.
10. Identify what is controllable, what is not, and believe in good outcomes.

Oh yes, and sleep well!

CHAPTER THREE

Enhancing performance through the science of positive leadership

In a nutshell

'What can I do if I want to become a more positive leader?' Building on the emerging science of positive leadership, this chapter offers practical strategies for cultivating a growth mindset, leading with curiosity and fostering a positive climate. It's not about ignoring difficult behaviour, but it is about your growth as a leader through recognizing what works and what is energizing for others.

What's the problem?

Simply put, the problem is that there is not enough positive leadership being practised across organizations.

If you think about positive leadership on a bell curve, with negative, narcissistic behaviour on the extreme left, and positively divergent behaviour on the extreme right, most leadership falls into the muggy middle. That is, sometimes you know you exude optimism, demonstrate appreciation and regulate your moods. Perhaps you've attended leadership courses where the theories promote being an authentic, transformational, charismatic, emotionally intelligent or servant leader, and you sincerely try to put the learning into practice. But at other times you are just a naturally flawed human being – stressed out, short of time, anxious and far too exhausted to embrace any notion of positive leadership.

And this shows. Current statistics emanating from leading UK, European and US organizational surveys suggest that leaders are simply not doing enough to stem the tide of increasing stress and disengagement at work – and these figures were collected *before* the impact of Covid-19 was properly investigated. Here is just a sample:

- Stress, depression or anxiety now account for 51 per cent of all work-related ill-health cases in the UK (HSE, 2020).
- 17.9 million working days are lost due to stress, anxiety or depression in the UK (HSE, 2020).
- Work-related stress costs European organizations some €20 billion per year (Roberts, 2019).
- 52 per cent of adults in the US are not engaged with their work, while 12 per cent are 'actively disengaged' to the point of misery (Harter, 2020).
- 79 per cent of British adults in employment report experiencing work-related stress (Perkbox, 2020), with 89 per cent observing 'presenteeism' (people working when unwell), and 73 per cent observing 'leaveism' (people working when on leave) (CIPD, 2020).

Of importance here is the question, *what causes such considerable distress and despair to so many working adults?*

Unfortunately, the top two causes of stress given by respondents across multiple surveys are (a) heavy workloads and (b) leadership/line manager style. Study after study report that senior leaders remain key to reducing stress through positive leadership practices, but just 15 per cent of companies believe their leaders are engaged in this process (CIPD, 2020).

So, what has this got to do with the science of positive leadership? Positive leaders create productive, superior performance (Cameron, 2012). This is not about blind optimism and just having fun (although more fun wouldn't go amiss in most workplaces). It's about recognizing the impact of positive emotions, of appreciation and of spotting excellence in action (Fredrickson, 2001). It is also not about ignoring problematic behaviour, poor performance or bullying in the workplace, but it *is* about noticing what works, what is energizing for others and leading through compassion and connection (Dutton and Spreitzer, 2014). As Cameron (2012) states in his book, *Positive Leadership*, the aim is to promote outcomes such as 'thriving at work, interpersonal flourishing, positive emotions and energizing networks' (p 4).

Put another way, the difference between positive and negative leadership is fairly simple. Positive leadership encourages, empowers and energizes people. Negative leadership drains, discourages and demoralizes people.

What all of this means is that leaders have to work harder than they realize to help people be the best they can be and fulfil their potential.

What does positive leadership look like in action?

As someone who straddles the worlds of academia and business, I'm often struck by the discrepancy between the language of science and the reality of day-to-day practice. According to Kim Cameron, widely seen as one of the founders of the science of positive leadership, it 'enables positively deviant performance, fosters an affirmative orientation and engenders a focus on virtuousness'.

Compare this with the survey I conducted when I was doing my Master's in Positive Psychology, with over 200 employees of a sizeable financial institution responding to the question, *what does positive leadership feel and look like to you?* Looking back at the answers today, I'm struck by their sheer humanity and simplicity:

- *I feel noticed and appreciated.*
- *More smiling, less crank.*
- *I know I matter and that feels good.*
- *Meetings start with what's working, before we talk about what needs fixing.*
- *They close their laptop when they're talking to me.*
- *They don't cancel, delay, postpone our 1:1.*
- *They show care and compassion.*
- *We laugh more than we worry.*
- *I don't receive an email from them with what's going wrong first thing in the morning or last thing at night.*
- *We have time to just talk to each other, person to person.*
- *It just makes everything better.*

This is down-to-earth stuff. Beyond the academic definitions, this is about your teams waiting to be heard, craving care and compassion, earning your full attention, having their time respected and wanting to be at work.

It's not hard, but it does take effort, and the science and practice of positive leadership deserves to be taken seriously.

The big idea: Cultivate positive habits

In this chapter, I'll outline practical ways you can nurture a growth mindset, lead with curiosity and foster a positive climate. These are all pragmatic ways for self-insight and leadership growth; however, to shift from the 'muggy middle' of leadership to a place of positive leadership, it will require intentional personal habit formation. For this reason, I've given you quite a few 'nudge lists' in this chapter so you can apply action easily.

In Chapter 5 you can explore further ways to utilize the science of leadership for motivating others through direction, progression and connection.

Cultivate a growth mindset

Let me differentiate between a fixed and a growth mindset. A fixed mindset is the belief that intelligence is a static trait that is unchanging (Dweck, 2008). On the flipside, a growth mindset is the belief that intelligence is a quality that can be developed and changed through effort.

Dweck's scientific work on mindsets had a massive impact on schools, where it was evidenced that growth-oriented mindsets had a superior result on students' performance. Interestingly, the same results are also showing up in organizations (Keating and Heslin, 2015), and although there is limited research on the link between growth mindsets and positive leadership, results from the NeuroLeadership Institute suggest that a growth mindset culture is key to transformation, engagement and innovation (Derler, 2019).

Listening to leaders over the last 20 years, I've learned that a fixed mindset actually stems from a lack of confidence and fear of getting stuff wrong. *What if I fail? What if I'm found out?* Those who have a growth mindset have become accustomed to making mistakes and being OK with that. They know their self-esteem is not damaged by 'failure', and the opportunity to embrace learning is much more interesting than limiting their potential.

FIGURE 3.1 Fixed and growth mindsets

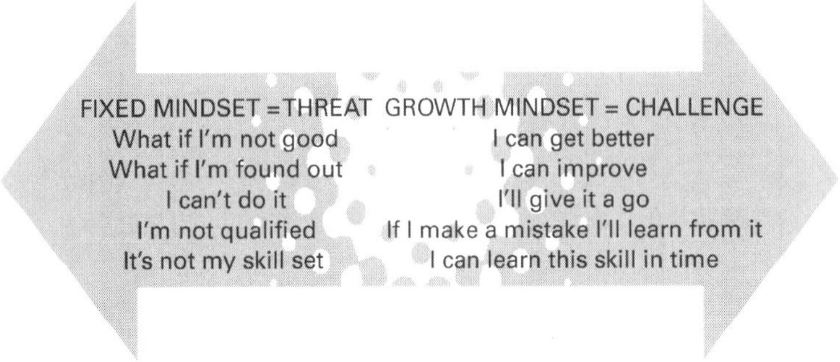

FIXED MINDSET = THREAT
What if I'm not good
What if I'm found out
I can't do it
I'm not qualified
It's not my skill set

GROWTH MINDSET = CHALLENGE
I can get better
I can improve
I'll give it a go
If I make a mistake I'll learn from it
I can learn this skill in time

Interestingly, I've also noticed that teams and organizations can have fixed or growth mindsets. You'll recognize an organization with a fixed mindset when you hear language around and about such as, 'we tried that before and it didn't work', 'we don't want any mistakes round here', 'good enough is not good enough, we need perfection!'

What I notice in leaders who recognize the energy-giving properties of a growth mindset is they promote learning, feedback and the power of mistakes. As a respondent in the NeuroLeadership report (2019) stated, 'If you truly embrace a growth mindset, you never have to have a difficult conversation. You're just having a series of conversations and you're doing them in a way that is authentic and humanistic and growth-oriented.'

So here are 10 ways to develop a growth mindset culture. A word of warning here! You want to be sure you're acting with integrity by role-modelling the right behaviours, so as you look at this list, make sure you are practising the same habits yourself.

Practical inspiration #1

10 ways to develop a growth mindset culture

1. Everyone has a learning programme, and development is seen as critical.
2. You talk about mindsets openly with personal stories of failure and success.
3. You publicly celebrate success and provide in-the-moment reinforcements.
4. Challenge projects that are 'out of comfort zone' are regularly allocated.
5. Learning from mistakes is noticed.
6. Strengths-based coaching is the norm (see Chapter 6).
7. There is a noticeable change in language, e.g. developmental replaces negative.
8. Weekly meetings are held with your team, incorporating what went well, hurdles encountered, what they learned, what they'll do differently.
9. Encourage expansive thinking, stimulated by 'what if' and 'yet' language.
10. You use growth mindset questions in coaching: 'How can you move beyond this?' 'What can you learn from this?' 'What will you do differently?' 'What's the next thing you'll do?'

> *Create space for other people to perform.*

The art here is to create space for other people to perform. As the leader, you're the architect for facilitating this culture, so stand back, give your people challenges, allow them to fail, and be there with the support.

Lead with curiosity

You might consider yourself a curious leader; indeed, I hope you do, as it's the first quality I look for when I'm on assessment panels for leadership positions. What I'm exploring here is not just the ability to ask great questions, but the skill to explore what is currently working across your organization, *before* you start fixing problems.

The root of the science lies in the field of what is called 'Appreciative Inquiry' (Cooperrider and Whitney, 2005), which explores organizational change from first understanding the 'positive core'. The assumption is that humans have a tendency to evolve in the direction of questions that are asked most often (you might remember from science classes the 'heliotropic effect', which means that all living things have a tendency to move towards sources of light and positive energy).

This is where I begin with coaching, leadership training and consultancy projects. Before you tell me all the problems and what needs 'fixing', I want to know first:

What are you like at your best?
What are your strengths?
What works and when does it work?
Who wants it to work?
When have you achieved extraordinary performance?
How did that happen?

Try this out

Curiosity through positive questions

Try this. Lead the way on any project, team meeting, coaching session by first understanding what works – you'll be surprised how rare a practice this is.

For example, a few years ago we were asked to design a new customer experience methodology for a client. The initiative started from the UK but was expected to have global reach across the client's 29 countries. The objective was to have a methodology that outlived a consultancy or a leader. Not a fad, but *just the way we do business*. This was not a new initiative – there had been a couple of expensive mistakes of imposed methodologies from external consultancies that had limited relevance to day-to-day business. We took a different approach of helping them with the starting point of understanding what already worked. We gathered teams from across the business, all levels, asking them:

When do you experience great internal customer service?
What does it look and feel like?
When does your customer service make you feel proud?
Who delivers fantastic external customer service?
Where are the pockets of excellence?
What makes a customer really happy with you?
What would a relevant customer experience methodology have to include?

The resulting methodology has lived and breathed across the organization (and all 29 countries) for eight years now, outliving most of the original leadership team and surviving recessions, cutbacks and multiple re-prioritizations of budget. It's because the starting point was one of excellence in action and owned by the organization, not my company.

Time to reflect

In your meetings over the next couple of days, when new projects are being discussed, listen to the starting point. How often does the discussion start with what's gone wrong and what needs fixing? Who asks, where it does work? When has our performance been exceptional? Who does it well? Who's a great role model for this?

Try asking some of these questions and see how the energy changes and the project direction takes a different, positive turn.

Foster a positive climate

The term 'positive climate' refers to a condition in which positive emotions predominate over negative emotions at work (Cameron, 2012), with multiple studies demonstrating that a positive climate generates 'upward spirals towards optimal functioning and enhanced performance' (Fredrickson, 2003, p 169). Essentially, individuals and organizations almost always flourish when a positive climate is present, and everyone benefits.

Importantly, positive emotions not only make people feel good in the present, but they also increase the likelihood that people will function well and feel good in the future. And more. Positive emotions broaden people's thinking, undo negative emotions, improve coping strategies, buffer against depression and build enduring psychological resources. In short, they help people survive and thrive.

You have such an astonishing opportunity as a leader to be a positive energizer. In every single communication you deliver lies the opportunity to energize or demotivate. Here are three exercises for you to practise, helping you develop those positive leadership 'muscles'.

Practical inspiration #2

A. Just one day

This might be wishful thinking, but I'd like you to imagine just one day to consciously radiate positive energy, emotion and appreciation! Indulge me and over 24 hours complete the following 10 actions:

1. One email expressing appreciation for a job well done.
2. One hand-written note to say thank you.

3. In one meeting you spot excellence in action and say so, then and there.
4. Praise someone in a function that flies under the radar and rarely gets noticed.
5. Publicize this praise in an internal message, citing their importance to the company.
6. Thank a customer with a meaningful, personal message.
7. Ask one person in your team, how are you? Show sincerity.
8. Close your laptop, put down your phone, and listen to one person with full attention.
9. Stay behind after a meeting, virtual or face to face, just to chat for a moment.
10. Ask someone about their family. How are they? What's important at the moment?

B. Positive responding

It's very common for positive feedback to barely register for the receiver. The giver is often really surprised: 'What do you mean they say they don't get much positive feedback? Only yesterday I said how great they are...'. Funny really. So much worry is expended over the delivery of criticism, but positive feedback is dropped into a conversation like a snowflake that fades away before hitting the ground. Shelly Gable et al (2004) produced some really interesting science around how we respond to positive news, called Active Constructive Responding. Most research is directed towards how we respond when things go wrong. Yet the complementary piece of the puzzle is how we respond when things go right and the subsequent benefits to the individual when you do this well. Let me walk you through an example:

Imagine your partner has just told you they've got a promotion. According to Gable et al, there are four ways of responding to positive news:

- ♥ Neutral + Positive: '*Great, well done...*' (as you go back to your work).

♠ Neutral + Negative: No response. *'Sorry, what did you say?'*
♣ Active + Negative: *'You have to be kidding me? Does this mean you're going to be travelling more and I have to juggle even more?'*
♦ Active + Positive: *'That's amazing. Well done. You worked so hard for that. What did they say? How did it go? Tell me more...'*

I'd like to think I respond to great news like a diamond. And then I remember all those times when my children were younger, brought me news and I only registered it with a sideways glance and an 'uh-huh' as I carried on typing. Oh, the shame of it! You get my point. You want to be mindful of how you respond to positive news, but also of how to offer positive feedback.

The reason positive feedback doesn't register is that you think you're giving great feedback because you've heard their news. In reality, you're giving 'heart' feedback, 'well done... you're great... terrific job... keep going' etc, before swiftly going back to what you were doing before. 'Diamond' feedback requires more effort – listening, positivity and curiosity. So, when your colleague tells you their presentation went well, stop what you're doing and be genuinely interested. Ask questions and allow them a moment of basking in your attention!

C. Emotional contagion

My final suggestion in this chapter is to remember the concept of 'emotional contagion'. That is, emotions and moods are catching. Employees are not emotional islands and will continuously spread their own moods and be influenced by others – namely yours! Unlike 'cognitive contagion' (the sharing of thoughts), emotional contagion is less conscious and more automatic.

Professor Sigal Barsade (2002), a pioneer researcher in emotional contagion, referred to those under the influence of emotional contagion as 'walking mood inductors'. It's worrying that some leaders still cling to worn-out beliefs that 'there is no place for emotions in the workplace', while unconsciously acting out and spreading feelings like anger, hostility and fear – all the while creating a toxic culture.

Fortunately, it works both ways. Increasingly, enlightened leaders will harness the knowledge of emerging brain science and recognize their ability to imbue a whole organization with enthusiasm, confidence and hope. As you do this, you'll transform work as we know it for the better.

Ten top tips for positive leadership

1. Maintain a positive perspective when difficulties arise, helping others to see what they can control and influence.
2. Show your appreciation, and then appreciate more.
3. Encourage high performance by building on strengths.
4. Role-model learning and have your own personal learning plan.
5. Regularly ask for feedback on your behaviour and take action on the feedback.
6. Have a clear leadership philosophy which guides your actions and will be recognized by others.
7. Communicate a genuine and sincere excitement for the business and the vision.
8. Practise ethical behaviour and follow through on what you say you will do.
9. Be trustworthy, and treat others with respect.
10. Give your team autonomy, allow room for mistakes and celebrate their growth mindset.

CHAPTER FOUR

Increase your confidence to accelerate your leadership growth

In a nutshell

It takes confidence to lead. The feeling of 'not knowing' or of 'imposter syndrome' will be familiar to many of you – ever-present challenges on the road to leadership growth. You are not alone in feeling vulnerable as a leader (indeed, it's essential at times) and so understanding confidence, extending your boundaries, and challenging your beliefs form the foundations for this chapter, alongside making sustainable changes to the way you think, behave and present yourself to others.

What's the problem?

The problem with under-confidence and overconfidence will be recognizable to you, as you see it every day and, in all likelihood, experience it yourself. Under-confidence can result in a leader stunting or limiting their career, as they 'play small', stay within their comfort zone and restrict their potential. Overconfidence comes with as many problems. Leaders who possess supreme confidence often act with self-importance or arrogance, taking hasty and overly optimistic decisions for themselves and their organizations. Hubris needs to be counterbalanced with prudence, as much as anxious uncertainty needs to be offset by assurance.

As Francisco Dao (2018) said in his *Inc* magazine column, 'Self-confidence is the fundamental basis from which leadership grows. Trying to teach leadership without first building confidence is like building a house on a foundation of sand. It may have a nice coat of paint, but it is ultimately shaky at best.'

But the concept of confidence is very hard to pin down and scientists have wrestled with it for decades (e.g. Bandura, 1977). Because it's such a slippery notion which can be fleeting or sustained, astonishing, surprising and career altering, it means that the word is overused and misunderstood. Confidence is one of the few words in the English language used as a noun, a verb, an adjective and an emotion. For example:

I'm not feeling confident about…
The experience gave me the confidence to start my own business…
I'm in a relaxed, confident mood…
I'd like to talk to you in confidence…

More limiting, it's also used to describe a state, or a whole way of being:

I'm not a confident person…
I don't have confidence.

As well as this, confidence is often seen as a gendered topic. With the considerable number of articles and courses dedicated to increasing women's self-confidence and 'imposter syndrome', you'd be forgiven for thinking this is solely a female issue. I notice that women more openly discuss their confidence levels to colleagues but I can assure you from experience that men and women equally want to discuss issues surrounding confidence, and science echoes my understanding (Brown, 2010; Catalyst Report, 2020). Indeed, the more we stereotype confidence as gendered, with men possessing high self-confidence and women 'suffering' from low self-confidence, the more we ignore systemic issues that need addressing.

The big idea: Confidence is an expectation!

Confidence is NOT genetic, universal or forever.
Confidence IS changeable, specific and personal.

Joyously, this means that confidence can be contained, so it's rare to feel under-confident or overconfident in every situation and much more common to experience your confidence levels depleting or increasing at specific times. For example, you might feel confident being decisive with your team, yet less so when asked for your opinion with the board. You might be an open and inspiring public speaker, yet tongue-tied when talking to a small group of your peers.

It was a revelation to me when I first read about defining confidence as an expectation. I had fudged around for years with my own definitions, but my real 'aha!' came after reading Rosabeth Moss Kanter's (2006) book *Confidence*. As she states, 'Confidence isn't optimism or pessimism, and it's not a character attribute, it's the expectation of a positive outcome.' Those of you with a healthy level of confidence expect something to work out well. With that expectation, you'll put effort in and anticipate a positive outcome. Leaders who lack confidence expect the worst and create a self-fulfilling prophecy.

And because confidence is an expectation, this means sustained confidence relies on you unravelling your thinking patterns and understanding how your thoughts create your feelings, your actions and the response you get.

It's a wonderful thing to understand. With control over your thinking, you can shift from an unintentional cycle of under-confidence, to a purposeful, positive cycle of healthy confidence. And the reverse is as true. By 'de-biasing' the thinking that creates overconfidence and impulsive behaviour, you're looking at a leader who possesses enough self-belief to lead others, combined with the ability to ask, be wrong, check in and lead teams through mutual respect, sharing and cooperation.

Try this out

Think about a situation when you experienced difficulty managing your confidence. Be specific about the event or trigger and answer the following three questions:

1 What was the trigger?
2 How did it make you feel?
3 What action did you take as a result?

FIGURE 4.1   Triggers and consequences

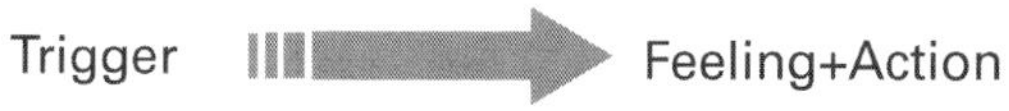

Trigger ⟶ Feeling+Action

For example, I remember well the exact moment my publishers advised me to start announcing on social media the imminent arrival of this book, creating an apparent 'raving fan base'! I felt so anxious, and delayed posting anything for at least two weeks.

After you've written out your example, add a fourth question:

4 After the trigger, what did you say to yourself in the moment?

FIGURE 4.2 Triggers and thinking

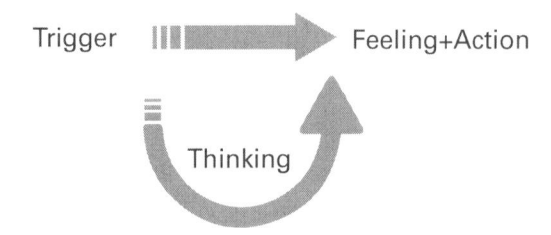

Trigger ➡ Feeling+Action ↑ Thinking ↺

If I'm being honest, what I was saying to myself was, 'you can't do this, you'll look so arrogant, what if the book's no good? What if you're found out? What if no one responds? You're going to look a fool' and so on. Therefore, I felt sick and anxious, and delayed.

You see, the art of getting to grips with your confidence is recognizing the role your thinking plays in the creation of positive or negative emotions and outcomes. If I expect the worst, I create anxiety and act in an unhelpful way. Ergo, if I change my thinking, I can shift the emotional balance, the action I take and the response I am likely to receive. Of course, I did post about the imminent book, and was overwhelmed with kind, helpful and encouraging comments. What a waste of negative energy I'd expended.

But you have to be brutally honest with yourself as your self-talk is unlikely to be kind, or something you want to show anyone else (unlike my example!).

Let's take a couple of business examples so I can show you how changing your thinking can change the outcome you create for yourself.

Example #1

Trigger: Lauren is presenting to the board. One of the directors says, 'Lauren, can you wrap up please, we're running short on time.'

Thinking:	*I knew I was no good in this role. I'm boring them. I can't operate at this level. Everyone is looking at me and thinking that I can't cope. What was I thinking that I could do this? What do I do next?*
Feeling and action:	I feel anxious, my heart's racing, I can hear myself starting to apologize and sounding hesitant. I say I'm sorry, and go through the following 10 slides really quickly.
Outcome:	The board start to notice Lauren panicking and are surprised that she finishes in the way she does. They were interested in hearing the strategic plan and wonder if it isn't as solid a plan as they thought.

Think again Lauren, with confidence...

Trigger:	Lauren is presenting to the board. One of the directors says, 'Lauren, please get to the point, you're digressing, and we're short of time.'
Thinking:	*Well at least they're interested. They're busy but engaged. I'll stop using the slides and just summarize the main points. I can do this.*
Feeling and action:	I feel in control. I say, 'I can see you're short of time. Let me summarize the main points of this plan in three points. Here's the action I'm looking for.'
Outcome:	The Chair thanks Lauren for recognizing their time issues and flexing on her presentation. They take the proposal seriously and discuss it after. Lauren gets the agreement she needs.

Example #2

Trigger: Kit is sitting on a new leadership committee, convened to respond to crises in a more effective way. He's received feedback that he needs to speak up more at meetings, as he tends to listen and take notes. At an initial meeting, he is asked for his contribution.

Thinking: *I haven't got enough information to add anything useful. I don't have all the facts. I don't know why they chose me to sit on this committee. They've made a mistake. Everyone else knows more than me. I'll look stupid if I say the wrong thing.*

Feeling and action: I feel annoyed with myself. I know I need to stop thinking about what to say, but I don't know when to talk. I say 'no, nothing to add' and leave the meeting without having made a contribution.

Outcome: Kit finds it harder and harder to contribute to the committee. The less he contributes, the harder it is to make his mark and add value. He comes off the committee after three months.

Think again Kit, with confidence…

Trigger: Kit is sitting on a new leadership committee, convened to respond to crises in a more effective way. He's received feedback that he needs to speak up more at meetings, as he tends to listen and take notes. At an initial meeting, he is asked for his contribution.

Thinking:	*Nothing bad is going to happen if I just add my opinion. It's not going to be wrong. We're all in the same boat here and everyone is learning, including me.*
Feeling and action:	I feel some anxiety but start to talk, building on one of the comments made by a colleague and showing what my last company did with a couple of crises they faced. I'm pleased with myself for speaking up.
Outcome:	Kit starts to enjoy being on the committee. He finds his voice and learns how to make a contribution, while calming his self-talk.

Name and tame your gremlin!

Like Kit and Lauren, we all have self-talk. Understanding it, accepting it and taming it is a wonderful practice. To help you start this process, it's useful to recognize that you have control over what you say in your head by giving it a name or shape. This might sound trivial, but it works. Steve Peters (2012), in his brilliant book, *The Chimp Paradox*, creates the image of self-talk as a 'monkey' you need to manage.

Instead of a monkey, I think of our 'self-talk' as gremlins. My gremlin is called Bob. He's small, hunched with a permanent scowl on his face. He sits on my shoulder and tells me when I'm going wrong, how people will laugh at me, what I should and shouldn't do. If I ignore him, he shouts louder. But I love Bob. He keeps me safe, keeps me sane, he keeps me grounded. He also needs to learn when to shut up!

Give your gremlin a name. Thank them for trying to keep you safe. Tell them you've got this and to sit there and be quiet.

Where does your thinking come from?

Once you understand where your thoughts come from, you can start to do something about them. You can expand them, love them, shift them and of course, dump them when they're redundant. Change can happen and that's why this simple matrix is so magical. Your levels of confidence will come from one (or more) of four sources as explained below and illustrated in Figure 4.3:

- You've been **told** who you are and what you can do (e.g. parents, teachers, colleagues, spouses, friends).
- You **see** other people and make self-comparisons.
- You have experiences, you **do** something and reach conclusions about your abilities.
- You **say** stuff to yourself and in your self-talk you create beliefs about yourself.

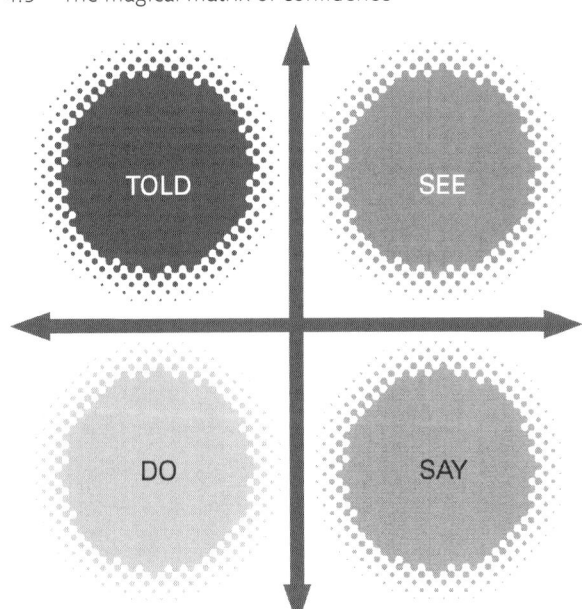

FIGURE 4.3   The magical matrix of confidence

The depth and breadth of your confidence will depend on how prevalent each of these areas is and how long you have held these beliefs about yourself. Let me bring this to light with an example of an internal job interview and four candidates with differing levels of self-confidence:

Noel: Since he was a child, Noel has been told to be strong, to not make mistakes and be self-reliant. As the new values of his organization include to 'embrace vulnerability', he had difficulty demonstrating this value in the interview.

Vanessa: Prior to the interview, Vanessa had pored over the other candidates' career histories, their LinkedIn profiles and their photos. She asked around about them and convinced herself that she didn't stack up in comparison to them. When asked how she compared herself to her peers on interview, Vanessa faltered.

Dev: This is the third time Dev has interviewed for a 'step up' leadership role. His feedback is consistent, that he is not as good in interview as he is face to face. Dev has come to believe that he is 'just not very good at interviews' and as a consequence comes across as anxious and hesitant.

Malia: Malia struggles to control her self-talk. As she catastrophizes, she imagines what will happen to her career if she doesn't get this role. Will she lose her job? Lose her self-respect? Be unable to get another leadership role elsewhere? Once this is out of perspective, Malia is poor at answering the questions about her future at the company.

If this seems like an exaggeration, with all four candidates having their own confidence crises, it's not. In fact, it is more likely that in any interview situation, thinking like this will be going on in the heads of most interviewees. Furthermore, it's healthy. I would far rather interview a 'confidently vulnerable' person than someone who believed they had all the answers, with little learning along the way.

But of course, to reach this sweet spot, you have to grab hold of your thinking, give it a good shake and ensure it doesn't overwhelm your actions. Which brings me to the next section to explore, which is how to shift your confidence.

Before we do that though, here's some reflection to do on this stage.

Time to reflect

Think about another time when you've struggled with your confidence. Don't generalize; be specific about the context, the situation and your thoughts and feelings. It might be an email, a difficult conversation, a decision you had to make or a speech you delivered. Now you have this situation in your head, I'd like you to explore where your thinking and feeling might have come from:

Told: Did your thinking reflect what you've been told in the past that you should do or feel, or how you should act?
See: Who were you comparing yourself to?
Do: When have you experienced this situation before?
Say: What were you saying to yourself in your mind?

Now reverse the context and think of a time when you felt confident. Again, be specific about the situation. Essentially, you felt in control of your emotions and actions, which is the goal here. And answer the same questions.

What differences do you notice?

When my clients observe the difference between the experience of high or low confidence, there are strong similarities. For example, when you experience low confidence, it is likely:

- You are behaving according to someone else's script of you from the past that you haven't resolved, and you are still

trying to please them. Your language often reflects this, with the word 'should'.
- You are comparing yourself to impossible or inappropriate role models. Or simply people you don't know. You've seen them on social media, you've heard them speak, you've looked at their profiles and you've reached the conclusion that you don't stack up. If you're constantly comparing yourself to others and feeling that you're coming up short – not smart enough, not successful enough, not advancing quickly enough – you can quickly spiral into self-doubt.
- You've been in this situation before and it didn't go well. You've decided that you're not very good at this and your language reflects this. You are likely to avoid the situation again.
- Your self-talk is unhelpful. Actually, it's downright unkind!

When you experience healthy confidence, it is likely:

- You've had great early learning or have resolved unhelpful scripts laid down for you in the past.
- You look towards healthy role models. Who has done this before successfully? Who manages to resolve difficulties, write respectfully, behave considerately and act with compassion? You reach out to these people for advice. You recognize that people you don't know probably have the same confidence issues going on in their head as you!
- When you experienced this situation before, and it didn't go well, you saw this as part of your learning. You sought feedback and acted on it. This is a learning loop you're prepared to invest in (see Chapter 3 for more on the growth mindset).
- Your self-talk is compassionate. You don't beat yourself up when you go wrong, you recognize mistakes happen, you move on from decisions without ruminating.

Practical inspiration

5 steps to expand your confidence

1 Change your state
2 Control the controllable
3 Challenge your thinking
4 Act 'as if'
5 Take action!

STEP 1: CHANGE YOUR STATE
To change your state, consider how you move and what you say. I'd go so far as to say that your physiology is the most important tool you have for changing your state. Picture yourself before a difficult conversation that you do not want to have and where you're feeling anxious. How are you sitting? What's the look on your face? How's your eye contact?

Now imagine the moment you're about to start a difficult conversation that you have prepared for. You know it might be hard, but you feel confident and equipped to handle it as effectively as possible. Again, how are you sitting and what's different about your facial expressions?

So, when you're feeling under-confident, even if for a fleeting moment:

> *move, make eye contact, sit up, lean forwards, open gestures, demonstrably relax and show a sense of openness.*

While people will believe what they see more than what they hear, once your physiology looks confident and impactful, you have to sound the part too:

> *Consider your breathing, the sound quality of your voice, your pitch, speed and tone.*

Listen to how you talk about yourself and your subject matter. Do you use confident words or is your language littered with 'clutter'? Do you sound hesitant or apologetic? Do you speak over people or are you actively listening?

STEP 2: CONTROL THE CONTROLLABLE
You can also change your state by changing your focus. You can do this by learning to only focus on the things you can control. Imagine you get an email on a Friday evening asking you to attend an important meeting on Monday morning. Your mind goes wild and you catastrophize. Before you know it, you've pictured yourself losing your job, your house and your future – and your confidence crashes. What can you control? You can email back asking for more details? You can distract yourself over the weekend? You can ask a colleague? Control what you can control, accept what you cannot control.

STEP 3: CHALLENGE YOUR THINKING
Astronaut Chris Hadfield (2015) describes in his extraordinary book, *An Astronaut's Guide to Life on Earth*, the power of negative thinking. As he says, 'I'm pretty sure I can deal with what life throws at me because I've thought about what to do if things go wrong, as well as right.'

To gain confidence, you have to control what you can and work to achieve the most realistic outcome for the situation. Coming up with a plan isn't a waste of time, it's productive and gives you peace of mind. This means you:

- think through the *worst* possible outcome;
- outline the best possible outcome (in as much detail as you've imagined the worst!);
- describe the most realistic, yet positive outcome (and act to make this reality).

STEP 4: ACT 'AS IF' SOMETHING ELSE WERE TRUE
Trick your mind. Pretend the person you find difficult is your best friend. How would you act then? Pretend the person who

is yawning when you're presenting is just tired. Act as if your blunt boss doesn't realize she is offending you. How different are the actions you take and responses you receive now?

STEP 5: TAKE ACTION!

The closest scientific term there is to self-confidence, is 'self-efficacy', defined by psychologist Albert Bandura (1977). Bandura held that self-efficacy, a sense of 'I can', can be most easily increased through experience and taking action. This means you have to stretchhhhhhh out of your comfort zone!

- You cannot get more confident as a presenter, without presenting more.
- You cannot sort out your difficult relationships by avoiding difficult conversations.
- You will not step up in your role without new experiences that probably scare you.
- You will only learn to be heard in meetings by speaking up more often.
- Toxic behaviour can only be addressed through your confident voice.
- Culture can only be changed by changing yourself first.

Have fun with expanding your comfort zone. Tackle things you never thought possible (I'm working towards stand-up comedy!) and learn to enjoy learning again. Remember that confidence is contagious, and so is failure, so learn to expect the former.

A final thought

What about overconfidence?

I'm aware this chapter has largely focused on those leaders who want to increase their confidence, as this is the issue that's presented in coaching. However, I want to leave this chapter with a final thought about overconfidence. At its extreme, here is the realm of toxic leadership, with bullishness leading to myriad business problems. You're looking at a leader who believes they are right, with little need to collaborate or check in with others as their way is the right way. Ultimately, such leaders create disempowered, unstable teams.

I'm hoping those of you who lack the confidence to tackle the behaviour of a toxic leader now feel more in control of your thinking, emotions and behaviour to have the right conversation. If you want further help with this, go to Chapter 10 for how to structure a difficult conversation.

If you know you're a leader who might act from the perspective of unrealistic optimism, brashness or impulsive action, I urge you to inject some vulnerability and humility into your behaviour. There is some great research which shows that the key for any healthy 'organism' (person, family, team, organization) is the mix of confidence and vulnerability (Brown, 2015; Morse, 2020).

Psychologists at Harvard agree that the best way to 'de-bias' thinking and broaden your perspective is through asking questions (Soll et al, 2015). And be careful not to lead FIRST with what you believe is the right answer, otherwise people will simply agree with you. Try questions such as:

- What haven't I thought of here?
- Why might I be making a mistake?
- What would our greatest competitor or critic say about this plan?
- What else should I consider?
- What further risks are possible?
- What would you do and why?
- Assuming we can't choose any of these options, what else can we do?

Ten top tips for confidence

1. Don't worry about being perfect. There are never right or wrong answers to complex business decisions.
2. The best that you can do as a leader is to gather the appropriate information, use your best judgement – and then go for it.
3. After you make the final decision – commit! Don't continually second-guess yourself or stay awake worrying about it.
4. Show courage on the outside – even if you don't always feel it on the inside.
5. Be comfortable with not knowing all the answers and ask for help.
6. Think of vulnerability as the *lever* for balancing under- and overconfidence.
7. Try doing new things – often! Stretch out of your comfort zone and continue to have new experiences.
8. Learn to live with failure and not being perfect. You are human. Learn from mistakes and move on.
9. Keep a journal of your thinking patterns and notice your negative thinking habits. Then start to change them by deliberately thinking differently.
10. Perspective (not perfection) is your best friend. At all times, keep your leadership role in perspective.

PART TWO

Leading your team

CHAPTER FIVE

Motivate me!

How to empower your team with a 12-step process

In a nutshell

To lead and empower people to perform in the way that suits them and achieves great results is the art and science of great leadership. This chapter will establish the importance of individual fulfilment and consider the 12 factors that enable motivation to flourish for an empowered team.

What's the problem?

The problem is that you cannot motivate anyone. Trust me. I'm the person who has stood on the stage at a corporate gig, having been asked to motivate everyone and 'build morale'. As I stare into the whites of the eyes of several hundred people, with their arms firmly crossed, I can almost hear them mutter, 'Yeah, sure, motivate me, just try.' It's a tough gig!

To be in a state of motivation is deeply personal. What inspires me (cold water swimming, stormy seas, hours writing alone, proper belly laughing, log fires) might not float your boat. Conversely, what turns me off (anyone in authority, still a teenage rebel!) might be the key to your uplifted morale.

BUT before you leap forwards a chapter in dismay, what you CAN do as a leader is create the conditions for motivation to flourish. Moreover, you play a critical role in establishing this environment. You are creating the space for people to perform.

To achieve this, it is worth understanding what motivation is, and why the motivation of your team will dip and dive. What makes this topic so complex is that motivation depends on multiple factors including the environment and task, their confidence and state of wellness in the current moment, as well as personal challenges (Pink, 2011).

You are creating the space for people to perform.

My job in this chapter is to simplify the science so that a) you have a good grasp of what motivation is and isn't, and b) you have a 12-point strategy that you can use to assess the level of motivation in your team and as a 'how to' tool for enhancing drive, so that your team can thrive:

> There's no trick to motivating others. It requires a clear, unbiased understanding of the situation at hand and deep insight into the vagaries of human nature at both the individual and the group levels. It requires, in other words, hard thinking and hard work. And when an organisation is under strain, the challenges – and the stakes – become that much higher (Fiorina, 2003).

The big idea: The Motivation Scale

Motivation is a combination of **Desire** (to achieve something), **Will** (to expend energy on it), and **Drive** (to persist despite setbacks). When scientists talk about motivation, they distinguish two different kinds: intrinsic and extrinsic motivation (Deci and Ryan, 2012).

Extrinsic motivation is triggered by external factors such as money, incentives and titles. As soon as those factors don't exist anymore, the motivation will stop. Extrinsic motivation (the traditional 'carrot and stick') has its uses but will only ever produce short-term results.

Intrinsic motivation comes from 'within' and has to do with the joy or fulfilment a certain job or task gives the person, rather than the reward it will bring. Intrinsic motivation brings long-term results. As Herzberg (2003) says, 'Forget praise. Forget punishment. Forget cash. You need to make their jobs more interesting.'

What this means in practice is that by understanding The Motivation Scale below, you get a deeper understanding as to what is and isn't motivating your team – and what to do next.

Won't do: The disengaged person. Comes to work but the 'lights are off'. Does what is asked but no more. You didn't recruit the person in this state, so what happened? At some point they fell out of love with the work, the team and their desire to contribute.

Have to: A very motivating state! And that's because it's driven by compliance, fear and deadlines. Rewards will be effective in this state but only for the short term. It's a survival state, and not one you want your team to be in for a long time. But they will be very focused.

Should do: The motivation stage of exercise, diets, new year resolutions, and to-do lists! There's a sense with this stage of 'this will be good for me', but no one is forcing you (unlike the stage before); this is all self-regulated. Hence the emotions of guilt and anxiety accompany this stage.

FIGURE 5.1 The Motivation Scale

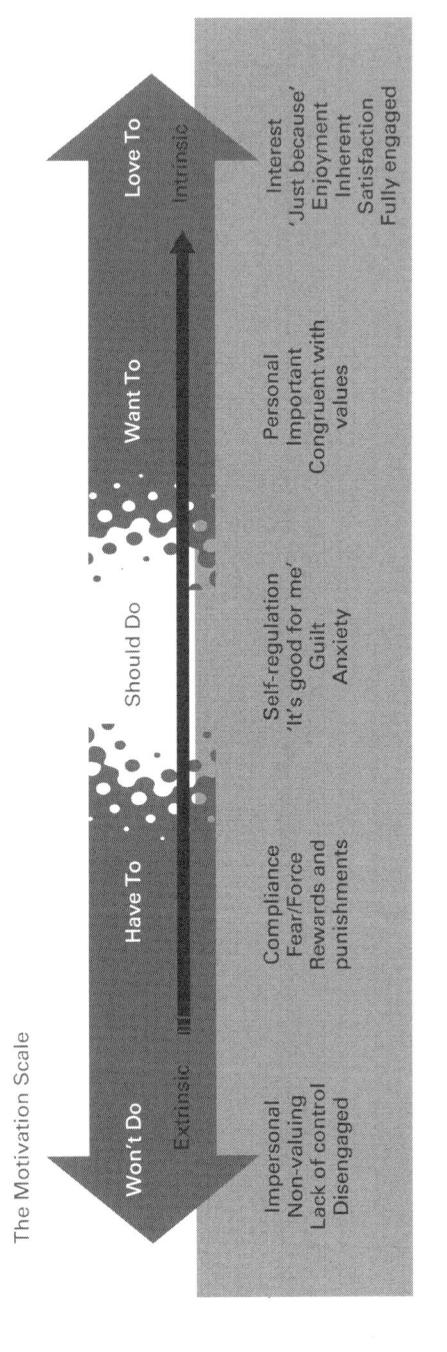

The Motivation Scale

Won't Do	Have To	Should Do	Want To	Love To
Extrinsic				Intrinsic
Impersonal Non-valuing Lack of control Disengaged	Compliance Fear/Force Rewards and punishments	Self-regulation 'It's good for me' Guilt Anxiety	Personal Important Congruent with values	Interest 'Just because' Enjoyment Inherent Satisfaction Fully engaged

Want to: We're moving into the state of intrinsic motivation. You'll achieve something because it feels good, it feels personal and congruent with your values and it is likely to feel exciting. You still want a reward at the end.

Love to: When you are fully engaged, interested and in flow (Csikszentmihalyi, 1990). You'd probably do this for no money and require no external reward. Interestingly, such reward can make you feel disengaged, because it is attaching a measurement to something you love doing, just because...

What's important to note about these five states of motivation is that it is as unusual to find someone fully disengaged at work, as it is to find someone fully in love with their work. Put another way, you can experience all five states just doing one task, or a variety of tasks across one day.

For example, when I was completing my PhD part-time over four years and needing to work every weekend, there were plenty of days when I would experience all five states in a few hours. For example, my mind would go, '*I don't want to do this... but I have to, I have a submission deadline... OK come on Lucy you really should get started... I really want to focus on this piece of research... oh I love what I'm reading here, this is exciting...*' and so on!

And so, what is the relevance of the Motivation Scale for you and your team? Here are three ways to start using it.

Try this out

a Understand the scale more effectively by applying it to yourself first. Think about the main tasks you accomplish in a 24-hour period, work and home:

When do you experience each of the five states (and what are you doing)?

What are you feeling in each of those states?

How do you motivate or reward yourself through the difficult stages?

How can you recraft your 24 hours to do more of what you love?

b   Listen to the language used by your team. Attune yourself to motivational language and you'll start to hear, 'I don't want to do this... I wish I could spend more time doing that... I should get through my to-do list...'

c   Share the scale with your team and find out where they are spending most of their day. I can think of an immediate example of this:

Nadene, previously seen as the 'star' performer of the team, had started to miss deadlines and not engage with other team members. Head down, she was quieter than normal. After a discussion using the Scale, Nadene said she was so weighed down with work, every day was a 'have to do' day. She was just getting through the to-do lists with no time for the work she loved – the induction presentations for new employees. After a good coaching conversation, Nadene and her manager re-arranged some of her workload to free up time for what she loved. It wasn't a big adjustment, but it was a worthwhile shift and Nadene appreciated that her manager noticed what was going on, took time for a good conversation and invested time and resource to reshape her workload.

Practical inspiration #1

Moving up the scale – shifting from won't do to love to

If your question is, *what can I do to help my team move up the scale?* this is the section for you.

Peak performance in teams happens when they are thriving, and 12 essential factors determine whether a team will thrive or not. The Motivation Wheel encapsulates these 12 evidence-based factors and I'll briefly outline them and then give you a host of ideas for putting them into practice.

Developing a thriving team

The 12 factors can be grouped under these headings:

Direction – a team needs to know where it is going and needs to care about getting there.

Progression – team members need to know how they are doing, to be in a learning environment and to recognize that they are getting better at what they do.

Connection – collaboration, great relationships and teamwork are essential to help a team thrive, as is appreciation for all their hard work.

Let's take a closer look at the different factors that come under these three headings:

DIRECTION

We need to know where we are heading and why (and feel something about it):

Vision
- Your team understands the vision and what you aim to achieve.
- Team members are optimistic about the future.

Purpose
- The team is proud of what they stand for.
- The team believes that their team matters and makes a difference.

FIGURE 5.2 The Motivation Wheel

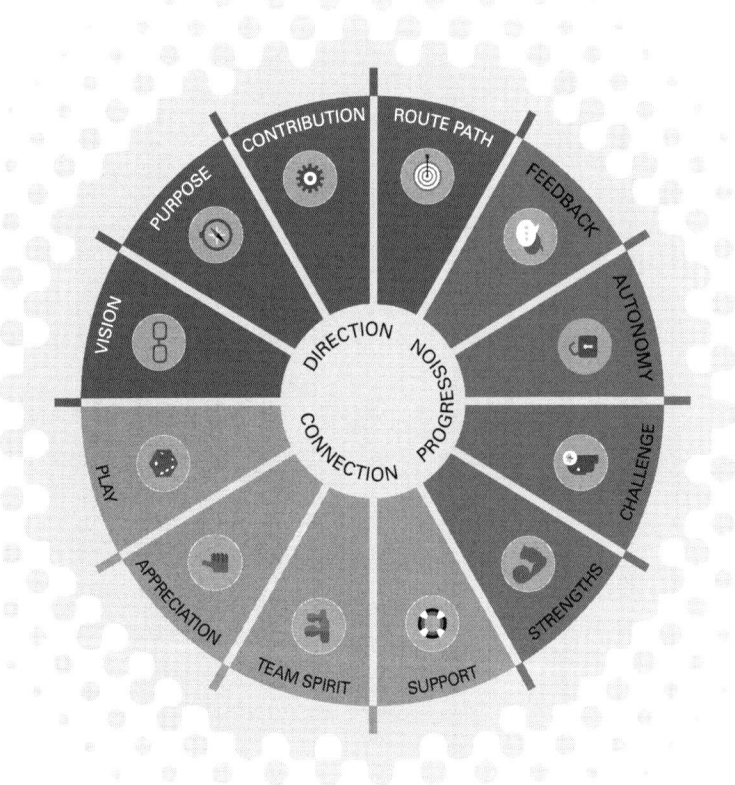

Contribution
- Team members know how they add value.
- The team wants to give their best.

Route Path
- Team members have clear objectives.
- The team knows what to do next and can achieve it.

PROGRESSION

We need to know we're getting better, each and every day:

Feedback
- Team members get regular feedback and give feedback to each other.
- The team believes they can be honest with each other.

Autonomy
- Team members are given responsibility.
- The team believes their voice is heard.

Challenge
- Team members have stimulating opportunities to advance.
- Learning is important to the team and is actively talked about.

Strengths
- Team members' strengths are recognized and valued.
- The team has opportunities to develop further strengths.

CONNECTION

We need to know that we're not alone and are appreciated for our efforts:

Support
- The team feel encouraged by you and are regularly coached by you.
- Team members can turn to each other for support.

Team Spirit
- The team like collaborating and are a great team.
- Team members look out for each other and share the same goals.

Appreciation
- Team members feel appreciated for the work they do.
- The team are rewarded for their efforts.

Play
- Team members say they have fun and there's a lot of laughter.
- The team knows that success and achievement are celebrated.

Time to reflect

As you reflect on the 24 statements above, use this blank Motivation Wheel to rate the current level of motivation of your team. I know it might be different for each person, but this exercise will get you started thinking about each of the 12 factors. With 0 at the centre, and 10 at the outside of the wheel, shade each area appropriately for your current team. Then use the 10 coaching questions to guide your thinking about your next steps.

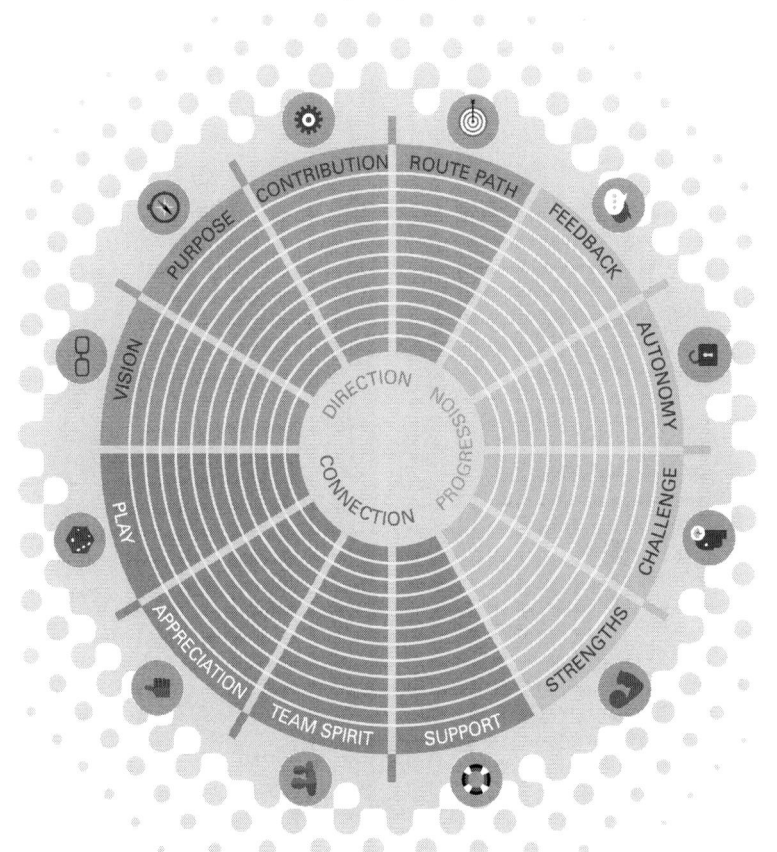

FIGURE 5.3 The Motivation Wheel worksheet

Coaching questions

1. When you look at the Motivation Wheel, where are your strengths?
2. What do you do with the team that makes this so strong?
3. How can you develop this area further?
4. Would your team agree this is an area of strength?
5. Where are the weaker areas of motivation?
6. What do you think are the reasons for this?
7. What do you believe you need to do 'more of' to strengthen this area?
8. Which other managers motivate their team effectively in this area of focus?
9. What are your 'quick wins' to inspire motivation right now?
10. What would be an effective longer-term strategy for you?

Practical inspiration #2

20 ideas for change

As you answer the coaching questions above, here are 20 ideas to help you strengthen the areas of motivation that will help your team to thrive. Pick and choose what's right for you; some ideas you'll like, some you won't and that's OK. Use the ideas as a springboard for you and your team to share and develop further inspiration.

Motivation is a shared endeavour.

I cannot stress more that motivation is a shared endeavour. Share the Scale and the Wheel with your team. Allow them to choose what will help them feel more motivated and go with their ideas. You don't have to impose yours, even if you think it's great! This is just a stimulus to help you on your motivation journey.

DIRECTION IDEAS

1. Vision: As a team leader, develop a five-minute 'Vision Speech'. In order to do this, visualize where you see the team in one year's time; describe how they are working as a team; what they are achieving; how they are demonstrating best practice; how their strengths are being employed; what the atmosphere is like in the team; what you will be hearing them say and why everyone is so pleased to be part of this team. Having done this, craft your vision speech and practise it with the team!
2. Purpose: A shared and compelling purpose helps a team pull in the same direction. Work together with your team to design this as the team is the most potent unit of change in your organization. Start this process by answering three questions:
   What does our team do?
   Who are we doing it for?
   Why does what we do matter?
3. Purpose: Collect 'Success Stories' – ensure you talk about them in your team meetings, distribute them round, link them in with the vision and purpose of your organization. Have a 'success story' of the week. Write an appreciation letter to the team member/s who contributed to this success.
4. Contribution: Keep employees informed and involved with the big picture at your organization and across the team. Show how their role serves the greater mission and increase their feeling of connectedness at work.
5. Values and Contribution: Look at your organization's values and choose one that is meaningful to you. Describe to a team member what this value means to you and how it plays out in your life. Share this with members of your team so they understand you at a deeper level.
6. Route Path: Take one project and visualize the project as a journey. Sketch out this journey and create visual milestones

along the route path. Have some fun with the team making these visuals fun and interesting. Sketch in the timeline and people you can turn to at each milestone. Plan how you will celebrate the achievement of each milestone.

PROGRESSION IDEAS

7 Personal Feedback: Ask for feedback on yourself. How often do you get useful, consistent feedback? Who can you get feedback from? How many different people do you currently get feedback from and how can you increase the quality and quantity of feedback? In order to do this, decide the skills or behaviours you specifically want to develop and choose two people who will give you honest, constructive feedback.

8 Feedback Practice: Practise your own feedback skills through using the Do/Think/Feel model. This means you are saying, 'When you do or say this, it makes me think…, which makes me feel…' Also, specific, on-the-spot praise is good! 'Praise in public/criticize in private' demonstrates respect and achieves results.

9 Autonomy: Look at your monthly planner and choose a task that will be important, new and challenging for a team member. Schedule a meeting with the team member to brief them on this challenge and schedule in times to check on progression of the task and to review progress (allow them to choose how they want this).

10 Autonomy: Instead of you running the team meeting, rotate ownership for this across the team. Each member 'owns' the meeting for that week and has five minutes within the meeting to talk about something they are passionate about this week.

11 Challenge: Look at your rewards system and develop it with your team. Thinking about each individual's personal strengths, develop new rewards that have mutual benefit, such as skills training or personal development. So, find training and skills courses that will feel like a reward to the person (while also

increasing the capability within the team) and after the course ask the individual to present back their main learning to the whole team, to increase team learning power.

12 Flow and Goal Setting: Ask every person in the team to tell each other when they are in 'flow' (that is, when their level of challenge meets their level of ability) – usually a hobby or activity they are passionate about. Lead a discussion about how you can bring elements of this into work.

CONNECTION IDEAS

13 Support: Take the time to meet with and listen to employees. One incentive or approach may not work with all, so it's important to find an individual approach. Don't be afraid to ask direct questions, like 'What motivates you to stay here?' 'What would lure you away?' and 'What kind of incentives would be meaningful to you?' Such questions give insight into the employee's values, and ensure that your approach to motivation is effective.

14 Support: Separate task coaching from personal coaching. Schedule time just to have a chat with one of your team. Have a coffee/tea together and don't let work intrude. Just catch up with them personally and let them know you value them.

15 Support: Improve your listening skills. Practise just asking 'what' and 'how' questions in your coaching sessions, without interrupting.

16 Appreciation: Say 'Thank You'. This might sound obvious, but nothing beats receiving personal thanks when an employee has put in extra effort on a project or achieved a goal that you mutually set. Giving immediate, specific acknowledgement ('Thanks for finishing the report I needed. It was critical for my meeting this morning') lets the employee know what they did and why their effort was of value. This could be followed up by acknowledging the employee at a team meeting.

17 Appreciation: Learn personal dates for every member of your team and record them, such as their birthday, anniversary, children's birthdays. Give cards or texts, or acknowledge in a team meeting.
18 Team Spirit: Encourage the team to give strengths feedback to each other that is useful and helpful, so that you build the team's capability and resilience to receive positive and constructive feedback from others. In a team meeting ask everyone to pick one other person to give feedback to. Ask each person to choose a strength that they value about the other person, and one strength that they would like to see 'more of'. Encourage the team to accompany the feedback with specific examples to deepen their feedback skills.
19 Team Spirit: Hold a competition for creating a new team awards programme or team people up to complete a project.
20 Play: How do your team want to play? It's very personal to a team! Look up 'icebreakers' in BusinessBalls (google this) and play some energy games at the start of the team meeting. Hold a themed day and raise some money for charity; bring in food and/or fruit for energy breaks or to link in with a theme for the day, e.g. Independence Day; St George's Day or Australia Day!

Ten top tips for motivation

1 Show a sincere, personal interest in each person's wellbeing and level of motivation. How has it changed over the last six months? Lead a coaching conversation.
2 When someone appears disengaged, rather than point the finger at them, ask yourself, 'What did we do to create this state of disengagement?' They didn't join you like this, so find out their motivation journey and what you need to do to put it right.

3. Share the Motivation Scale and the Motivation Wheel. What ideas do your team have? What interests them? What would they like to do differently?
4. Know the purpose of the team. Use the three questions above to craft a motivating purpose statement and make this visual and important within the team.
5. Provide challenge for your team and ensure that the level of challenge meets their perceiving ability. Too much challenge with little support is demotivating. Too little challenge is just dull.
6. Research shows time and again that the most motivating factor in an employee's career is their relationship with their boss. Make sure you are the person that your team will point to and say, 'They were really inspiring. They understood me.'
7. Encourage innovative thinking. All ideas are good ideas and allow time for a small team to work on them until you know if it is worth taking further or not.
8. Never underestimate the power of appreciation! The informed, sincere 'thank you' is worth more than any clever incentive.
9. Reward extrinsic motivation (see the scale) and give time to intrinsic motivation. Rewards can diminish tasks people 'love to do' because they will do it to the best of their ability without any reward.
10. Pay your team well enough, so that the 'pay and reward' conversation is taken off the table. Then you can concentrate on all the great stuff this person wants to contribute.

CHAPTER SIX

Strengths-based coaching

*Leverage the strengths
of your team through every conversation*

In a nutshell

Strengths-based coaching is about helping individuals to recognize and explore what they do well, so they can perform more effectively and experience a sense of energy while doing this. As high performance is leveraged through the development of strengths, how do you have strengths-based coaching conversations that work?

Success lies in practice, so in this chapter there are over 50 strengths coaching questions for you to ask, to respond to and reflect on.

What's the problem?

There's considerable science to confirm that high performance is leveraged through the development of strengths (e.g. Linley,

2008; Rath and Conchie, 2019). Yet three factors make this surprisingly hard to achieve in your leadership coaching. Firstly, evolution has gifted us with a *negativity bias*, ensuring we're attuned to any threat. That is, we are attuned to notice what is wrong with us, what mistakes the team is making, or the difficulties experienced in a day. You'll know this when you've had an interesting, positive day, but when you get home, your conversation can get fixated on the poor weather, parking, difficult people, delayed meetings, excessive talk, and so on!

Secondly, post-World War II, the broad field of psychology reacted by directing resources to helping those suffering from anxiety, stress and depression. Much was usefully learned, but the direction proved remarkably 'sticky', so much so that the field of psychology became fixed in the problem-focused 'pathology' model, which fed through into the organizational world. What is 'right' with us, or how we can develop the psychological resources towards feeling good and functioning well, was pretty much ignored until Martin Seligman rebalanced the field at the turn of the 21st century with so-called 'Positive Psychology'.

Lastly, there's a view that working with strengths is flimsy, even dangerous, and for real change to happen, we need to get to grips with weaknesses. As Chamorro-Premuzic (2016) wrote in his *Harvard Business Review* article, 'It seems a little odd, even intellectually irresponsible, to ignore our limitations and shortcomings. We cannot solve the severe problems we face in leadership with wishful thinking.'

Chamorro-Premuzic has a good point to make, if coaching is used to simply deliver positive messages at the expense of more difficult conversations (see Chapter 10). However, great strengths-based coaching is *not* about giving people an inflated view of themselves or ignoring weaknesses. It's about first paying attention to what we are good at. As Seligman wrote in *Flourish* (2011), 'Being in touch with what we do well underpins the readiness to change and develop.' Or, as one of my clients said to me recently, it was the 'golden key' to transforming the performance of his team.

The big idea: Exercise your coaching muscles

In the same way you train for a marathon, developing your fitness and muscles slowly but surely, it's the same with strengths coaching. You've got to exercise and build your coaching muscles so that:

your **mindset** is confident +
you **listen** for strengths +
you have the **willingness** to practise.

Mindset matters

Before any coaching session, the mindset you hold about yourself as a coach, the process and the other person, ultimately directs the outcome. It's that important. Take three examples from a recent coaching programme:

Sarah: 'I'm a technical expert. I haven't done their job before. I've got no idea what their strengths are or even if it matters.'

Namir: 'We're friends. We're IT experts. They'd laugh if I suddenly started "coaching" them and "exploring their strengths".'

Rachel: 'We're so busy and time stretched. It's easier to tell my team what to do, than lean into coaching for strengths. I know I have to do it… be less directive, more of a listener, I just don't have time.'

All three of these beliefs will have an unhelpful impact on the outcome of the coaching, no matter how good a coaching model is. I understand the problem here. Of course, at the beginning it feels awkward to coach team members who are friends, and yes, coaching takes time, even if you know it will pay you back in the long term. And everyone questions their confidence as a coach, no matter how experienced.

Don't let this stop you. In my experience, even the most hardened, cynical colleague finds strengths coaching surprisingly useful, relevant and practical – even if they don't tell you immediately! So here are three mindset positions worth holding for a good outcome:

1. Our areas of greatest potential are in the areas of our greatest strengths.
2. We succeed by fixing our weaknesses *only when* we are also making the most of our strengths.
3. Coaching through strengths is the smallest thing you can do to make the biggest difference in your team.

Listening for strengths

Open any good coaching book and there will be an emphasis on listening; unsurprisingly, as listening is the critical skill for engagement. However, not everyone is skilled at listening for strengths (again, the effect of the negativity bias) and often the desire to be helpful or give the answer gets in the way of good listening. Equally, our interest in the problem can blind us from seeing strengths. Derailers to listening can be summarized in three ways:

- **Distractions**
  As Janie van Hool suggests in her book, *The Listening Shift* (2021), 'Listening is hard because we are so distracted – our bodies, our thoughts, our emotions and our environment are constantly calling out "NOTICE ME!". Being a great listener is not magic, or talent – it's self-awareness, discipline, challenge. You have to find a way of silencing all that noise.'

- **The tug of tell!**
  Most leaders I know REALLY want to give their advice! You might recognize this. What happens is that you start by asking some great open questions: 'How do you go about this?' 'What do you want to do next?', etc. but the moment you hear a problem you can solve, you leap into the conversation and offer an explanation, a solution, an answer. Coaching is over – we've moved back to the management circle (see Chapter 1).
- **Listening for problems**
  Coaches are usually trained to ask problem-focused questions, for example, 'What stops you…?' 'What's the real problem here?' 'What are the barriers?'. These are all good questions that shed light on past issues, barriers and problems, but they are not helping your colleague understand, explore or reflect on their strengths.

Willingness to practise

And so, like many leadership skills, it comes down to practice. Here are three exercises to help you learn to exercise your strength coaching 'muscles'. I'm suggesting you practise in three ways: with your team; with your peers and with an individual.

Try this out #1

The timeline exercise

This is an invaluable exercise for drawing out your team's strengths resources, and my starting point in any team-based coaching practice.

On your next Monday morning team meeting, ask each of your team to draw a rough timeline from the last week or month, highlighting the peaks and troughs. This can be very rough, as shown in Figure 6.1:

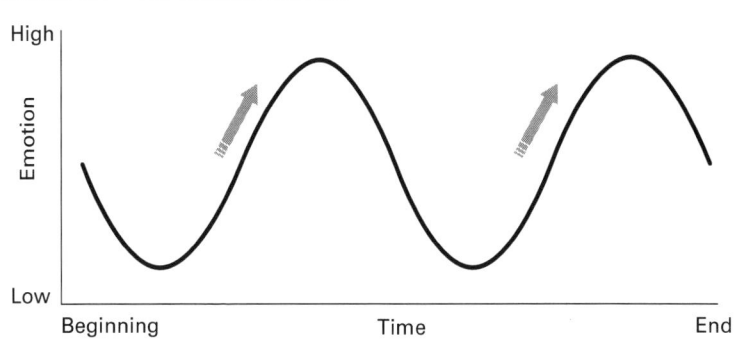

FIGURE 6.1   The timeline exercise

Emotion (High to Low) plotted against Time (Beginning to End), showing a wave curve with upward arrows on the rising sections.

These upward curves show you how people have come through a difficult time and learned something important

You might be drawn to the specific highs and lows, but I want you instead to concentrate on *how* your team has come through the troughs each time. Where the arrow is in this diagram is the place of resourceful strength. Here are some questions to practise asking:

- What strengths did we as a team draw on to come through the downturn?
- What have we learned about ourselves as a team?
- What matters? What's useful for us to take note of?
- How will we draw on this learning again in the future?

What you are doing here is helping your team recognize that they already have a mighty resource of strengths they are naturally drawing on. Once this is recognized, it is repeatable for the future. Very powerful learning.

Try this out #2

Discovering strengths

Buddy up with a peer and ask to share a strengths-based guided conversation with them. Just 15 minutes either way. Focus on *asking* the questions (not chatting), *listening* for the strengths and *reflecting* on the information to ask further questions. There are two edifying outcomes from this exercise: a) it is hard but worthwhile to focus on just asking, listening and reflecting, and b) you will learn so much about your colleague by focusing on their strengths.

Here are my TOP 10 strengths questions for you to practise:

1. What makes you feel like you have had a successful day at work?
2. What are you doing when you feel at your best? Why do you think that this is so?
3. When do you feel most alive and energized?
4. To what extent do you use your strengths at work?
5. How could you utilize your strengths to a greater extent at work?
6. What gives you a sense of pride?
7. What would you say that you are most passionate about?
8. Can you describe what it feels like to enjoy this passion?
9. When do you feel that the 'real you' is coming out?
10. Which situations do you find yourself in when you are expressing the 'real you'?

Try this out #3

Dialling up/dialling down

I encourage you to introduce a strength psychometric to your team, such as the CliftonStrengths Talent Assessment, the Strengthscope tool, or the VIA (Values in Action) Character Strengths Survey, the latter being the only one that is available at no cost, with a strong evidence base (there's a list of these strengths in Chapter 12). Alternatively, you can give your team a pack of Strengths cards from my website.

Once this person has chosen their top strengths (and an idea of their middle to low strengths), support them to reflect on their findings with the following questions. The purpose here is threefold: a) to help the individual recognize the power of their top strengths, b) to relate this to their performance in the workplace, and c) to learn how to flex their strengths.

Top strengths:

- When do you use your top strengths?
- What does each strength offer you?
- How does this strength make you feel?
- What other novel ways can you think of to use this strength that would serve you?

The workplace:

- How well do you use your strengths at work?
- How else can you use your strengths in your role that would energize you?
- In what ways are your strengths not utilized? How can this be changed?
- How can I as your manager employ your strengths more effectively at work?

Dialling up/dialling down:

- What strength/s would you like to DIAL UP this week to help you cope with the challenges you are facing? How can you dial it up?
- What strength/s do you need to DIAL DOWN this week so you can more effectively face your challenges?
- What strength/s can you DIAL UP to improve your relationship with 'X'?
- What strength/s can you DIAL DOWN to enhance this relationship?

Practical inspiration

SABAT – a coaching model

After committing to practise, how do you incorporate this learning by holding a good strengths-based coaching conversation from start to finish? If you are new to coaching, start practising this model from the beginning. If you're an experienced leadership coach, look at the 'B' of SABAT, so that you complement your existing practice by building on the positives and broadening their knowledge:

- Set up
- Agree
- Build and broaden
- Affirm
- Take action

FIGURE 6.2　The SABAT coaching model

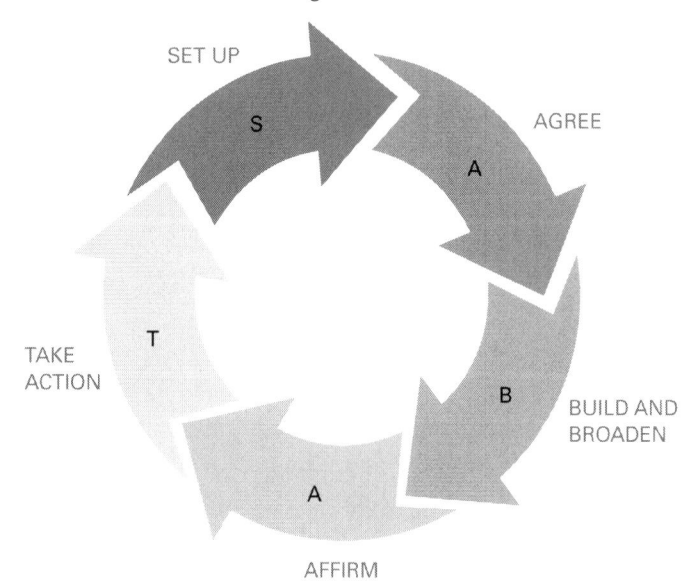

SET UP

For any coaching conversation, there are three essential questions to ask yourself before you start. Strengths work is no different:

a Am I sure this is a coaching conversation? (Or am I just trying to lead them to my decision and tell them what to do?)
b How do our personality styles differ? (And what does this mean I need to flex about my behaviour for a positive outcome?)
c Is my intent positive? (Am I in a good state to hold this conversation?)

ASK AND AGREE

Open questions are the building blocks for any coaching conversation. So, if you're new to coaching, just stay with 'how?' or 'what?'. If you find yourself asking, 'don't you think...?' you're leading the conversation. Go back to the questions above (and Chapter 1) and check your intent.

The main purpose of this stage is to ask and agree the boundaries of the conversation, and the desired outcome from the coachee. Think of this conversation as a contract, and a vital starting point to keeping the conversation on track. In strengths-based coaching you are asking the coachee to think through the differences they want as a result of the coaching:

Where do you want to start?
What will be most useful to focus on for this conversation?
What is going to give you the most value today?
What do you want to be different as a result of our coaching?

BUILD AND BROADEN

This stage is beautifully simple and subtle yet will make a real difference to your leadership coaching practice. Rather than starting with problem-based questions, your starting point here is to **Build on the Positives,** by first asking someone to think through what already works:

When does this go right for you?
When has this already worked for you?
Where have you experienced some success with this before?
What did you do differently?

In their book, *The Solutions Focus* (Jackson and McKergow, 2006), the authors suggest adding in a scale at this stage, which gives you and the other person a benchmark for progress. If you want to use a scale, ask the person to rate themselves on a scale, 10 being the ideal outcome and 0 being the opposite. Then ask the individual what they have already done successfully to reach that number.

This stage is so important there are two parts to it, and the second part is to **Broaden your Knowledge.** The purpose here is to help the individual broaden their capacity to strengthen their capabilities by finding who else can add value to this potential solution:

What else works?
Who does this already in the organization?
Who would be a good role model?
How can I help?

Think of this stage as adding *Breadth and Depth* to the coaching conversation.

AFFIRM

This is a small stage, often skipped, but invaluable to the success of your strengths practice. Not only do you affirm this individual's resourceful choices, broad thinking and positive direction, but it shows you have listened and can reflect back their language:

What I'm hearing that's great...
What I really like about what you've been saying is...

TAKE ACTION

There are some specific questions to ask at this stage. Firstly, small steps matter! If you're using a scale, just nudge one step forwards. If not, ask the question below. Remember to find out what progress is going to look and feel like – to themselves and to others. And take note of the last question: '*How do you want me to support you further?*' Lastly, keep in mind that coaching gives ownership and autonomy to the other person. So, find out how they want you to review their progress:

What small step will take you forwards positively (in the direction you want to go)?
What action will move you forwards one number on the scale?
What do you want to do next?
How will you notice progress has been made? (How will others notice?)
How do you want me to support you further?

SABAT in practice

J is a new senior leader, and this is her first month in role. J has an expressive personality, is easy to talk to and has an open willingness to coaching. Below are the barebones of your conversation with J, with the stages of SABAT on the right-hand side.

FIGURE 6.3   SABAT in practice

You: What do you want to focus on in this conversation?	**Ask**
J: Lots. I barely know where to start. Getting to know my team, building trust, assessing personalities... yes?	
You: OK. We have an hour together. What focus will give you the greatest value in our time together?	**Agree a focus**

FIGURE 6.3 *continued*

J: I'd like to start talking about N. He's the most senior leader in the team and I'm struggling to build trust here – you've worked with him before. Advise me here?	
You: Talk to me first about what you have already done as you're adept in this area, with great emotional intelligence. When are your efforts at building trust working? When do you feel you are laying down the foundations of trust?	Don't leap to advising here. Patience. **Ask first** Build on the positives
J: It works when I slow down, ask for lots of information and give the 'why' of the decision. I guess when I make the effort to give the evidence behind the decisions. I don't always have that time, so I talk with pace and get frustrated at the critical response.	
You: It's great you can identify when it works, when it doesn't and what the difference is. So, what do you need to do more of, to get more of the positive behaviour from N?	Affirm Build on the positives
J: I guess more time, more detail, more evidence until the trust is built.	
You: OK. Great. Who else can help you here? Who has a great relationship with N? What do they do differently?	Broaden their knowledge
J: C and A have worked together for years, they're different but work together very efficiently.	
You: Good. What else?	Broaden their knowledge

FIGURE 6.3 *continued*

J: OK, as I think about this, at our next 1:1, I can ask N how he would like it structured, rather than doing it my way. Give it more time. Set an agenda... yes?	
You: Sounds great and what I'm hearing is that you're working this through really effectively, understanding the differences between your personalities and flexing yours to build trust and get a better outcome. Good to hear, well done. So, what small step do you want to take next?	Affirm Take action (1)
J: I think the easiest next step that'll make the greatest difference is the 1:1. I'll set it up this afternoon.	
You: Good. And how will you know you've made a positive difference in the relationship with N?	Take action (2)
J: I'm not sure yet, but I think when he starts to talk to me more openly and when I notice that I'm flexing towards him. It'll be give and take for a while I think.	
You: You're right, it will. Thanks for working this through with me and I'd like to hear how you'd like to review this with me going forwards?	Take action (3)
J: I'm happy to take this forward now on my own, but I'll review progress again with you at our next 1:1. Many thanks.	

Time to reflect

In closing this chapter, a final word on reviewing progress. Progress is fundamental to our motivation and core to the philosophy of any strength work. And it's up to you to **notice** progress, **reward** improvement and **celebrate** success.

Ten top tips for strengths-based coaching

1. With your coaching, start with the premise that people already have the resource of strengths. Find out what they are through your questions.
2. Practise listening for strengths. Work with your team, your peers and colleagues. Ask to have a strengths-based conversation until your focus naturally shifts.
3. Shift your language from problems to a solution focus. Instead of 'why does this go wrong?', shift to 'when does this go right?'
4. With your questions, think Breadth and Depth. Build breadth by building on the positives, expand depth by broadening their knowledge.
5. Adults need appreciation. Affirm their answers and reward individuals for thinking problems and solutions through autonomously.
6. Avoid 'The Tug of Tell!' Sit back, contain yourself and ask another question.
7. Small steps matter. Encourage the person you are coaching to make the least change to gain the greatest result.
8. Progress is motivating. Notice it, reward it and celebrate it.
9. Self-assess your own progress regularly. *Did you help someone improve their performance today? Did you ask great questions that enabled someone to fulfil their potential? Did you recognize and acknowledge someone's achievement? Did you focus on someone's future potential?*
10. Keep on doing what works (and stop doing what doesn't work!).

CHAPTER SEVEN

Less talk, more walk!

*How to lead a diverse team
and drive a culture of belonging*

In a nutshell

Having a diverse workforce is good business and leading a team who feel they belong is motivating for everyone. While diversity is everyone's business in your organization, in this chapter I'll guide you through an action plan for increasing your own capacity to lead on diversity, energize others and make meaningful progress, together with practical strategies for driving a culture of belonging.

What's the problem?

Diversity is not 'a problem', it's the solution. Having a workforce that is representative of a blend of gender, age, cognition, ethnicity, sexuality, disability and social background should be as natural as breathing. It's what the world looks like, it's what your customers look like, and it's what your staff want you to stand for. Yet despite a multiplicity of diversity initiatives, the results remain underwhelming. For example, white women and people of colour remain seriously underrepresented in many industries and in many companies' senior ranks (Ely and Thomas, 2020); one in three people in the UK, and one in four in the US say they don't have a sense of belonging at work and, pertinent to this chapter, less than half the workforce in the UK (and only slightly more in the US) believe their leaders take personal responsibility for diversity (Jacob et al, 2020).

So, what is the problem? Broadly, there are five issues:

1 It's not part of the culture.
2 We have an unconscious desire for similarity.
3 There is a broad fear of getting it wrong.
4 There remains an underlying threat of a 'zero-sum game'.
5 The road to diversity can be messy!

I'm passionate about diversity and have read, studied, consulted and actioned it, and I understand why so many people tiptoe around this subject. If you look at the five problems above, 'fear' and 'threat' are big hairy emotions that people want to avoid. Equally, our desire to be liked and for similarity is as strong, meaning that existing patterns of recruitment, promotion and talent diversity remain entrenched in so many organizations. Let's explore the organizational problems associated with diversity further, as by raising the lid and looking under the surface, we'll be able to craft sustainable solutions. The desire to lead, and belong to, a diverse and inclusive organization needs to shift from functional to cultural. I recently interviewed Kathryn Jacob and Sue Unerman (2020), who (together with Mark Edwards) co-authored the inspiring, practical book, *Belonging*, tackling diversity in the media industry. I was struck by Sue's suggestion to ask random people across your organization, 'who owns diversity?' 'If you get the answer, "HR (human resources) are dealing with it", you've lost it.' Her point is well made.

For the subject of diversity to be anything more than tokenistic or a tick box exercise, it has to be owned by everyone, embedded in the culture. That means the practice has to move from the functional aspects of diversity, through to the behaviours of inclusion and then further embedded in the feeling of belonging. As Sue further suggests, 'belonging is not something the CEO or head of HR can impose. It has to be something that everyone who works in the organization truly believes, and truly feels. It's everyone's job.'

But pay heed to the lure of our desire for similarity! As Herminia Ibarra's (2015) research indicates, similarity is the primary determinant of chemistry in a professional relationship. Meaning, we're attracted to people with whom we have something in common, as they remind us of ourselves. And who doesn't want to work with people with whom you feel comfortable? An easier and safer life, yes, but a less successful and inclusive one.

And what of fear? Or as a client recently said to me, 'What if I make it worse?' There's a fear associated with diversity, for saying the wrong thing, using incorrect language, or perhaps messing it up. And when that fear is mixed with the potential of a zero-sum game, that is, a win/lose threat (if you win, I lose), it's little wonder that so many diversity initiatives have fallen on stony ground.

So, yes, the pursuit of diversity can be messy. But perhaps that's your special job – to lead through the messiness? As Dan Brooke (2017) says, 'It's hard and sometimes it feels like diversity of thought is not leading you to the promised land. But keep going – the milk and honey will come.'

Time to reflect

Your starting point

Whatever your starting point is on this diversity journey is OK; you're here and you're on it! Here are some questions to get you started:

1. Why do you care about diversity?
2. What does your business currently do about diversity?
3. In what ways have you got involved?
4. What more would you like to do?

The first question is the most important, as without a meaningful connection to the issues surrounding diversity, inclusion and belonging, this will always be a functional project for you. Perhaps you put your team on a training course (which you don't attend), or recruit a minority of people who look, sound or think differently to most of the team, and you feel you're playing your part.

The fact that it's good for business matters, and there's enough evidence for you to feel confident that by leveraging diversity and taking action, you can reap real and full benefits for the workforce, your team and the customer, as well as economic gains. As Harvard's 15-year review of diversity efforts stated (Ely and Thomas, 2020), 'Diverse teams are more effective than homogenous teams, produce higher quality work, make better decisions, and are more engaged at work.' Put another way, I like Dan Brookes' (2017) sentiment, 'People with different identities have different ideas, and different ideas have a knack of being successful.'

To make this work, you have to undergo the same shifts of heart, mindset and behaviour you're looking for your organization to do. Hence, less talk, more walk!

The big idea: Less talk, more walk!

So, a successful diversity strategy that reaches beyond numbers and embraces inclusion and belonging, takes many people. It's everybody's business. But this chapter is about how *you* can make a personal difference, so through reflective questions and practical exercises I'll help you influence action and show you mean business. It's much less onerous (and much more joyful) than you might think. Here is a four-phase action plan for leading the way:

Awareness: Start with curiosity
Energize: Lead from every seat
Empathize: Demonstrate understanding
Action: Show you mean it

FIGURE 7.1 From awareness to action, a four-phase strategy

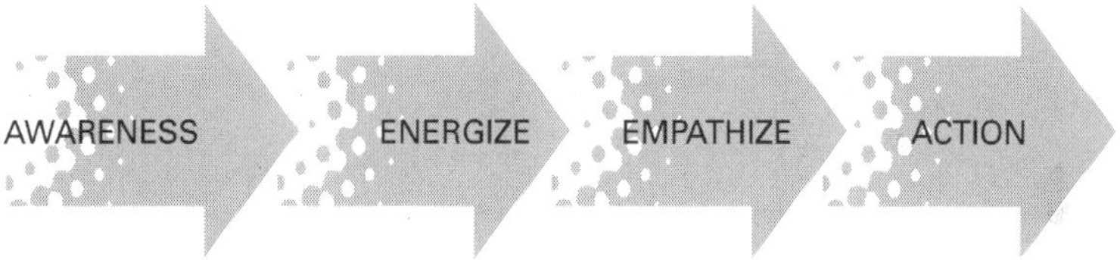

AWARENESS → ENERGIZE → EMPATHIZE → ACTION

Try this out

Awareness – start with curiosity

The first step to build your awareness is through three simple reflective exercises:

a Look around you in the office (if you're working virtually, do the same on your next team call). What do you see? A healthy blend of gender, race and age, or a homogenous group of people who look and sound alike?

b   Notice what happens in your meetings. *How much diversity of thought happens?* This is the beating heart of diversity. Beyond what you see, you're looking for people who have different points of view, who feel safe to disagree, challenge and confront. And how do people listen to this disagreement? Do they open up the conversation and demonstrate curiosity, or close it down and move on?
c   Next, imagine someone is coming for a job interview and they do their research beforehand. They google the leadership team and explore manager profiles on LinkedIn – what will they see?
    ○ Does everyone look the same or is there diversity across gender, race, religion, region, etc.?
    ○ Is there a diverse board of directors?
    ○ Does your mission statement explicitly state your commitment to D&I?
    ○ Is there recent news about progressive stances you've taken in this area?
    ○ Will they feel they belong in your organization?

After you've started to build your awareness, the next stage is to use your influence to energize senior leadership towards action and not just because great diversity will bring economic gain to your organization. That's unlikely to be motivating to someone who wants to join you and might think, 'so I'm a token figure who'll improve your diversity numbers?' This is what scientists call an 'add diversity and stir' approach (Ely and Thomas, 2020).

Diversity, inclusion and belonging work when the purpose is greater than economic gain. In other words, a sustainable strategy works when it embraces a broader vision of success encompassing learning, creativity, flexibility, equity and human dignity.

Energize – lead from every seat

While every article and book written about diversity stresses that it's everyone's responsibility, if it's not role-modelled from

the top with the subject given the airspace and action it deserves, your company's efforts will fail. To drive an inclusive culture for your teams, change needs to be embedded on three levels of the business: the organizational, team and individual levels. In the next two sections of this chapter, we'll explore team and individual changes you can affect, but first it's worth asking yourself, what role do you take in leading systemic change?
Consider the following case study.

CASE STUDY

Having been highlighted in a report for their poor ranking in national diversity tables, the CEO and executive leadership of Company Inc. have made a public commitment to driving diversity. They have committed funds to a diversity strategy, 'together we're better', and a research project to understand their numbers. When they released their current statistics, the CEO admitted they 'had a lot to do' and vowed to do better. And positive efforts were made with a diversity survey, mandatory diversity training courses, and an increase in the diversity demographic. But, in a recent engagement survey, the response to the statement, 'I feel I belong here' was disappointing, with 32 per cent answering 'disagree'. It was a recognition from the leadership team that diversity of people will not necessarily translate into diversity of thought or a sense of belonging. This was an issue that holds real meaning to the leadership team, and after a brainstorm about how to unearth a real sense of awareness of the issues at heart, a more radical approach was taken.

With everyone's permission, they recorded employees, in their own voices, and then the leadership team listened back in the dark, allowing them to truly hear and internalize their colleagues' sentiments. The comments were moving and dismaying in equal measure, such as:

The first time I felt I belonged was when all our department wore a rainbow lanyard during PRIDE month.
There's virtually no woman in this company who is my age. If anybody. I mean presumably somewhere there's somebody my age but I'm not aware of them.

> *I think about the people who sit round the table with me; there are no other black people. Not one. And in the level below me there are probably two out of 40 or 50. I'm definitely an outsider with no role models.*
>
> *Organizationally the culture is very bullish, it is all kind of go down the pub, sort it out, we're all mates, we're all 'sorter outers'. I'm a 'wanna go home' kind of guy and it's hard to fit in.*
>
> *Belong? Not when you think about this comment last week: 'You know for an older bird, you're quite attractive.'*
>
> *To celebrate mental health week, our department had a get-together called 'Dare to Belong'. I've never been so proud of this organization than at this event. People shared their experiences of difficulties with their mental health, including senior leaders, and it's sparked an openness and compassion in our function I've not seen before. I felt I could be myself for the first time working here.*
>
> The result was a breakthrough conversation where most senior executives shared their own stories and decided to make belonging a core element of their culture going forwards.

This is how you can spearhead interest and energize action. The first stage for this business was to demonstrate action. Writing about inequality in the workplace, Raval and Amphlett (2021) suggest seven ways to energize the organization to diversity commitment:

1 Carefully consider the barriers to diverse recruitment by refreshing the language of your job advertisements and advertise in places that will attract a broader potential recruitment pool. For example, asking for a candidate with 'cultural fit' carries an implicit bias; words such as 'fearless, dominant, driven' repel many female applicants, and your 'work hard, play hard atmosphere' can shun parents.
2 Emphasize your desire to listen through staff appraisals, surveys, questionnaires.

3 Capture your current diversity data, setting inspiring targets and publishing progress.
4 Set up and encourage participation in diversity networks.
5 Hold a mandatory programme on diversity training that's regularly reviewed and updated.
6 All managers and leaders to have a responsibility for diversity and inclusion, with diversity KPIs as part of their objectives.
7 Commit to zero tolerance of harassment and bullying.

This stage can still be pretty hands-off for many leaders, and therefore the second stage is to become personally involved and responsible. The case study highlighted above shone a very acute light on the issues at hand and, importantly, demonstrated that the leaders were prepared to be part of the solution beyond demographics. Ask yourself:

- What conversations about diversity are had around the senior leadership table?
- How does your organization celebrate difference?

Let's turn the lens now from reflection to practical action. In the next two sections we'll explore down-to-earth ways you can role-model compassion and empathy for difference in your team and spearhead diversity of thought across your function.

Empathize – demonstrate understanding

Great intentions around diversity often feel abstract, or too big and intractable to take action, yet your team deserve to feel included and have a sense of belonging. Karen Blackett, OBE, is a force to be reckoned with. CEO of media giant GroupM, Karen was appointed by the UK prime minister in 2018 as Race Equality Business Champion and is non-executive director for the UK Cabinet Office. She uses the example of Marvel Avengers as her role models for building a successful, diverse team (Jacob et al, 2020):

I believe the best teams are made up of very different people, all excellent in their varied ways. Just as the marvel avengers are. You need teams that complete each other, rather than compete. You wouldn't want a whole team made up of Incredible Hulks, but a Hulk, with a Captain America, with an Iron Man, Black Widow and the Scarlet Witch, that could be exactly what you need!

Practical inspiration #1

What's it like to be you?

When I'm facilitating programmes designed to expand team understanding and develop cognitive diversity, this is the first exercise I turn to. It's based on the premise that most individuals, instead of welcoming diverse thinking, secretly wish that everyone else was more like them! This set of eight questions acts as a catalyst to a better conversation on diversity of thought and empathy for different ways of responding to each other.

Let your team know you'd like to introduce an exercise on diverse thinking and appreciation for difference, and why you think it's important for your team. Perhaps share Matthew Syed's (2020) book, *Rebel Ideas*, with the team. Syed's premise is that 'Teams that are diverse in personal experiences tend to have a richer, more nuanced understanding of their fellow human beings.' He argues that diverse teams that are able to genuinely work together and question their leaders produce the best decisions.

Firstly, I suggest you send these questions to everyone prior to any form of team get-together. Give people time to think through their answers – especially the more introverted reflectors who will want time for initial reflection.

You can share the answers together in a team meeting, but I prefer to start the reflection in pairs. Allow people time to talk and share, then you can ask the pair to feed back their shared learning to the team. It's a more elegant way to gain insight than putting an individual on the spot and asking them to share their deep feelings!

1. At my best, I am…
2. To get the most from me, you can…
3. I prefer to communicate by…
4. When I'm stressed, I feel…
5. When I'm under pressure or in conflict, you'll recognize this because I…
6. You can make things better by…
7. You can make things worse by…
8. One thing I would love you to know about me is…

Action – show you mean it

As a leader who wants to step up to diversity initiatives, here are a plethora of pragmatic ways you can increase a sense of understanding, and belonging, in your team and organization.

Practical inspiration #2

Make it meaningful

- Mentoring. When mentoring is discussed, the assumption is often made that this is about building a relationship with a senior leader you admire. I suggest you reverse this process and ask senior leaders to build a relationship with a junior team member they admire. Start this process of reverse mentoring so that you're showing inter-generational understanding and interest. As the *Belonging* authors stress, 'By empowering younger members to ask questions, offer opinions and work closely with a more senior person, you start the opportunity to open up ideas and interests.' Meetings. Work hard to build psychological safety into your meetings,

emphasizing the value of every voice. To do this, set clear expectations with the team. Rotate ownership of the meeting and encourage everyone to offer a point of view. Practise active listening and summarize frequently: 'When you say this, what I think I'm hearing is…?'
- Avoid HIPPO thinking – Highest-Paid Person Overrides all (Syed, 2020). Don't give your opinion first!
- Nip negativity or unwanted 'banter' in the bud. If you have a team member who speaks negatively about peers, or excludes others through inappropriate jokes, talk to them about it. Be clear, let them know you work together as a team and negativity will not be tolerated. If you allow negativity to stand, it can become contagious and spread to others.
- Practise using ACE with points of view you either don't understand or disagree with. Role-model this three-point practice first, and then coach the team to use it too. It's one of the simplest, yet most powerful means of increasing understanding and empathy:
  - **Acknowledge** – that the person has an interesting point of view.
  - **Clarify** – with questions.
  - **Explain** – your point of view. For example:

    (Acknowledge) John, clearly you feel passionate about the way we're working, and I'm interested in hearing more.

    (Clarify) When you say we're slowing the process by involving everyone, what do you mean? What do you want instead? How can we achieve this?

    (Explain) My aim was inclusivity of thinking. Let's discuss how we achieve this, while respecting the need for pace in some discussions.
- Put diversity and inclusion on the agenda every month. Don't skip it, or quickly move on to the next point. Make it meaningful and listen to the actions everyone is taking.
- Share your stories and insight. There is nothing more powerful than sharing your own stories. Think about times when you

have felt like an outsider, or someone who didn't belong. Lead the way and find an appropriate time to share your insight.
- Ensure your talent is sponsored. Instead of letting this process be informal (chat at the pub, golfing together, etc), recognize that it's your responsibility to get individuals in your team noticed and formalize this process. Plenty of extremely talented people who don't have a natural sponsor go unnoticed and eventually leave.
- Show that failure is OK. Make it a regular feature of meetings as long as it's accompanied by learning. Avoid blame and welcome the learning from mistakes. Instead of 'What happened and why?' ask 'How can we make sure this goes better next time?'
- Think about activities that exclude others, e.g. parties in the evening, golf days, after-work drinks, and find different ways to enjoy getting together.
- Celebrate diversity success. Notice the difference in the team when people feel they belong and be proud of the efforts and progress you and your team have made.

This chapter is about helping you increase your awareness about diversity, energize others to action, demonstrate your empathy for different opinions and make meaningful progress, so that you drive a culture of belonging. Each week, I recommend you ask yourself in your reflection journey, *'This week, how have I created conditions where every person can contribute in their unique, meaningful way and feel safe and secure doing this?'*

Ten top tips for building diversity, inclusion and belonging

1. The benefit of diversity has to be felt by everyone. Ensure you don't set up a zero-sum game (I win/you lose). Everyone can win through building cognitive diversity.

2. Allow different voices to come to light in your meetings. Work hard to develop a fair share of voice where all contributors feel welcome and appreciated.
3. While diversity is everyone's business, it's your responsibility as a leader to be a role model. Stand up for difference, speak out when you recognize others being excluded, through language or action.
4. Diversity takes effort, and it'll be worth it. So, move from a rhetoric of 'diversity is good', to 'diversity is good, *and* it takes effort'. Galvanize people towards effort.
5. Maximize joy and connection. Don't be po-faced about diversity. Show how bringing different-minded people together to solve problems can be a joyful part of belonging to your team.
6. Be open to feedback yourself. And take action on that feedback. Ask '*What would you like me to do differently?*'
7. Ensure people feel comfortable to make a mistake. Celebrate the learning that comes from mistakes and build confidence to try different approaches.
8. Get your team to problem-solve on an issue according to their specific strengths. Notice the results of people approaching a problem with a different creative dimension.
9. Not belonging renders people silent. Belonging has the power to liberate ideas. Think of it as a gateway your team pass through to bring 100 per cent of themselves to work.
10. Educate yourself. Here are some favourites: read articles (*Forbes*, *Inc.* or *HBR* magazine are great), listen to podcasts (The Will to Change, or Inclusion Works), explore blogs (Greater Good Science Centre is one of my go-to's), and feed your brain with TED talks. There are so many beautiful talks on this site, I'll let you choose!

CHAPTER EIGHT

Become a customer-focused leader, really!

In a nutshell

Many leaders urge their staff to place the customer at the heart of everything they do. Yet for all the passion and conviction, genuine customer focus remains elusive, with the experience wrapped up in data processing, rather than a human interaction. This chapter outlines five principles for humanizing the customer experience, giving you practical guidance to make it a positive reality in your organization.

This chapter was developed with the invaluable contribution of Jo Hale, a customer-focused leadership expert, with 25 years' experience of transforming global call centres, influencing board-level strategy decisions and galvanizing corporate action in the service of the customer.

What's the problem?

Here's a hypothetical scenario.

CASE STUDY

'Glow!' is a retail business specializing in women's activewear. Four values are published on their website, visible across the business and emphasized to all employees: Think customer; Better together; Be passionate; Drive innovation. In the light of these values, the decision is taken to relaunch their popular yoga app and make it truly customer interactive, so that customers can post their own yoga sessions and receive real-time feedback on their progress. The IT team have been delighted with the product, with deadlines achieved, and positive early feedback from users.

And then the Covid-19 pandemic spread, forcing people indoors and doing more solo yoga. Response to the app went wild, traction increased beyond all forecasted data, but functionality began to falter, with customers having problems logging on and receiving feedback. Calls to the small contact centre increased by 67 per cent. Each team reacted differently to the customer response, with no 'joined up' solution. Here's a snapshot of the departmental reactions:

The IT team are enthusiastic about their product and consider it a 'big win'.

The customer call centre team are understaffed and overwhelmed by calls. They need more resources and call for temporary staff.

HR (human resources) believe numbers are high in the call centre and cannot be increased.

Finance want to cut costs due to issues with retail outlets and are not in favour of employing more staff.

Management decide to cut off the phones, respond to customers by email only, letting them know they will receive a reply within 28 days.

Customers shift their emotional response from 'excited' to 'frustrated' and 'annoyed'.

Without a response, customers take to social media to publicize their negative feedback, warning other customers against using Glow!

Customer NPS (net promoter score) scores plummet.

The board takes notice. Their bonuses are linked to the NPS score. Now it's business critical!

A consultant is brought in, who puts the phones back on, employs temporary staff, clears the backlog and involves IT back in functionality. Within three weeks, issues are solved, but trust has been dented, reputational brand damaged and many customers have just drifted away, never to return.

The board blames management, management blames HR, HR blames finance, finance blames the contact centre and everyone blames IT.

There is a paradox here. While everything has changed in business, from technology to communication, through to globalization, nothing has changed for the customer. Even though Peter Drucker (1954) wrote his infamous words, 'the purpose of a business is to create and keep a customer' some 60 years ago, many businesses are still struggling to understand this fundamental concept.

Yes, you need great products, but most of all you need a customer experience that drives loyalty and a long-term relationship, starting well before they receive the product or experience your service and lasting through the entire life cycle. Customers still want ease of finding, using (and returning) your products and services. They want to interact with you and sometimes see you. They like the opportunity to upgrade on demand and differentiate their experience based on the relationship. They want an interactive and in-control experience and they want to know they matter. This hasn't changed.

But it's become remarkably easy for leaders across an organization to become divorced from the reality of the customer, operating in silos like the example above. Even though leaders exhort their followers to place the customer at the heart of everything they do, scribed in blood through the cultural model, the customer is often little more than data – a complaints figure to be reported upwards, a churn or retention percentage, a profit marker, or a visual for behavioural economists. The customer is there to be measured, mapped and modelled – and knocked into organizational shape.

The big idea: Humanize the customer!

To prevent the scenario outlined above from repeating itself within your organization you need to be unafraid to bring the customer experience back to basics. Five principles sit at the heart of customer-focused leadership. This involves immersing yourself in the customer journey, embracing the emotional experience (internally and externally) and connecting this with business strategy and measurement.

FIGURE 8.1   The five principles of customer-focused leadership

#1 LISTEN AND LEARN

#2 SHOW YOU CARE

#3 LOOK INSIDE — IT'S EVERYONE'S BUSINESS

#4 ENGAGE THE BOARD

#5 MEASURE WHAT MATTERS

5 PRINCIPLES OF CUSTOMER FOCUSED LEADERSHIP

Principle #1: Listen and learn

Every day you will hear something about the customer. Do you listen? Do you help others to listen?

The first stage in engaging with customer-focused leadership is to educate yourself. Before you embrace the later principles of strategy and measurement, take a step back and into the customer's shoes. Use the questions below to reflect on your current levels of awareness.

Your goal is to be in touch with what it's like to be a customer and connect with the emotion of the experience. This isn't some touchy-feely mumbo jumbo – the customer experience is the sustenance of your business, not an indulgence. And it's worth emphasizing at this point that by 'customer', I mean your internal customers, as much as your external ones.

Once you've answered the questions below, share your learning with your team. Don't let this be a blame game: 'Well if it wasn't for sales/HR/IT/ExCo* (*delete where applicable), we'd be fine!' This is about listening and learning. What does your customer say, feel and do when they interact with your business? Then share your learning with your senior leadership team and ask them to answer the same questions. The shared learning experience will be invaluable for understanding the customer.

Time to reflect

How customer-aware are you?

1 What is it like to buy from your organization today? (And I mean this literally – go and buy from your organization, ring the contact centre, report a service issue, return a product.)

2   From a customer point of view, what's easy and what are the barriers?
3   What one lesson have you learned from a customer this week?
4   What emotions do you want a customer to feel when they interact with you?
5   What is the root cause of customer defections in your business? (Where do they go?)
6   With regards to customer focus, what behaviours are you rewarding?
7   What's the most frustrating barrier that prevents your customer-facing teams from giving the customer great service?
8   What's the last thing you personally did to improve the quality of the customer experience?
9   What place does the customer have in your leadership meetings?
10 How often do you discuss the internal customer relationships in your leadership meetings and address silo mentality?

Principle #2: Show you care

Let's start addressing your answers to some of these questions by considering the emotional experience your customer is having with your organization. Your goal here is to shift the customer interaction from being a transactional activity to one of emotional engagement – and to shift your own perspective from the customer being a slice of data, to a beating heart deserving of a relationship.

Most leaders I work with understand the language of the customer journey and touchpoints. That is, all those precious moments when the customer interacts with your company, from when they first hear about you to the end of the relationship. I'd go further and suggest that many of you reading this chapter will have the customer journey mapped out, with crucial data points and the process supporting those data points.

But there are two important things to consider when you are looking at your customer's relationship with you. Yes, you might understand the data touchpoints, but where is the customer in this process? What really matters is not what the customer does, it's what they say and how they feel. And it's important because it will be the emotional experience that will drive loyalty and trust – ultimately determining your net promoter score (or your own customer satisfaction measurement) and repeat business.

Research in Colin Shaw and John Ivens' (2005) book, *Building Great Customer Experiences*, states that 69 per cent of all consumers say that emotions account for 50 per cent or more of every customer experience they have. This makes sense given that, as human beings, when we experience something it passes through the emotional side of our brains before it enters the logical side. And you'll know yourself that if you think about poor or exciting customer experiences you've had, the more stimulated your emotions (for good or bad), the more memorable! As Shaw and Ivens say, 'Emotions are a major differentiator and are the most underestimated assets available to businesses today. They can be used to put colour back into our grey world.'

> What really matters is not what the customer does, it's what they say and how they feel.

For example, let's take a closer look at our earlier fictional scenario. Customers using the new Glow! app might have the simple data touchpoints shown in Figure 8.2.

FIGURE 8.2 Physical customer touchpoints

PHYSICAL CUSTOMER TOUCHPOINTS

OPEN APP → LOAD OWN VIDEO → ASK FOR FEEDBACK → WAIT FOR RESPONSE → PROMPT 4 RESPONSE → FAILURE CLOSE APP

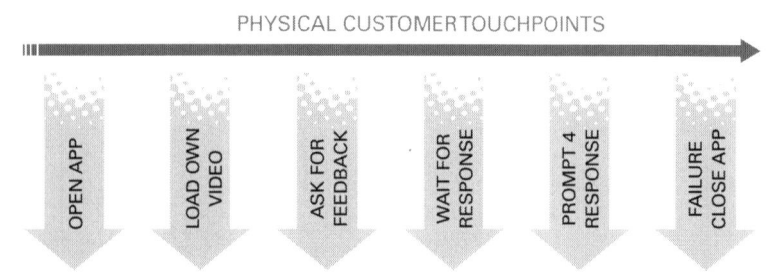

This is useful and stimulates discussion over functionality adjustments. But look at what happens when we overlay this with the emotional experience (Figure 8.3).

FIGURE 8.3 Emotional customer touchpoints

EMOTIONAL CUSTOMER TOUCHPOINTS

OPEN APP → LOAD OWN VIDEO → ASK FOR FEEDBACK → WAIT FOR RESPONSE → PROMPT 4 RESPONSE → FAILURE CLOSE APP

EXCITED   EXPECTANT   HOPEFUL   CONCERNED   BORED / FRUSTRATED   ANNOYED / ANGRY TELL OTHERS

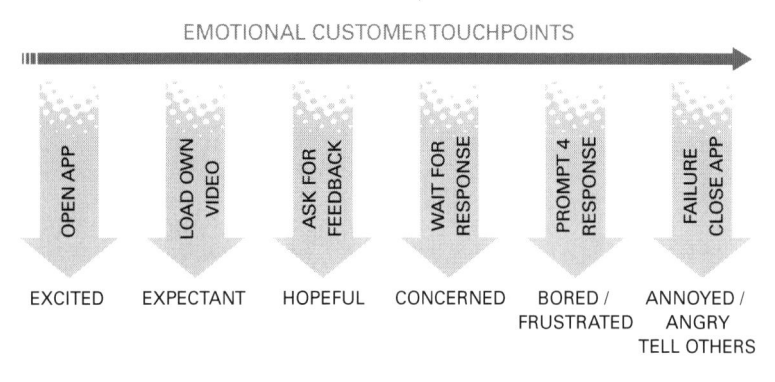

Now *this* is meaningful data as it clearly shows something important about the emotional impact on the customer – the consequences. In 2013 Colin Shaw wrote an intriguing blog about this topic, titled '15 statistics that should change the business world – but haven't', and included these four relevant statistics:

- It takes 12 positive experiences to make up for a single bad experience.

FIGURE 8.4 Changed emotional customer touchpoints

CHANGED EMOTIONAL CUSTOMER TOUCHPOINTS

OPEN APP	LOAD OWN VIDEO	ASK FOR FEEDBACK	WAIT FOR RESPONSE	PROMPT 4 RESPONSE	FAILURE CLOSE APP
EXCITED	EXPECTANT	HOPEFUL	APPRECIATIVE	PATIENT	ENGAGED WILLING TO TRY AGAIN

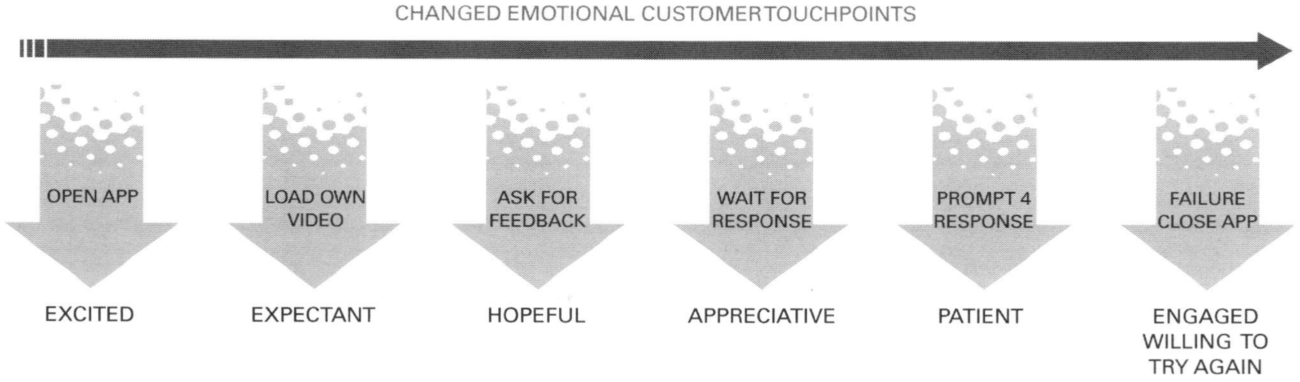

- Negative interactions with a business are spread to twice as many people as positive ones.
- It costs over six times more to get new customers than it does to keep one current one.
- For every customer who complains, 26 others don't speak up.

The obvious answer for Glow! is to fix the functionality of the app. But sometimes this isn't possible in the immediate future, so fix the emotional impact first. Instead of turning *off* the phones while you fix the app, turn the phones back *on*, get people in to talk to the customer and concentrate on the emotional impact. Yes, this might cost you more in the short term, but it's better than losing customers while you wait for a technology fix. So, interrupt the emotional impact before it turns negative, knowing that if you involve your customer, people will be more understanding in their response.

Try this out

This is a quick, useful exercise I've done with many leaders as they explore the emotional impact of their customer service.

FIGURE 8.5   Customer emotions

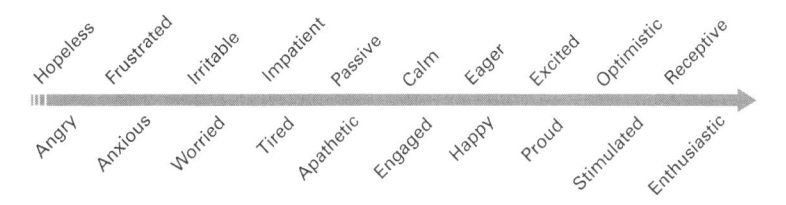

Hopeless, Frustrated, Irritable, Impatient, Passive, Calm, Eager, Excited, Optimistic, Receptive

Angry, Anxious, Worried, Tired, Apathetic, Engaged, Happy, Proud, Stimulated, Enthusiastic

a   Look at the list of emotions in Figure 8.5.
b   Take a slice of your customer journey, internal or external, with 4/5 customer touchpoints.

c At each stage of the customer journey, what do you *want* the customer to feel?
d From your experience or research, what *does* the customer feel?
e Where there is a negative discrepancy, what action is under your departmental *control*?
f What small *actions* can you take that would transform the experience for the internal or external customer?

Principle #3: Look inside, it's everyone's business

'Many hands make light work' was one of my mum's favourite phrases, basically urging me and my siblings to get off our bums and do some clearing up. Given the vigorous and continually accelerating pace of technology and change, you would think mum's phrase would be the obvious solution, with functions pulling together and finding new ways to collaborate and execute the perfect customer experience. Yet it's still surprising to me how entrenched silos can be across organizations, with Glow!'s experience above remarkably common and functions operating from a position of self-protection.

To test the strength of silos within your organization, ask various people across multiple functions this question:

Who owns the customer experience?

If your answer is, 'we all do', hurray! If the answers range from 'no idea', to 'sales… customer service… complaints team' or worse still, 'not me', you have a 'silo syndrome'. And it's worth some self-reflection here. If you find yourself saying:

I don't make the strategy
I don't define the customer experience
I don't make the customer journey
It's not my problem

then you're part of the problem.

It's a truism that the experience the external customer receives from your organization is a direct reflection of the internal one. With embedded silos, the external experience will be fractured – and no amount of money you throw at process solutions will change this. With fluent communication across functions, a shared purpose and commitment to the customer, you stand a fighting chance of transforming the experience. The customer of course doesn't care about your silos or power battles. They want a seamless experience that satisfies their expectations (and occasionally delights them).

The answer to this lies in shared end-to-end ownership. Focusing on 'fixing' individual touchpoints can provide a distorted view of what is happening to the customer. As customer experience experts suggest (Rawson et al, 2013):

> Most customers aren't fed up with any one phone call, field visit or other interaction. In fact, they don't much care about those singular touchpoints. What enhances satisfaction is something few companies manage – cumulative experiences across multiple touchpoints and in multiple channels over time.

Practical inspiration #1

Smashing silos with two ideas

1 Your quickest route to dispersing silos and creating shared ownership is through shared metrics. That is, everyone's objectives across the business linked to the NPS score, or customer satisfaction measurement.
2 Engage the entire organization in redesigning the customer experience, through shared understanding. Jo has led this exercise multiple times to great success, from board level across all levels of the organization:

- Ask each member of your team to sit in the call centre for at least a couple of hours. Listen to the customer calls, hear the issues and note potential solutions. Bring the team together for a shared customer experience session and pose three questions:
  How do we as a team contribute to the customer's problems?
  How can we as a team provide a solution to these problems?
  What's the simplest thing we can do to make the biggest difference?
  Then ask the same three questions to your internal customers! Your bravery will be rewarded with invaluable data to improve the way your team operates internally.

Principle #4: Engage the board

Every customer leader asks how to influence the board more effectively, so they can have the investment to address functionality, recruit the right people, increase the product offering and ultimately improve the service for the customer. From a leadership perspective, shift a mindset from analysis of data, to humanizing the customer interaction. Peter Massey (2018) leads a customer experience consultancy and suggests, 'Once senior management talk the same language as the customer, it's harder to ignore the frustration of the customers' requests for help, and a cultural shift occurs'.

Practical inspiration #2

Six ways to engage the board

It's possible your board is fully immersed in customer data (perhaps complaint, service levels or retention numbers) but this is not the human being! So how do you bring the customer alive? Here are six tried and trusted ways to achieve this:

1. Play live customer calls at board meetings and lead a discussion about three common factors they noticed in the calls.
2. Influence senior leaders to call or visit customers themselves: to join the call centre, the escalation team or the complaints team. Get to the heart of what the customer wants you to do, not what you want to do to the customer.
3. Introduce customers to the board. Customers who have complained and happy customers. Let them talk about their experience, what works and vice versa.
4. Involve each senior leader in the actual customer buying journey. Walk the talk.
5. Get senior leaders involved in talking about the customer to the organization. Urge them to blog, to vlog, to show they care.
6. Show your senior leaders all the customer metrics available. Together, choose one single metric that links to the business strategy and make this public and owned by everyone.

Principle #5: Measure what matters

Here's a common scenario: a company selects 'delighting the customer' as a strategic objective and decides to track progress on it using customer survey scores. The surveys do tell managers something about how well the firm is pleasing the customer, but somehow employees start thinking the strategy is to maximize survey scores, rather than deliver a great customer experience (Harris and Tayler, 2019). It's a common outcome in call centres when call times are measured for the experience to decline and NPS concomitantly decrease.

There is a growing trend in customer-focused organizations to remove measurements where they are a barrier to the customer experience. It's certainly been my experience in our training organization that evaluation scores at the end of the course damaged the experience. As customers demanded scores of plus-80 per cent 'happy' scores at the end of a course, trainers concentrated on having a 'nice time' and stopped providing a challenging, albeit stimulating experience. Once the immediate measurement was removed, replaced by a more genuine in-house measurement one month post-programme, the experience increased all-round.

Don't get me wrong. I'm not suggesting measurement is a bad thing, as it's often the only way to make sense of your environment, results and delivery on strategic objectives. Metrics provide direction and can indicate desired behaviours and actions. But you have to decide what intended outcomes you want from your measurements, and whether it is going to hinder or help the customer.

So, use the following five questions to explore your measurement strategy and ensure what you measure has the right intended consequences.

Practical inspiration #3

Five measurement questions

Before you ask these questions, gather all your customer metrics and the different measures being used to measure the customer experience. There might be quite a volume here from churn/retention rates, customer lifetime values, first customer resolutions, customer complaints and satisfaction scores. Then ask:

1. Why do they matter to the customer?
2. What measurements help the customer experience and what measurements hinder it?
3. What behaviour does this measurement drive internally?
4. What is the one metric that is critical to your business strategy?
5. How do you get that measurement at every level?

Time to reflect: bringing it together

Customer-focused leadership in practice

Julie-Ann Haines is the CEO of Principality Building Society, previously Chief Customer Officer, and providing an awesome customer experience to her members has always been at the heart of her leadership philosophy. In her own words, this is her experience of customer-focused leadership in practice:

'Thinking about customer-focused leadership, some of the issues we faced were colleagues feeling remote from the customer, unable to see the whole picture and solve problems on behalf of the customer. And although we've always been proud of our customer satisfaction and customer focus, we've recently put into place three major interventions to transform the engagement of our people and improve our business performance. What links them is leadership setting a common purpose, providing the frameworks to encourage learning, and empowering our people to do what matters to our customer and colleagues.

'Firstly, we changed our measurement approach so that customer-facing colleagues received customer feedback within hours of us receiving it, directly to them. This changed the feedback from being a 'marketing thing' received two months later, to a hugely important voice of customer in a coaching session between the colleague and their manager.

'Secondly, we changed our whole remuneration approach so that all colleagues across the organization were incentivized on the same simple measures – profit and Net Promoter Score. This galvanized our organization to solve the blocks in each other's way.

'Thirdly, we empowered colleagues to take ownership for the whole customer journey, for instance, a savings account opening. Colleagues across numerous departmental silos worked together to listen to calls, read letters of complaint and analyse the purpose of the customer requests. They used that insight to ask really simple questions, such as 'What is the minimum we have to do to meet regulatory requirements?', 'What stops us making that simpler?' or 'Why so many handoffs to other teams?' Our systems thinking approach led the teams to design a new way of working and to huge improvements in their engagement. It reduced the number of mistakes, increased their productivity and led to improvements in our core customer metrics.

'Overall, we have seen our NPS increase from 68 to 81 per cent, we've seen engagement increase from 74 to 85 per cent, and some of our core teams dealing with 100 per cent more customer requests within the same headcount.'

Ten top tips for being a customer-focused leader

1. Every day you will hear something about the customer. Hear it and take action!
2. Ask yourself the most important question: 'As a leader, how do I influence the customer experience?'
3. Involve your team, visit places where best practice is evident, and role-model similar practices back in your team.
4. You don't need to reinvent the wheel; brilliance will already exist in your organization – find it and replicate it.
5. Become customer curious and ask great questions across the business.
6. Bring the customer alive in your meetings. Give them a seat and a voice!
7. Agree what single metric is key to your strategy and use technology for simplifying data, trending and visibility.
8. Ensure measures are understood, shared and visible across the organization, and in the customers' words.
9. Make customer satisfaction a common purpose that is motivating for everyone.
10. Celebrate and publicize positive customer feedback.

PART THREE

Hitting roadbumps

CHAPTER NINE

Be a brilliant change leader

In a nutshell

Not everyone experiences change in the same way and leaders need to understand their proactive role in creating the team's experience of change. By understanding the role of the change leader, your mindset and the three simple phases for brilliant change – Why? What? How? – you will gain considerable flexibility in your change leadership.

What's the problem?

Being a leader in today's ever-changing business world demands an extraordinary level of pace and energy, and you would have to be superhuman not to be overwhelmed by the amount of information, jargon, models, podcasts and books about change. So much so, it is hard for many leaders to know how to act, how to lead and how to galvanize their teams to face yet more change.

The volume of advice is understandable given that change happens every day and in every pocket of your business. It's global yet local. Fleeting and lasting. Innocuous and momentous. And our shared experience of change through the pandemic of 2020/21 was a stark reminder of the volatile, uncertain world we live in, and the need for leaders to respond with courage, agility and compassion.

The concept of change is also enveloped by assumptions. Let's take a few sticky ones:

- change is hard and lengthy;
- it requires big budgets and special talents to see it through;
- everyone goes through a 'grief cycle' when they experience change;
- those who resist change are 'fossils', 'dinosaurs', 'die-hards', 'lazy' (or any other negative label you want to apply to people who are not yet on board);
- if you lead with a change model, everyone will follow!

We'll examine these assumptions through this chapter, but the last point throws up an interesting problem with change leadership. Because no matter how much you inspire, persuade, cajole, threaten or encourage, human beings are solo creatures who ultimately do what they want to do, even if that means leaving their roles.

But before you throw your hands up in despair, we can cut through the volume of material on change and explore two important aspects for change leadership that have stood the test of time, that keep replaying in the coaching room, and remain relevant today:

Be a change leader, not a change manager.
Simplify complexity and make change as easy as possible.

As anyone knows who has been through a major change programme, change is rarely straightforward (no matter what your plan suggests!), but is an iterative process, requiring strong leadership, input from across the organization and consideration of 'course correction' as you go along. And that's where a change leader is important. Change management is usually recognized as being reactionary, working through a linear process, with a beginning and end point. Change leadership requires different skills: the need to be visionary and forward thinking; able to influence and inspire action; agile and responsive to your changing business environment.

Time to reflect

Are you a change manager or a change leader?

Draw five lines on a piece of paper, marking them from zero to 10. Think about these five differences between a change manager and a change leader and score yourself.

Change manager		Change leader
Do I control	or	do I inspire?
Do I follow process	or	do I win hearts as well as minds?
Am I functional	or	am I strategic?
Do I work on a finite project	or	on cultural transformation?
Do I challenge performance	or	do I change behaviour?

From change manager to change leader – what really matters?

If you look at the above and know you want to shift your behaviour to be more of a change leader than manager, read through this section. As I've echoed across many of these chapters, your mindset is of critical importance, and that's where we'll start.

THREE MINDSET POSITIONS OF A CHANGE LEADER

1. My beliefs shape my behaviour (and create the reaction from others).
2. Change is about process, transition is about people (head and heart).
3. Everyone is unique (and I need to flex my behaviour to reflect this).

BELIEFS SHAPE BEHAVIOUR

Leo Tolstoy (1900), the Russian novelist, famously wrote, 'Everyone thinks of changing humanity, but no one thinks of changing himself.' In other words, as you can see from Figure 9.1 below, change efforts often falter because the beliefs you hold about change invariably dictate your behaviour and what you deliver.

FIGURE 9.1 The impact of mindset

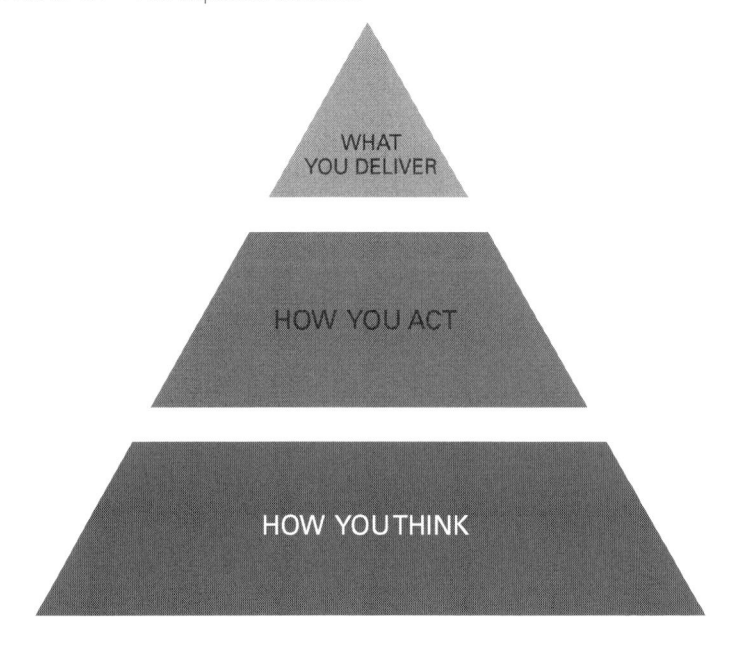

- WHAT YOU DELIVER
- HOW YOU ACT
- HOW YOU THINK

Writing for McKinsey research, Boaz and Fox (2014) suggest that 'If companies can identify and address pervasive mindsets at the outset, they are four times more likely to succeed in organizational change efforts than are companies that overlook this stage.'

Use the statements below to explore your mindset. If you notice unhelpful beliefs that could hinder the way you lead people through change, make a note of these in your journal, e.g., *'it's going to be difficult'*, *'people won't buy into this'*, *'I'm not good at leading change'*, and then try out some different beliefs (that's the beauty about your own thoughts, you can change them in an instant!). Notice how your actions change over time once you learn to habitually, and authentically, shift your mindset.

Try this out

Let's start by exploring your mindset. Grab a piece of paper and fill in the blanks

Lasting change is...
Another word for change is...
The visual image that comes to mind when I think about change is...
I'm good at change when...
I'm bad at change when...

Change is about process, transition is about humans

One of my go-to books that I gift to clients is *Managing Transitions* by William Bridges (2017). It was a revelation to me when I read Bridges' work and read that startling reminder that great change requires human transition. No magic steps and no financial incentive will ensure that your team will embrace change – it always has been (and always will be) a psychological transition. And while change can happen very quickly, transitions usually occur more slowly. As Bridges says: 'When a change happens without a transition, it is just a rearrangement of the chairs.'

This might sound obvious until you stop to think about a recent change project you've been working on. In the planning phase of the project, where did you spend your time? What percentage of time was spent on the process? And what percentage of time was spent on people?

Everyone is unique (and it's not always bad)

Change models assume that everyone will act in the same way, with probably the most ubiquitous change model being Kübler Ross's (1969) change curve. It's remarkable this change model is so prevalent more than 50 years since its inception, given it was designed to mark the five stages of grief for partners of those with a terminal illness.

If you don't know the model, it guides you through the five stages of grief: Denial, Anger, Bargaining, Depression, Acceptance. What concerns me about its predominance is how employees presuppose they will react to change. I cannot tell you how many times I've walked into an organization and heard the conversations about change going something like, 'I suppose we'll all go into denial... it'll be a while before we accept the change... I don't feel very angry, but I guess it'll happen.'

People will react emotionally to change, and for some people change is akin to the stages of grief and the model will really help them understand how to lead people through this. But not everyone, and not all the time. What can often happen is that those people who LOVE change and flourish in the wake of its chaos, remain quiet or operate under the radar. And they're often the people you need on side, helping you to influence others through the transition.

It's worth reflecting on the notion that those people who do not embrace your change programme immediately become the ones with a negative label attached to them. As I mentioned above, the labels attached to such people are not pretty and remain consistently negative. But what would happen if you challenged your perspective?

What if the people who are not embracing your change project do not understand why you're doing this?
What if they feel forgotten or left out, within the change process?
What if they wish they knew what was happening?
What if they are just plain scared or fearful for their future?
What if you, as a change leader, flexed the way you communicate about change with the different personalities to gain their engagement?
What if you, as a change leader, reacted with curiosity and compassion to those not embracing change?

Time to reflect

Different person: different approach

Think about the diverse personalities in your team. They will be reacting to any of your change projects in different ways, and your behaviour to them needs to be equally personable. Here's a snapshot for ways you can approach different personalities going through change:

If the individual has a preference towards analytical data:

Give them more information than you might want to receive.
Ensure the 'why' is clear and the outcomes fair.
Allow them time to reflect on the change, and praise for autonomy.

If the individual has a preference towards speed and achievement:

As far as possible, give them a position of control, let them lead.
Praise them for speed and visible achievement.
Notice and reward incremental change and improved performance.
Talk to them about what the change will improve.

If the individual has a preference towards relationships:

Talk to them about the change, more than you might want to.
Pay attention to feelings and be aware of potential anxiety they and others will feel.
Praise for openness and show you care.

If the individual has a preference towards sociability and teams:

Involve them in the change as much as possible.
Praise for their ability to hold the team together.
Be creative with strategies for change projects.

The big idea: Simplifying complexity – why, what, how?

Every company is in a different place when it comes to their position, their market and their current needs. So, there's no fixed, magic way that every company can use to implement change successfully. But fortunately, there are three components that remain consistently essential to every change project, small or large.

FIGURE 9.2 The road map for change

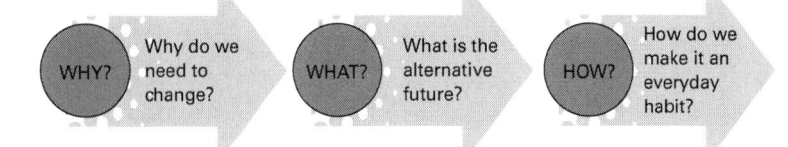

WHY? → Why do we need to change?
WHAT? → What is the alternative future?
HOW? → How do we make it an everyday habit?

Phase 1: Why?

WHY DO WE NEED TO CHANGE?

FIGURE 9.3 Start with why

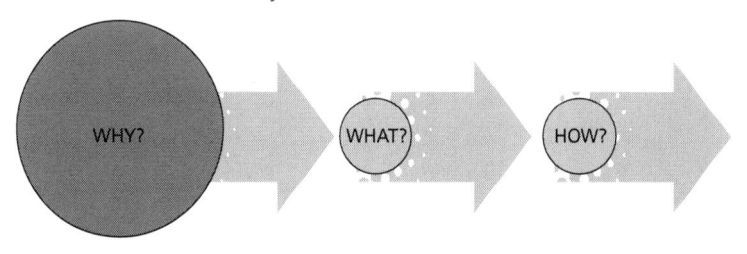

Just one look at the extraordinarily swift changes people incorporated into their lives in 2020, from homeworking to home-schooling, tells you what you need to know about this first step. When the need for change is clear, people will embrace it. Of course, when the need is urgent and external, often people have no choice but to comply and shift.

But what happens when the change is not being driven by an external urge? What happens to most organizations is that one big question lingers when the change initiative is announced:

> When the need for change is clear, people will embrace it.

WHY ARE WE DOING THIS?

And this simple question left unanswered can stifle even the most important new project:

As Head of People, Leila was in charge of rolling out the organization's new values. With a new CEO, a shift of organizational emphasis from 'command and control' to that of 'taking responsibility', the six values that had been in place for 20 years were being modernized. The new three 'R's, Respect/Responsibility/Reward, were launched with a fanfare. Values forums and workshops took place across the company, supported by brand values literature and posters. Considerable budget had been allocated to the brand design, corporate launch and leadership follow through. Yet six months on, the values were not resonating through the organization, with the majority of the employees (at the six-month values survey) expressing either scepticism, outrage at the investment, or worse, indifference.

At the senior leadership team meeting, the learning was clear. The senior team were clear in their vision with a modernization of the values. They understood what the shift could do for the business, how teams could interact differently, thereby offering a transformative customer experience. But few others could see this. By skipping the foundation stone of communicating the 'why we need to change', the new values were just another expensive piece of corporate change that, in the minds of the workforce, would soon go away.

The story didn't end here though, with a return to the old. Instead, the senior leaders decided to look outside of their team, look to their employees and start with insight. And the next practical inspiration section reflects their next actions.

Practical inspiration #1

Start with insight and find your WoWs

Appreciative Inquiry is a well-documented, strengths-based method for exploring stories of moments where teams are at their very best (Whitney and Trosten-Bloom, 2003). As well as being vital in your coaching (see Chapter 6), it is also your starting point for any change project. You will gain invaluable insight by finding out What already Works (your WoWs). Take any new change initiative and find out:

Who is already doing this?
How are they doing it?
What makes it work?

When you do this, you'll find extraordinary examples of best practice already happening across your organization. Whether you are looking to transform your customer experience, revolutionize your technology, change behaviours or develop organizational resilience – whatever changes you're looking to make at an individual, team or organizational level, you'll find beautiful examples hiding in plain sight.

And then work with these people as your change advocates.

Find your change advocates

Your change advocates will come from three areas:

- They're already practising the change you want (but don't always know it).
- They're excited about the change initiative (and will influence others).
- They understand the data (and can explain it to you and others).

All three types of people are vital to your enterprise. You will need practitioners, influencers and data-driven techies. If you miss any of these three, you'll run the risk of criticism, such as 'it won't work in practice', 'nobody's behind the project', or 'there's no good underlying data'.

Now involve your change advocates in the next step of communicating the change.

Communicate x 10

Once you've completed your insight phase, start to communicate 'why we're embarking on this change'. And if you think you've told people the 'why', do it again. I was once given great advice to 'communicate to the power of 10' through change, which has stuck with me. Find every mode of communication to do this – videocast, podcast, internal newsletter, forums, change champions, meetings, 1:1's. Any and all of this will work, and do not underestimate the power of the gossip mill – for good and bad. In *Managing Transitions*, William Bridges offers four wise pieces of advice:

i   Don't rationalize *not* communicating.
ii The grapevine already has the news.
iii You told them once, but it won't sink in.
iv Say what you know, say what you don't know and commit to a time to give them more information.

Time to reflect

What change project have you got coming up? Write it down and answer these six questions that follow on from the learning above:

1 Where in the organization does best practice already exist?
2 If you don't know, how can you extend your insight and find out?
3 Who will be your change advocates?
4 How are you going to reward them for standing alongside you in the change project?
5 What mediums of communication are you comfortable with?
6 Who can help you extend your communication to methods unfamiliar to you (but relevant to others)?

Phase 2: What?

WHAT IS THE ALTERNATIVE FUTURE?

FIGURE 9.4 Build a compelling future

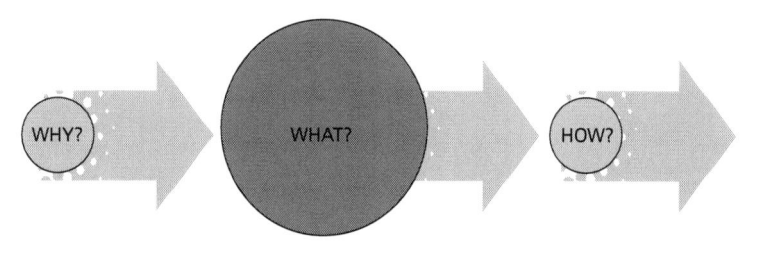

You've explained the 'why?' and now it's time to consider the 'what?' That is, you have to lay out an alternative future that is more compelling and appealing than the past. I should add that this needs not only clarity, but also simplicity. A complicated future mapping process might appeal to a minority, but most people will want to grab hold of an inspiring vision. To let go of the past, the future needs to be more appealing.

> *To let go of the past, the future needs to be more appealing.*

When Steve and I moved from the village we'd been living in for 17 years, and where we'd brought up our children, I created a simple, visual postcard to remind myself of our reasons for the move (which included a lido, a café and no car!). If this sounds simplistic, you're just scaling this up. Everyone will need consistent reminders as to what the future holds – and the easier it is to visualize, the higher the take-up.

So, if your tendency is to reach for a fabulous 14-tabbed Excel spreadsheet accompanied by a very complicated mind map and 60-strong slide deck, start reading the next section!

Practical inspiration #2

Think head and heart

There are two fundamental elements of a powerful and compelling vision:

- *It is simple and easy to understand.*
  Ideally, when written down, it should fill no more than half a page of paper and take around 30 to 60 seconds to explain. This means it can be communicated quickly and effectively and, more importantly, it is likely to be remembered and passed on to others. Or make it visual on one page.
- *It is logical, but also has emotional appeal.*
  A powerful vision is logical: it is reasonable and works intellectually. It must, however, also make a conscious appeal to the emotions. In other words, it must 'grab' people, and make them want to follow, but can also clearly be achieved and is a reasonable thing to aim towards.

Try this out

If you're like most leaders, the logical vision is clear. But what about appealing to people's emotions? Free your mind here, put away your judgement mindset and have some fun:

If your vision was an animal, what would it be? (Not as daft as it sounds. A client of mine likened the toxic culture he was trying to change to a pack of hyenas. It led to a creative wilderness vision that the company raved about.)
If your vision could be summed up in three emotion words, what would they be?
What metaphor describes your vision? It is like…?
Draw your vision, however rudimentary. What stands out?

Phase 3: How?

HOW DO WE MAKE THIS AN EVERYDAY HABIT?

FIGURE 9.5   How to build a habit

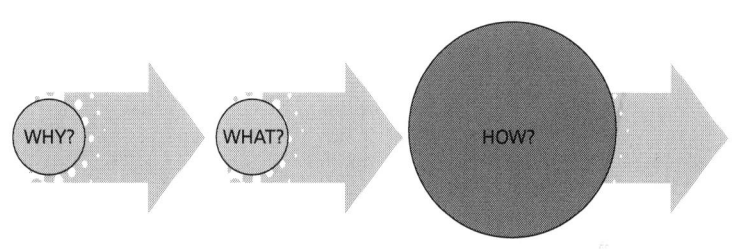

Do not let all your hard change work fizzle out due to lack of **consistent commitment**. Given that research from the Society of Human Resource Management (Meinert, 2018) suggests that up to 70 per cent of change initiatives fail as a result of bad leadership or poor implementation, this is the stage that will test you the most. Your team needs to know you mean it and you're prepared for the long haul.

Practical inspiration #3

Here are the top five ideas suggested by clients to me for sustaining change:

1. Show that you mean it

If you want people to embrace the future picture, you have to show you're prepared to take action to sweep away old habits in order to reach that future goal.

What behaviours are being rewarded now that will change or need to change?

Or as brothers, Chip and Dan Heath (2011) suggest in their readable book *Switch*, 'You've got to design an environment that makes it more likely that reform will happen.' This will undoubtedly include difficult conversations, highlighting behaviours that are no longer acceptable. Even letting people go as a result, as well as tangible changes to the situation:

Tom leads a 400-strong contact centre, heading up the customer experience transformation. There are many factors to this, but let's take one critical change – talking to the customer like a human being. The 'why' was clear, and very appealing to the customer teams who found their conversations strangulated by unwieldy scripts and bureaucratic measurements. In the first stage of 'how', Tom's management team simplified the scripts and extended the timescales for customer talk. But it wasn't working as well as they'd hoped. It took a leap of faith to abandon all scripts, time measurements and affiliated reward and place trust firmly in the hands of the agent, allowing them free conversation and in the time required to solve the customer's issue. The feedback most prized from a customer, and celebrated on the wall, says, 'For the first time speaking to a contact centre, I felt like a human being!' Mission accomplished.

2. Be consistent

All of your communication, prioritization actions and recruitment appointments send a message. Make sure you're consistent, as conflicting messages are confusing and give people the opportunity to be sceptical about the reality of change. And ensure your own behaviour is consistent with the new values you're championing.

3. Help people let go

'People don't like endings. Yet change and endings go hand in hand' (Bridges, 2017). Before your team embrace anything new, they will have to let go of what was before. And this can take time, as some people can hang on to old ways of doing things for a remarkably long time! There is an attraction in familiarity, and like an elastic band, people will bounce backwards when possible.

If this is happening, it is likely the future is not counterbalancing the old:

- Show how the new is a progression of the old.
- Demonstrate this isn't going away, it's not a fad or fashion. It's the new reality.
- Don't just add to people's 'to do' list with more new stuff. Help them delegate or dump what can be left behind.

4. Don't expect too much

Over to Chip and Dan Heath again: 'When you hear people say that change is hard because people are lazy or resistant, that's just flat wrong. In fact, the opposite is true: change is hard because people wear themselves out.' What looks like indifference is often just tiredness. Don't overpromise output and set realistic expectations of what can (and can't) change.

5. Celebrate success

Change doesn't need to be earnest, or just one long, difficult slog. It can be involving and interactive, fun and oftentimes swift. It can be fascinating and bursting with opportunities for people to grow and develop.

I read this morning that the pace of change will never be as slow as it is today. That's a breathtaking thought. So, given that 'change as the norm' is likely to be your mantra going forwards, celebrate each milestone, communicate the positives and appreciate everyone's progress.

Ten top tips for being a brilliant change leader

1. Inspire other people with your passion, energy and belief so that people want to follow you.
2. Show compassion. Letting go of the old is subjective and some people will find it harder than you.
3. Set the bar at a realistic level and celebrate small wins.
4. Describe the change in as much detail as possible. Make it visual, verbal and tangible.
5. Embrace creativity and innovation. Celebrate new ways of doing things.
6. Be trustworthy and do what you say you will do, behave as you want others to behave.
7. Provide training, coaching and mentoring so you help people embrace the new reality.
8. Role-model momentum. Set the pace for change and ask 'What needs to be done now?'
9. Regulate your emotions and stress points. Remain calm.
10. Always return to the 'why?', the 'what?' and the 'how?' to keep you grounded and on track for success.

CHAPTER TEN

How to master difficult conversations with compassion and confidence

In a nutshell

What makes some conversations so difficult for you? And how can you hold these conversations so that you achieve the outcome you want? This outcome has to work for you, for the other person and for the relationship – instead of being a 'muddle' where no one is sure of the next step. Learn how to prepare your mindset and craft your skills by using the POEMS model. This will help you create a safe space for difficult conversations and achieve mutually agreeable outcomes.

What's the problem?

What's so difficult about a 'difficult conversation'? If this is a topic that causes you apprehension, you are not alone! In coaching leaders, it's the one subject that results in clammy hands and high levels of anxiety, and everyone has stories of feedback going wrong – whether being on the giving or receiving end.

If we reduce a difficult conversation to its essence, it's one where you:

> *anticipate a problem (and are uneasy about reaching a mutually positive outcome).*

And it's made difficult by the fact that the conversation matters to you, emotions run high and, if you are anything like most leaders, you have replayed this conversation again (and again!) in your head.

It's the anticipation that causes hesitation, doubt and anxiety. As Holly Weeks, author of *Failure to Communicate* (2010), says: 'A difficult conversation tends to go best when you think about it as just a normal conversation.' Just framing the conversation as 'difficult' leads to an abundance of 'what if' thinking, such as:

What if it goes wrong?
What if they cry/shout/walk out (pick your emotional fear)?
What if I do it badly?
What if I hurt their feelings?
What if they reject the feedback?
What if it escalates and gets really serious?
What if we ruin the relationship?
What if I get triggered and behave badly?
What if it's 'career limiting'?
What if it doesn't get resolved?

What's so pernicious about this thinking is that it causes the very outcome you were hoping to side-step! Because such thinking causes five different leader behaviours:

1 Avoidance. Just hoping the problem will go away or resolve itself if you just ignore it.

2. Minimizing the problem. 'It's probably me, not you'; 'Don't worry, this really isn't a big issue'; 'It's just a small, minor concern'.
3. Blame. Yourself ('I didn't manage them well enough') or Them ('They didn't take responsibility').
4. Triggered behaviour. Your leadership style under stress shines out. How do you react when faced with potential conflict? With aggression, passive aggression, withdrawal, defensiveness, humour?
5. 'Winging' it. You don't know how to prepare, and what can go wrong?

The big idea: Balancing compassion with confidence

What can go wrong indeed? Quite a lot really! Taking a difficult conversation seriously really does matter as the consequences of a poorly handled exchange can be far-reaching. Thankfully, there's an alternative to a muddled exchange with confused outcomes, and the POEMS model will guide you through a step-by-step confident conversation.

Before this, we need to talk about preparation and your mindset. Without mastery of this, no model can be effective. Like the old adage said, 'Fail to prepare, prepare to fail'.

Renowned coach Mary Beth O'Neill urges executive coaches to hold the tension between Backbone and Heart. I echo this, and further suggest that the balance you are looking to strike is that of Compassion + Confidence.

Let's start with compassion

Two factors are important about compassion. The first is empathy, the ability to understand how someone else might be feeling and thinking – so, compassion for someone else. The second factor is your ability to manage the tension between caring deeply about the people you lead, while understanding that at times you will be unpopular, so compassion for yourself.

IF ONLY YOU WERE MORE LIKE ME…

Robust scientific findings across decades of social science research suggest we go through life wishing everyone was more like us. If you were more like me, thought like me, talked like me, there'd be no more difficult conversations – so the thinking goes. The primary determinant of chemistry in a professional relationship is similarity or attractiveness, or, put another way, we are drawn to people who are like us in ways that are important to us. Herminia Ibarra, in *Act Like a Leader, Think Like a Leader* (2015), calls this the Narcissistic Principle of relationship formation.

Why does this matter in a difficult conversation? It means you are more likely to be negatively triggered in a difficult conversation, because the person doesn't react the way you do to a stressful situation. Perhaps they reflect while you talk; or they cry while you sit there in stony silence. Or they fold their arms, utter the deadly word '*fine*', as you urgently try to find a way forward.

THE TIGHTROPE OF CARE

Kim Scott's *Radical Candor* (2019) describes compassion as to 'Care Personally'. She suggests that in our efforts to 'keep things professional' in a difficult conversation, we deny something essential about being human: 'We are all human beings, with human feelings, and even at work we need to be seen as such. When that doesn't happen, when we feel we must repress who we really are to earn a living, we become alienated.'

The difficulty lies here in the tension between caring personally about the people you lead, while being prepared to be unpopular in return. Not an easy tension to manage, but one I'll help you manage with the POEMS structure below.

The Confidence Continuum

Confidence lies on a continuum as you can see in Figure 10.1 (which you can explore further in Chapter 4). Humility at one end, and arrogance at the other extreme.

FIGURE 10.1 The Confidence Continuum

Humility --------------- Confidence --------------- Arrogance

This means you are neither apologizing for holding this conversation, nor do you think you are right above all else. And so, confidence in this context is a belief in your ability to handle this conversation in an acceptable way, without undermining the other person.

It's also useful to know that like many leadership skills, confidence is not an innate, fixed characteristic. It can be acquired and improved over time – just like the skill of mastering a difficult conversation. For this reason, I often suggest to clients in coaching that they adopt some of the following confident beliefs before a difficult conversation:

- This conversation needs to be had.
- I am OK, they are OK. This is not about winning.
- I have prepared as much as I can.
- I have the experience to manage any challenges that arise.
- I understand myself well enough to remain calm.
- I might not get it all right, but that's OK. It's human to make mistakes and I'll learn from this.
- I feel compassion and know how to make it safe to talk.

Time to reflect: what might derail you?

For the balance of Compassion and Confidence to remain steady, it's important to know what might derail you. And by this, I mean what emotions or behaviours might set you off course?

Marshall Goldsmith, in *Triggers* (2015), emphasizes the need to decide how to respond rather than react, so breaking the chain of long-held and often counterproductive instincts.

Four clients shared their 'derailing' moments with me and the impact:

The person started to cry, so I started to apologize saying I was sorry, it wasn't important, it really wasn't a big issue. I felt dreadful and then worse after when I knew we hadn't even started the difficult conversation.

My colleague slightly turned their back, closed their eyes, and said, 'fine, whatever you want me to do'. I didn't know what to do. I just muttered 'OK' and the meeting ended.

Roisin and I have a great relationship. As I gave her the difficult news, she smiled and told me not to be so serious. Had I been on a course? Just let it go and she'd be better next time. Come on, take a break. We just went and had a coffee and never had the conversation.

They stood up (I was still sitting), said 'you have to be kidding me?' in a really loud voice. Kind of banged the table. Seriously! Everyone could hear in the outer office. It felt threatening and I just didn't know whether to shout back, shut up or how to find the middle ground. In the end, I just delayed the conversation.

As you read their stories, consider the following questions:

1 How do you react under stress?
2 What emotions or behaviours will trigger you and set you off course?
3 What do you need to do to remain confident?

(If you want to read more about this, go to Chapter 7 where we explore bias, different personalities and styles under stress.)

Practical inspiration #1

Six mindset questions

By now, it'll be clear that your mindset to this difficult conversation matters! Indeed, it's the only way to maintain the delicate balance of Compassion and Confidence. Let me help here with preparation questions designed to understand your intent and move your mindset to one of growth and openness. By answering these questions, you're introducing some 'grey' thinking into what otherwise might be too rigid.

So, here are six questions to get your mindset in a useful place before you hold your difficult conversation:

1 What is **difficult** about this conversation for you? (What problem are you anticipating? Why are you uneasy about this?)
2 What's the **problem for them**? (Start building your flexible thinking for this conversation by considering the other person's point of view.)
3 How are you **feeling**? (*All* difficult conversations are emotional. What emotions are going on for you? Name them, so you are not hijacked by them.)
4 How might you have **contributed** to this problem? (This isn't an easy question to answer, but it can shed a different lens on the direction of the conversation. Perhaps you haven't been timely with your feedback? Or entirely honest in an earlier conversation, which means the issue has now escalated?)
5 What **outcome** do you want for you, for them, for the relationship?
6 How do you need to **behave** to realize your relationship outcome? (E.g. what's the best way for this person to hear this message?)

The last two questions are suggested by the authors of *Crucial Conversations* (Patterson et al, 2011) and what I particularly like is the focus on the relationship. It's standard to think through your outcome for a difficult conversation, but rare to effectively think through the outcome for the relationship, and then translate that into shifting your behaviour.

Try this out

Think about a difficult conversation you need to have and work through the six questions. I urge you to write down your answers, as the act of writing, as opposed to just thinking, will give you clarity. In answering the questions, what insight to your mindset did you gain? What did you notice needs to shift in your behaviour for a more successful outcome? What is your contribution to the problem?

Practical inspiration #2

After you have got your mindset in a good state, it's time to plan this conversation. POEMS is a five-step model for you to use as a planning tool for difficult conversations. It's not a script as no difficult conversation will go exactly the way you plan it, but I've given you examples to help you make sense of each step. It's designed to help you slow down, with structure, as described in Figure 10.2.

Slow down, with structure.

Prepare

- Prepare yourself. Write out your answers to the six mindset questions above and check your attitude towards the issue – if you're annoyed or frustrated right now, it's not the time to have the conversation.

FIGURE 10.2 The POEMS model

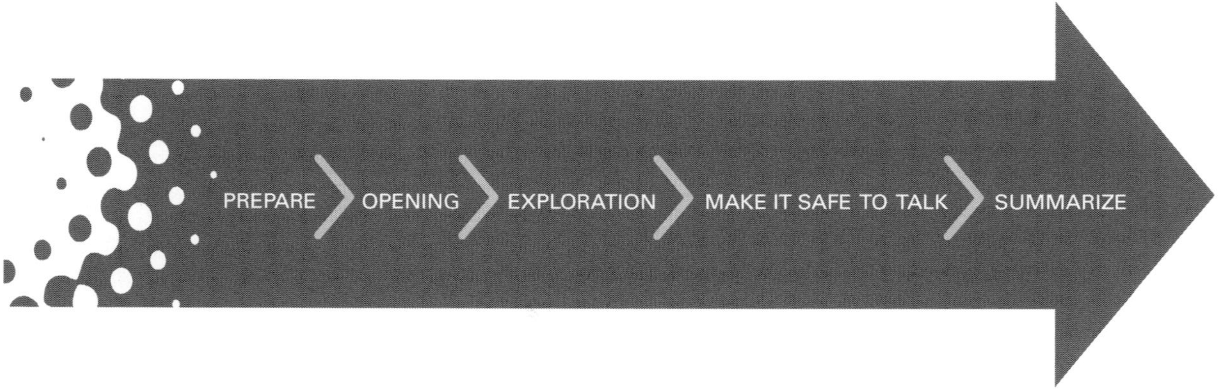

PREPARE › OPENING › EXPLORATION › MAKE IT SAFE TO TALK › SUMMARIZE

- Breathe. Be calm.
- Have the factual evidence with you – whether seen, heard or written.
- Book a safe space – virtually or face to face. Where are you going to have the conversation? The middle of a hotel lobby is not ideal, nor is an office with open access to all. If it has to be held virtually, ensure you are both sitting somewhere comfortable and private.
- Ensure you have scheduled enough time for the meeting – if you haven't enough time, postpone it until you have. Difficult conversations are never successful when carried out with speed.

Opening

- Frame a strong, assertive reason for the meeting by creating a 'mutual purpose' statement. For example, 'We need to discuss your performance, so that we're both clear on the way forward.'
- Start with facts. This is critical. Facts cannot be argued with (or if they are, take a pause in the conversation, find out the facts and start again). For example, 'Over the last three months your performance has dropped by 24 per cent'; 'In the last board report you wrote, there were six errors.'
- Tell your story. The facts alone are not enough. It's the facts plus your conclusion that make this a two-way discussion. Use 'I' to show that this is your story, not someone else's. This is a critical psychological step, as you are demonstrating to the other person that this is just *your* version of the facts – and they might have a different story. You are opening the door to an honest, mutual conversation, not just presenting a slam-dunk version of the facts. It might help to frame your story in terms of what the facts made you 'think + feel'.

    For example: 'At our leadership meeting this afternoon, you interrupted me twice, even though we talked about this last week. It makes me think that I haven't been clear enough about the impact of your behaviour, as it makes me feel undermined and frustrated.'

Explore

- Explore the other person's point of view – allow them to talk about their interpretation, their 'story' situation from their point of view. Sometimes people need to make excuses or vent their feelings before they can accept the necessity for change. Writing in the *Harvard Business Review* in 2017, Monique Valcour suggests reframing the purpose of the conversation from Convincing to Learning. As she says, 'No matter how well-spoken and logical we may be, we can't understand and solve the problem without exploring how the other person sees it.'
- You can listen without necessarily agreeing. It is the only way to find out where the motives for their behaviour lie.
- Avoid closed and 'why?' questions. These will only cause defensiveness. Instead ask 'what?' and 'how?' questions. In Chapter 6, I describe the 'Tug of Tell', the human desire to tell someone what to do, think, behave – or just act the way you do. So, stay open and stay exploring for far longer than you think you need to:
   - *What do you think about this situation?*
   - *How does this feel from your point of view?*
   - *What makes you say that?*
   - *What else matters here?*
- Your goal here is to get the best possible outcome for you, for the other person and for the relationship. To do this you need as much information as possible. Encourage them to express their facts, stories and feelings. Listen and be willing to reshape your story as you learn more facts.

Make it safe to talk

- In any difficult conversation, there will undoubtedly be *Roadbumps* or *Flashes*, which indicate the conversation has just become 'unsafe'. And it can happen very quickly. Flashes are speedy reactions, verbal or non-verbal, and can include a sigh, a turning away, a shrug, watery eyes or closing of the eyes. They might be expressions: 'fine... right... you would say that... I can't believe you're saying this', etc. Teenagers specialize in this – a toss of the head, a raise of the eyebrows, a 'whatever' and you're triggered! Breathe, remain calm.

- *Roadbumps* tend to be new information, a more serious behavioural reaction, or strong emotion. You need to slow down, listen and take it carefully to get the conversation back on track. Going back to the example above where you open the conversation with the impact of someone interrupting you:

  'At our leadership meeting this afternoon, you interrupted me twice, even though we talked about this last week. It makes me think that I haven't been clear enough about the impact of your behaviour, as it makes me feel undermined and frustrated.'

- Ideally, you will get a thoughtful response to this opening. But you might also get:

  'Seriously Lucy? Aren't you just being a little sensitive here? I'm sure there are times when you interrupt others? What do you want me to do, just let you talk on and on...?'

- Roadbump or Flash, you have to *make it safe* for someone to talk openly to you – rather than act in a defensive or hostile way. Don't get sucked into a silly game or battle. *You do not need to win anything.* We feel safe when we believe that someone has our best interests at heart; we respect that person's opinion and trust their motives and ability.
- To handle critical flashes, you need a blend of confidence, humility and skill. Here are the five best techniques to help you:
  a **Contrasting**. My preferred technique for the moment a difficult conversation is in danger of escalating. Contrasting

is a 'don't/do' statement which addresses any misunderstanding and provides context and proportion: 'No John, I'm not saying that I want you to let me talk on and on. I am saying that I would like to finish what I'm saying without interruption.'

b Stay **curious**. However provocative the response is, just ask yourself, 'I wonder why they are reacting in this way', which gives you a moment to think. Open questions are your best friend in a difficult conversation: 'How can we best resolve this between us?' 'What do you think?'

c **Step in and step out**. Step into the conversation while you are talking but remember to also step out and LISTEN. Remain calm. As I mentioned earlier, you can listen without agreeing.

d **Say what you see in the room**. And then move back to Explore:

'You sound really frustrated? What's causing this?'

'I'm noticing a sense of unease in your body language. I'd really like to hear more about what you are thinking and feeling.'

e Say **sorry**. At times, a simple apology is all that is needed to get a conversation back on track. 'I'm sorry, I phrased that in a clumsy way...' But make sure this is not a shift back to humility in the face of aggression, so use your apology sincerely and at the right time.

Summarize (with a solutions focus)

- Summarize first. When you summarize, you show you have listened, reflected and heard their point of view:

'This is what I'm hearing...' 'This is what I believe you're saying...?'

- After all this good work, the best next step is for mutual agreement for the way forwards:

'How would you like to resolve this?'
'What would you like to see happening next?'
'What do you suggest as the next step?'
'What do you want to do going forwards?'
'What support would you like from me?'

- Work out a win/win change: negotiate the next steps to be taken. What are the actions on which you can both agree? Look for the choices that will correct the problem, both now and in the future, focusing on the win/win approach. Expect to make changes yourself and demonstrate this is a two-way street.
- Unfortunately, not all difficult conversations end with a mutually positive agreement. So, if this is not going to happen, state what behaviour you expect to see in the future instead. You have two options here:
  a Decide not to escalate, but state specifically what you expect to happen in future (plus the consequence of this not happening) and get agreement.
  b Decide to escalate, explain why and what will be happening next.
- Always summarize your conversation in writing.

You may already be asking yourself, do I really need to do this for one 15-minute conversation? While this may take time (it will get easier with practice), I guarantee there's a huge payoff. You'll go into the conversation feeling prepared, acting with compassion, maintaining perspective and confidence to achieve a good outcome.

Ten top tips for mastering a difficult conversation

1 To maintain the balance between Compassion and Confidence, master your mindset first with the six questions.

2. Breathe, remain calm. Ensure your emotional state is steady before starting this conversation.
3. Avoid the Tug of Tell! Stay open, stay curious.
4. Plan, but don't script. Write out your POEMS framework to help you stay on course:
   - Prepare
   - Open
   - Explore
   - Make it safe to talk
   - Summarize
5. Know your intent. If it's negative, this will seep through to your verbal and non-verbal language. Look for your positive intent.
6. Maintain perspective for yourself and the other person. If you are thinking this conversation is difficult, it is likely to be more so for the receiver.
7. Know your triggers, your style under stress, and what might derail this conversation for you.
8. Slow down the conversation when you hit Roadbumps. It will help you find the right words and show you are listening.
9. Reframe the conversation from Convincing to Learning. What is going on here?
10. Prepare, prepare, prepare. Need I say more?!

CHAPTER ELEVEN

From survive to thrive

How to embed a resilient culture

In a nutshell

The need for a resilient workforce was tested under a global spotlight with the challenge of the 2020/21 Covid-19 pandemic, leaving many business leaders asking the question, 'How do we embed resilience across our organization?' This chapter explores a model for embedding cultural resilience, helping you take a proactive look at what's needed to develop thriving teams through trust, purpose, flexibility, support and space.

What's the problem?

Terrence Deal and Allan Kennedy (2000) gave clarity to the many complex definitions of culture, with the statement: 'Culture is the way we do things around here.' I'll add to this by outlining culture as the stories told behind your back or in the pub, about your organization. When your colleagues are asked, *What's your company like? What's your boss like?* do they give stories of survival (it's tough, grim, difficult manager, impossible clients, late nights, burnout) or stories of thriving (it's creative, challenging, looked after, great manager, tough but fair)?

We can usefully define organizational resilience as 'a company's capacity to absorb stress, recover critical functionality, and thrive in altered circumstances' (Reeves and Whitaker, 2020). This sounds straightforward, yet scientists are only recently noticing the paradox between the definition and the reality (Moss, 2021).

Resilience is needed when the climate is unknown, changeable and unpredictable. At such times, it requires leaders to operate with speed and trust, cross-functionally. Yet, too often, leaders are working in siloed, economic islands, on short-term solutions that maximize shareholder value. This complex, uncertain environment also requires teams to be supportive, resourceful and full of rejuvenated zest! And if that sounds impossible, it's because many organizations are designed to achieve the precise reverse of this. How many of these practices seem familiar to you?

- Back-to-back meetings.
- Unsustainable email inboxes.
- An attitude of 'lunch is for wimps'.
- Low tolerance for mistakes.
- Time dedicated to the immediate and urgent, trumping what is important long term.
- Abundant silo mentality.
- Few opportunities to recharge through the day.
- Overwork is celebrated.
- Learning squeezed into brief courses and rarely revisited.

It's not that wellbeing strategies are ignored. Indeed, they're starting to become a welcome mainstay objective springing from the human resource function. But it is common for the theme of resilience to be addressed through 'self-care' training and coaching. The message is clear – this is an individual issue, and we'll help you to cope. It's led scientists to argue that everyone has been attacking the issue of organizational burnout and resilience from the wrong angle: 'Let's just recommend more yoga, wellness tech, meditation apps, and subsidized gym memberships — that'll fix it' (Moss, 2021).

In my experience, embedding cultural resilience is neither exclusively an individual concern nor solely the responsibility of the business. We need to address resilience from all angles, and as Chapter 2 addresses how individuals can revive their energy through physical, mental and emotional recharge, so does this chapter offer concepts for broader organizational solutions.

The big idea: From deep roots to flourishing teams

A revolution has been taking place in the scientific understanding of trees (bear with me, I have a point here!) and Peter Wohlleben (2018) is the first writer to convey its amazements to a general audience, with his book *The Hidden Life of Trees: What they feel, how they communicate*. Since Darwin, we've generally thought of trees as disconnected, isolated and competitive – battlegrounds for survival of the fittest. There is now substantial scientific evidence that refutes this idea (Grant, 2018), showing that trees are cooperative and interdependent, relying on a symbiotic relationship underground, and above our heads, sharing the space and light.

The analogy to organizations is striking. Resilient teams have a deep connection to their roots, the vision and purpose, balanced with an ability to respond and flex to new situations. Space is prioritized to learn and grow. And these skills are achieved through a network of supportive relationships, based on empathy, realistic optimism and a 'can-do' confidence. And these four factors – roots, flex, space and support – are grounded in trust. As trees need water and sunlight, trust is critical to:

- believe in a company's vision and the purpose;
- accept change and work swiftly to problem-solve through challenges;
- take time to enjoy learning and growing;
- be vulnerable and empathic to others.

FIGURE 11.1   The roots of resilience

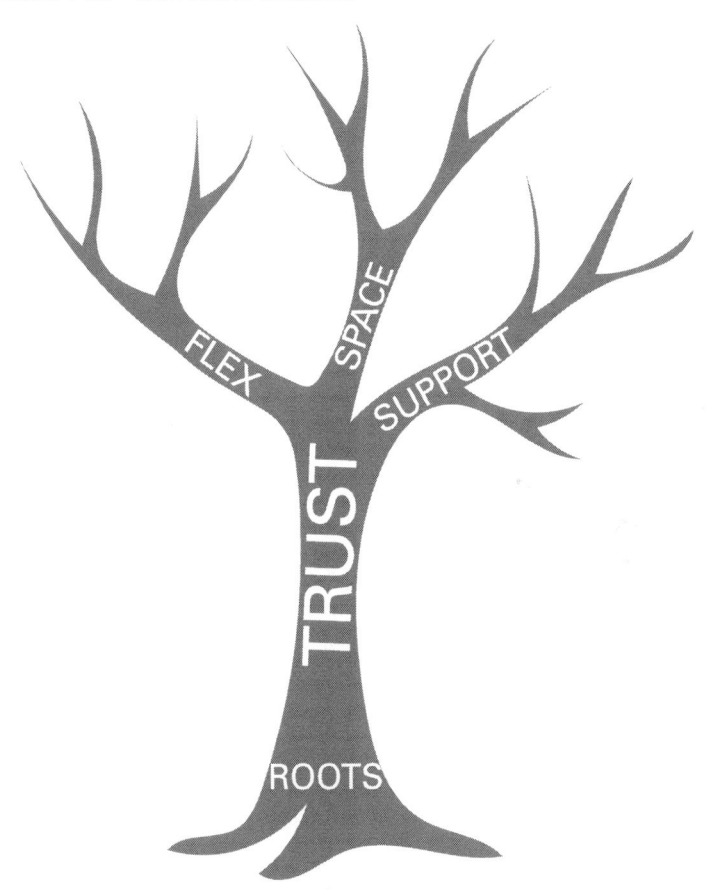

Strategy 1: Have firm roots

The National Star College in Cheltenham enables young students with complex disabilities to realize their potential through education and learning. There are always complex decisions to be made at the college, but during the Covid-19 pandemic 2020/21, these decisions became more acute and to be executed at speed. When I talked to their Principal, Simon Welch, about their response, I was struck by his focus on 'roots':

> Establishing a culture of resilience doesn't happen overnight but instead is built on a sound foundation of organizational purpose and vision. At National Star that means bringing each of our decisions back to their primary purpose: the students and young people we educate and care for. Every year the students change and their needs change, but the purpose and vision doesn't – even if how to achieve it does. The more we recognize the need to change and experience success as a leadership team who trust each other, the more resilient we've become to deal with our fast-changing landscape.

Practical inspiration #1

Test your purpose

Having a vision and purpose is integral to leadership practice, which most leaders can articulate. But are you convinced that your vision (where we're heading) and purpose (why we do it) are crystal clear to everyone else? The first thing that happens under pressure is to question your purpose: *Why am I doing this? Why am I getting out of bed this morning? How do I matter? How do I make a difference?*

While you're not responsible for individual sense-making, you are responsible for ensuring the vision and purpose of your organization is rich, exciting and ingrained. If you're unsure, here are eight questions for you to hand out to your team and find out.

TABLE 11.1 Test your purpose

	Agree	Disagree
1. I know and understand our organization's vision		
2. I believe in what we aim to achieve		
3. I am optimistic about the future		
4. I am proud of what the organization does for its customers		
5. I know the purpose of my team and how we make a difference		
6. I know how I add value and help achieve the goals of the team and company		
7. I fit in and want to give my best		
8. I have clear objectives with visible milestones		

Strategy 2: Lead with trust

In *The Speed of Trust*, Stephen Covey (2008) suggests, 'Trust is the one thing that changes everything. It is the least understood, most neglected and most under-estimated possibility of our time.' I've certainly not encountered any organization or team that's able to function with speed and respect, particularly in the face of adversity, without the underpinning of trust. In my world, the theme of trust sits at the heart of every leadership team programme and it's no surprise that trust forms the basis for Lencioni's (2002) five principles of a functioning team. That is, without trust, nothing else in the organizations operates in a satisfactory way.

Try this out #1

The importance of trust

You'll understand the importance of trust to embedding a culture of resilience when you try this simple exercise. Just fill in the different columns in Table 11.2 and go with your instincts.

TABLE 11.2 The importance of trust

	When I trust a person, I...	When I don't trust a person, I...
Believe...		
Feel...		
Say...		
Act...		

You're likely to notice that your behaviour is completely different based on your level of trust for someone else. Here's what other leaders notice. Without trust, they:

- hide their weaknesses and mistakes from one another;
- hesitate to ask for help or provide constructive feedback;
- delay offering help outside their own areas of responsibility;
- jump to conclusions about the intentions and aptitudes of others;
- hold grudges.

With trust, leaders:

- admit weaknesses and mistakes;
- ask for help;
- accept questions and input about their areas of responsibility;
- give one another the benefit of the doubt before arriving at a negative conclusion;

- take risks in offering feedback and assistance;
- offer and accept apologies without hesitation.

Imagine extending these cautious distrustful behaviours across a whole team under pressure, and you have a recipe for fragility, weakness and rigidity. When Google set up 'Project Aristotle' to research why some Google teams stumbled and others soared, the importance of 'psychological safety' was the surprising answer (Duhigg, 2016). The composition of the team wasn't important. What mattered was a climate of interpersonal trust, mutual respect and the confidence to speak up without recrimination. As Duhigg reports from the team, 'We must be able to talk about what is messy or sad, to have hard conversations with colleagues who are driving us crazy. We can't be focused just on efficiency.'

If you're left asking, 'Yes, but *how* do you build trust?, you're not alone. And that's because it's not easy, or simply a case of following one of my many '3 steps to success' plans!

But I can assure you that if you start with trust and act with trust, you will engender it from others. If you are vulnerable and willing to share something personal with your team, you'll indicate an understanding of the importance of openness and compassion.

When I'm leading team leadership training that needs a high level of trust, we start with this exercise:

share something personal that the team don't know about you

and I'm always humbled by the vulnerability and speed of trust among the team.

Strategy 3: Flex, bend and adapt

Most organizations I work with have change, 'blue sky' or innovation teams – teams of people dedicated to exploring and predicting the future, to testing and trying different approaches, to improvising with novel tactics. Unsurprisingly, they're exciting, creative teams to work with. Yet, it's still surprisingly common for the rest of the organization to act in a habitually inflexible way. You can see this through the language people use and the actions they take. For example, how often have you heard:

We never do things that way.
We've tried that before.
The customer won't budge.
The board aren't interested in that approach.
It won't work.
It's always been this way.

Or seen teams lurch from crisis to crisis, week in week out, not stopping to learn from mistakes, celebrating what works, and rarely questioning the assumptions behind the actions they take (Suarez and Montes, 2020).

What this means is that the opportunities to flex, bend and adapt to the ever-changing environment are missed. Let's explore both shifting language and learning to further embed cultural resilience.

Practical inspiration #2

The language of optimism

The word 'optimism' is flung around so much, it's easy to forget that in actuality it's an 'explanatory style'. That is, how do you explain away adversity or setbacks? When difficult things happen, do you use words like 'always', 'never' or 'everything'? So, for instance, if you don't get a desired promotion, how do you talk to yourself? 'I'll never get promoted… This always happens to me… I'll be stuck here forever.' If you have a difficult relationship with someone, how do you explain it away? 'It's always been like this... it'll never change... He's like that with everyone.' Even if good things happen to a pessimist, they write it off as a fluke.

The ability for a team to be mentally flexible and open to possibility, is core to cultural resilience (Seligman, 2011). Optimistic teams explain away adverse events in specific, temporal and impersonal ways, e.g. not always, not forever, not across everything (and not always our fault). In other words, when they encounter a setback, they are able to view it as specific to a certain situation, temporary and thus able to be changed and not related to a team deficiency. This enables the team to be positively energized and able to change the problem situation to their advantage. I talk to my clients about 'containing' adverse events – put a box round it and don't let it leak out to everything else.

Try this out #2

Pessimistic vs optimistic thinking

Think about a situation your team faced that didn't go well or remained unresolved; for example, a critical deadline missed, an outraged client or an IT collapse. As you think about the situation, what language was used across the team – pessimistic or optimistic? Try this for yourself first before sharing this learning with your team; write out pessimistic thinking sentences, and then train your brain to write out an optimistic version. I've taken an example in Table 11.3 – the rejection of a budget for a new project.

TABLE 11.3 Pessimistic vs optimistic thinking

	Pessimistic Thinking	Optimistic Thinking
Always	It'll always be like this	It's not great news, but we can rewrite and repropose from the feedback
Never	We'll never get this through the board	We did get a proposal through six months ago. We can try again
Everything	Perhaps this team just doesn't function well	There's lots we do well as a team, and this outcome doesn't change that
Us	We don't have enough resource. The system's set up against us	We need to rethink how we allocate our resources to adapt to the system

Practical inspiration #3

From crisis to opportunity

Too often, leaders focus on the negative aspects of a crisis and don't perceive the opportunities in the situation (Wooten and James, 2014). Crises are opportunities for organizational change and revitalization, with possibilities abounding for innovation and systemic improvements. They can enable you to get better, act with greater integrity or enhance your customer experience. Here are 10 questions you can use with your team to enable resilient, flexible learning:

1 What new strengths have materialized in the last couple of months?
2 What new ways of working have become evident that we can recognize and retain?

3. What positive, attitudinal shifts and beliefs have become apparent?
4. How can we capitalize and build on these strengths?
5. What weaknesses have become obvious?
6. What/who/which functions are holding us back?
7. What new opportunities and needs have emerged in our marketplace or in our culture?
8. What feels exciting? What's worth getting out of bed for now?
9. Who is not capitalizing on these emergent marketplaces/product/services (and can we fill this gap)?
10. What new threats are evident and where do they come from? (Locally, globally? Health and wellbeing? Turnover and cultural change?)

Strategy 4: Space vs pace

When any team is under pressure or facing considerable adversity, the pace picks up. Just take one of my clients in 2020. Within one week they had moved 85 per cent of their 1,000-strong staff to homeworking, while ensuring the other 15 per cent who remained in head office or the call centre were operating in safe environments. IT systems were adapted, ergonomic furniture ordered, and flexible working practices swiftly put in place. The human resource function worked overtime to furlough appropriately, and employees learned to home-school. Together with the senior leadership team, the HR, IT, Finance, Customer and Change teams were busting themselves to make purposeful, swift change happen. Astonishing outcomes were achieved in an extraordinary time in our history.

The necessity for space must equal the urgency given to pace.

But there's a paradox here. Because to embed sustainable, cultural resilience, the necessity for space must equal the urgency given to pace. What do I mean by 'space'?

I mean the ability to reflect on and consider your week's work.
I mean getting to the end of the working day with energy still in your tank, and more to give to your family.
I mean looking at your email inbox and not feeling sick.
I mean finishing a meeting and having time to linger and talk to others.
I mean closing your laptop when someone wants to talk to you.
I mean scheduling 'time to think' in your calendar – and sticking to it!

That's space.

Chapter 2 is dedicated to individual resilience and self-care, and I've equated resilience to five batteries (body, mind, heart, soul and connect) that need continuous attention and recharging. Organizational resilience is no different. Indeed, some scientists (Loehr and Schwartz, 2003) insist that 'the most important organizational resource is energy', with organizational energy capacity increasing as individuals increase their collective capacity. It's worth returning to Chapter 2 and doing the first 'Drains/Energizers' exercise from an organizational perspective and I'm willing to bet that top of your list of organizational 'drains' will be meetings. I've known executives attend some 15–20 meetings a day, which only increased when work went virtual.

Practical inspiration #4

Better meetings, more space

What if you made your meetings more productive, so that you released more space across the organization? What a fine goal that would be! While much of the written advice on making meetings productive is standard fare, e.g. have a purpose-driven agenda and know your objectives, it's still great advice. Stephen Rogelberg's (2019) scientific book on meetings is an enjoyable read and he quotes Andy Grove, the former CEO of Intel, as saying, 'A poorly conducted and unnecessary meeting is indeed a form of time theft, a theft that can be prevented.'

Here are 10 strategies you might not have tried, and I've experienced their practical success:

1. Don't schedule one-hour meetings. Schedule them for specific, unusual times, e.g. 18 or 43 minutes.
2. Always start on time, no matter who is missing (and put your most important information first, so people learn to be on time).
3. Short is better. Go for a 15-minute 'huddle' or a 10-minute walk instead.
4. Assign people to different parts of the agenda and give them the heads-up to prepare (with timing).
5. Don't re-use the same agenda. It's lazy and people fall into poor meeting habits.
6. The more complicated the meeting, the fewer attendees should be invited.
7. Try a silent meeting. I love them! At the top of the meeting, assign your brainstorming topic and give everyone 10 minutes in silence to write their thoughts. Then start the conversation. If this feels a stretch, just ask a question, and give everyone two minutes to write down their thoughts.
8. When you're invited to a meeting, ask 'why?', or perhaps more politely, 'what are you hoping I'll contribute?'
9. Use a timer in the meetings. In my experience, people resist at first but it's great at keeping everyone to time, particularly when you want to give all attendees a share of the voice. You'll soon find you won't need it once people learn what three-minute input really means!
10. Get the right people in the room, less is more, and ensure everyone takes part.

Strategy 5: Support – 'lean on me'

For 50 years, it's been fashionable within evolutionary theory to regard human beings as basically selfish. Richard Dawkins' (1976) book, *The Selfish Gene*, is illustrative of the philosophy that natural selection works through solitary individuals edging out the competition – akin to early theories of trees.

More recently psychologists, social scientists and historians have broken with this theory. For example, in his beautiful book, *Humankind*, historian Rutger Bregman (2020) demonstrates that it is our basic instinct to cooperate rather than compete, to trust rather than distrust and to look for what is good and positive in others. Put another way, Brene Brown (2015) suggests, 'we're hardwired to connect with others'.

It's natural, so the science says, to demonstrate acts of kindness, gratitude and empathy to others in the face of extreme adversity (Seligman, 2011). But for cultural resilience, you need to know that in all directions across your organization – upwards, downwards and horizontally – people can pull together. Not just in the face of a crisis, but through a desire to support each other entrenched in your organizational DNA.

Time to reflect

Who is the real team?

The remarkable female combat veteran, Michelle Dallocchio (2017), wrote in her book, *The Desert Warrior*, 'Adversity has the remarkable ability of introducing the real you to yourself.' This is such a thought-provoking statement, suggesting that adversity and pressure strip the façade away to reveal the true person – or in the case of this chapter, the real team. So, in terms of support, are the basics in place for your team? How ready is your team to cope with adversity? What's the real team like under pressure? I use the acronym CORE to start this process of understanding and here are four questions to start your reflection:

Compassion: Do your team care for each other and share both success and failure?

Openness: Is the team able to have honest, frank conversations with each other, giving and receiving constructive feedback?

Resourcefulness: When under pressure, do the team pull together, sharing resources and creating new ways of approaching problems?

Expectations: Does everyone know what to expect of each other, with crystal clear clarity of roles, and of team unity and support?

Practical inspiration #5

Extend your coaching practice to embed support

When leaders talk about coaching, they usually mean coaching their team. There are ideas for this in both Chapters 5 and 6, and if you've got to the point where coaching is a consistent, positive skill in your leadership toolbox, rather than a cautioning 'fix', well done! It's going to be worth your time extending your coaching practice to the leadership team you belong to – and by this, I mean peer coaching.

To embed 'support' as one-fifth of cultural resilience, all levels of your organization should feel there are people they can be vulnerable with, people they can trust and people they can be honest with. I know for some leaders it can feel awkward to start peer coaching, but I can assure you that once practised, it's a mutual win/win. Clients who experience this say that it's a great way to work through what is troubling them; they get a trusted colleague to bounce ideas around with and it lessens isolation.

Here are five ways to get you started:

1. Identify a peer you trust (they need to be able to maintain confidentiality) and invite them to explore peer coaching with you. Explain what you hope to get from it. Perhaps share this chapter with them?
2. 20 minutes each is a good amount of time to start with. If it needs to be shorter, OK, just don't use 'lack of time' as a reason not to start!
3. Choose a topic you want to focus on, e.g. it could be a project you're working on, a relationship that's difficult, juggling struggles. Keep it focused and specific. Try not to just moan! Remember, you are asking for perspective, questions and input, but you're not asking them for solutions (although this might naturally arise).
4. When it's your turn to be the coach, listen with your full respectful attention.
5. At the end, it's a good habit for both of you to identify one piece of insight and one action.

In summary, you can see that the skill of resilience is not something you can just graft on to your organizational agenda! It takes a proactive approach and a desire to ensure all levels across your workforce embrace your purpose, act with trust and empathy, maintaining mental flexibility. Your teams will thank you for the space you create to think and develop, and the support that is engendered cross-functionally will place you in a great position for a resilient response to the next adversity.

Ten top tips for embedding cultural resilience

1. Take a good look at how your organizational set-up acts as a barrier to resilience. What systems are unhelpful?

2. Generate a team climate characterized by interpersonal trust and mutual respect.
3. Practise conversational turn-taking at meetings, ensuring everyone has a voice.
4. Foster multiple ways of doing things, taking diverse approaches to problem solving.
5. Role-model the strengths of optimism, curiosity and perspective.
6. When you notice the pace of work is stretching to uncomfortable levels, enable more space.
7. Balance your firm roots with flexible attitudes and teams who are able to stretch and recover.
8. Bounce back from adversity, but bounce forward to new learning and adaptation to a new environment.
9. Notice what is praised across the organization. Instead of rewarding overwork, reward resourcefulness, support and growth. Take a lunch break!
10. Start with trust, act with trust, reward trust.

PART FOUR

Leading with influence

CHAPTER TWELVE

Build your leadership brand

(And be remembered, for the right reasons!)

In a nutshell

Whether you like it or not, you have a brand. And by your brand you are known (just think about what people say about you behind your back!). Whether you're starting from scratch, refreshing your brand or reinventing yourself through a leadership transition, two simple questions – a) what do you stand *for?* and b) how do you stand *out?* – will guide you through defining and delivering a brand that works for you.

What's the problem?

It's time to accept you have a personal brand and that your reputation is key to your leadership. You are the brand that leads the brand and often your reputation is the reputation of the company. If you aren't managing your brand and your reputation, then someone else will. So, it had better be you. Two issues lie at the heart of branding. Firstly, it's not taken seriously enough, and secondly, you can get 'stuck' with your brand. For example, do you know what your leadership brand is? This isn't a trivial question, because by your brand you are noticed, remembered and promoted. By your brand, or lack of brand, you are also overlooked, undervalued or static in your career (while you are left wondering why). So, while some coaching clients are keen to increase their visibility, their brand and their presence, there are still many leaders who dismiss branding as a fad, or some cynical jargon that will quietly go away while they get on with the day job.

When you factor in globalization, increasing competition, the need to manage your career and the pace of organizational change, your ability to stand out from the crowd becomes even more important. If you heard, like I do, how you're being discussed behind your back, you'll reach for a pen, take charge of your brand and be proud of the words people use to define you. I still remember waiting in a breakfast queue at a client's office overhearing two people discussing me (they were about to attend a course I was leading). 'What's she like?', went the question. 'Think Julie Andrews crossed with a meerkat' was the (remarkably speedy) response. Well… at least it was distinctive, but definitely time to take control!

You are the brand that leads the brand and often your reputation is the reputation of the company.

What about getting 'stuck' with your brand? I can immediately think of three clients who realized they'd been labelled with a brand they want to shift. Luca was known as a 'people pleaser', Ellie as 'technically competent' and Matt as a 'driven salesman'. Nothing is wrong with these labels, except when they want to make a step up in their careers and their brand comes with a 'but'. Here's what happens in discussion:

> '*Luca's great, he puts people first, BUT I'm not sure he's commercial enough for a bigger role.*'
>
> '*Ellie's intellectual stance and technical competence put her ahead of others for this next role, BUT I'm not sure she's emotionally competent enough.*'
>
> '*Matt's results-driven orientation is vital to this business, we need this drive leading the sales teams, BUT I'm not convinced he is a broad strategic player.*'

I'm sure Luca, Ellie and Matt can offer countless examples to demonstrate their commerciality, emotional intelligence or strategic direction. But if this is perception, then, as the saying goes, perception equals reality. As Longfellow (1847) said in his epic poem, *Evangeline*, 'We judge ourselves by what we feel capable of doing, while others judge us by what we have already done.'

So, it's going to happen, like it or not. Other people will sum you up in a couple of sentences, yet few of us manage our brand strategically, working out a careful plan of our values and aspirations, how we want to be perceived and how to turn this into action.

The big idea: Stand for/stand out

A big idea in its simplicity, as just two questions will frame and realize your brand:

1 *What do you stand for?* (Your authenticity.)
2 *How do you stand out?* (Your distinctiveness.)

What do you stand for?

As a leader, you are defined by your values and character strengths, shaped by your personal beliefs, developed through study, reflection, coaching and feedback, and a lifetime of experience. These values form your moral compass, often called 'authentic leadership'. When I asked a professor to sum up authentic leadership to me, he said, 'You, Lucy, only better'! I describe authenticity as the common threads of passion that have run through your life. For example, I've had multiple changes of career, including being a singer, salesperson, training director, psychologist, PhD student, leadership coach and author. Despite career highs and dives, there are three common threads of passion that run through my life: a love of learning, a tenacity to achieve and a passionate desire to make a positive difference to others. These three areas of passion matter deeply to me, I wouldn't feel like 'me' without them and they are therefore wholly authentic. You might be able to answer what you stand for immediately, but if not, here are two ways to help you access and answer this very important question. The first way is through the questions below. They're big, hairy questions, so take some time and enjoy the reflection.

Time to reflect

Authentic you

Passions and values:

- When do you stand your ground and on what issues?
- What do you talk passionately about?
- What are your most deeply held values?
- What makes you mad/switch off from other people?
- Why do you do your job?

Achievements:

- As you look back over your career, what achievements are you really proud of?
- In what ways do these successes show you at your best?
- What do you do better than anyone else?
- What would other people say are your key achievements?

Practical inspiration #1

Equally, you can use a list of character strengths. We're often unused to talking about our strengths, wary of people considering us arrogant if we did. Not only this, but we also all possess, to some degree, an inherent negativity bias that causes us to focus on the negative, on what's wrong, on what isn't working. As psychologist Roy Baumeister (2001) said in his popular article, 'Bad is stronger than good.'

If you are one of the people who find it difficult to attend to strengths and what is working, finding yourself being pulled back to focus on weaknesses, problems and difficulties – you are not alone. So, use this list, and focus on you at your best. Which strengths feel natural to you? Which ones energize you? Which ones excite you and would be recognized by others if you gave them this list? Choose up to five, as these will be your superstrengths (Peterson and Seligman, 2004):

- [ ] Creativity (originality, ingenuity)
- [ ] Curiosity (interest, novelty-seeking, openness to experience)
- [ ] Judgement (open-mindedness, critical thinking)
- [ ] Love of learning (mastering new skills, topics, and bodies of knowledge)
- [ ] Perspective (wisdom)
- [ ] Bravery (courage)
- [ ] Perseverance (persistence, industriousness)
- [ ] Honesty (authenticity, integrity)
- [ ] Zest (vitality, enthusiasm, passion, energy)
- [ ] Love (capacity to love and be loved)
- [ ] Kindness (generosity, nurturance, care, compassion, altruistic love, 'niceness')
- [ ] Social intelligence (emotional intelligence, personal intelligence)
- [ ] Teamwork (citizenship, social responsibility, loyalty)
- [ ] Fairness (justice)

- ☐ Leadership (encouraging a group of which one is a member to get things done and at the same time maintain good relations within the group)
- ☐ Forgiveness (mercy)
- ☐ Humility (modesty)
- ☐ Prudence (being careful about one's choices)
- ☐ Self-regulation (self-control)
- ☐ Appreciation of beauty and excellence (awe, wonder, elevation)
- ☐ Gratitude (being aware of and thankful for the good things that happen)
- ☐ Hope (optimism, future-mindedness, future orientation)
- ☐ Humour (playfulness)
- ☐ Spirituality (meaning, faith, purpose)

© Copyright 2004-2021, VIA Institute on Character. Used with permission. All rights reserved. www.viacharacter.org

As you explore both these exercises, what you're looking to recognize are those common threads of passion I mentioned earlier. Put them into your words, it can be as down to earth as you like, as long as you read it and know it's meaningful to you.

For example:

Luca: At my core is a passion for leadership and teamwork. When my team thrives, I thrive, as building genuine relationships matters to me, with trust forming the foundation to my brand. For me, leadership is all about resilience and courage, so I aim to inspire optimism through challenging times and celebration through the good times.

Ellie: What matters to me is leading through an authentic, collaborative and open-minded approach. I listen and learn, building networks across the different teams in our organization. What this means is I hold the space for our team to know that our contribution means something bigger. I feel really motivated when I feel seen and heard, and when I can help other people feel seen and heard. Just like everything, it has a ripple effect.

Matt: *I'm self-determined and tenacious, leading strategic projects through from beginning to end, always with a commercial eye for profitable results. As a leader, I'm a doer, an energizer, a motivator for getting stuff done. With a passion for our business reflecting our diverse customer base, I'm an advocate for inclusion and celebrating difference.*

How do you stand out?

Aha! The big question. *So what?* What's the difference here? As Goffee and Jones (2006) wrote in their hugely popular article, 'Why Should Anyone be Led by You?':

> Another quality of inspirational leaders is that they capitalize on what's unique about themselves. Anything can be a difference, but it is important to communicate it. Most people, however, are hesitant to communicate what's unique about themselves, and it can take years for them to be fully aware of what sets them apart.

Differentiating yourself comes down to two things:

- your image, *and*
- your actions.

Let's talk image

As you develop your brand, it'd be remiss not to consider the impact of your image, and naïve to think it doesn't matter. I'd like this to be unimportant and for your values and competence to be the lens through which you're judged, but, as Italian fashion designer Miuccia Prada once said, 'What you wear is how you present yourself to the world, especially today when human contacts are so quick. Fashion is instant language.' (Galloni, 2007)

Practical inspiration #2

The style questionnaire – my brand image

Take a look at the questionnaire below and reflect on your image – your look, your sound and your 'feel'. Remember, you're answering the question here, 'How do I stand out?', so circle a maximum of three words in each of the categories (or use your own words below) for how you **want** to be viewed in the business – this is your future brand.

STYLE QUESTIONNAIRE

What's my 'look'?

Tailored edgy bohemian relaxed minimal androgynous modern comfortable youthful dishevelled dynamic stylish elegant casual sporty quirky dressy dramatic powerful sophisticated simple colourful bold understated expensive arty polished coordinated fun timeless sharp trendy individual messy chic

_____

_____

_____

How do I sound?

Breathy animated quiet persuasive powerful thoughtful high-pitched softly spoken unassuming strident dominant friendly knowledgeable authoritative deep unsure animated anxious breezy quick bubbly calm casual relaxed serious firm matter-of-fact warm lively monotone bright mild informal

_____

_____

_____

What's the 'feel' of my brand?

Creative adventurous energetic pessimistic dominant dynamic successful extroverted introverted polite trusting reserved sensitive modest easy-going approachable motivated ambitious risk-taking collaborative focused independent energetic fun impulsive optimistic assertive authoritative supportive serious inspiring humble

_____

_____

_____

Try this out

Now give the questionnaire to at least **three** people you trust to give you honest feedback on your **current** style (this only takes five minutes, so doable in your lunchtime). Using the Style Questionnaire, ask them to circle three words in each of the three sections for how you currently come across to others.

Having got this feedback, it's time to take a reflective breath. What you're aiming to explore is the discrepancies between your current and future desired brand image. As you look at your answers, and compare them to those who gave you feedback, ask yourself the following three questions:

1. *What do you already project that is working?*
   What you are looking at here is congruency between what other people have said about your current brand, and what your desired future is.
2. *How will you strengthen this and gain consistency?*
   Strengthen what works first before you look for the gaps.
3. *What do you not project that you would like to?*
   In other words, what do you wish to be known for as you develop this year? What words did you circle that no one else

did? Where is there incongruency? Do you want to be seen as collaborative, but there's words such as impulsive or dominant highlighted?

For example, if you look again at Ellie's brand statement, you'll see it is all about inclusion and collaboration. Responses from her questionnaire showed congruity in her look and sound, with a polished, timeless appearance and a thoughtful, knowledgeable approach. Ellie is comfortable with this. However, there was a disconnect in the 'feel' of her brand. Ellie hoped that words such as motivated and collaborative would be reflected but instead, words such as independent and reserved were noted. Additional notes on the form suggested that Ellie needs to work harder at motivating and celebrating with the team, and networking across the different silos. 'More head up, than head down', one person noted.

Taking action

Communicating your brand

Living your brand is about congruity and consistency. What we're talking about here is trust, that's why we buy into a brand. For example, we're cynical about an organization that espouses 'putting the customer first' yet ignores the customer service team. We applaud the business that champions environmental causes and supports this with rewards for car sharing. And, according to the Edelman Trust Barometer (2020), trust is built through competence **and** behaviour, with less than a third of people worldwide trusting their leaders. Such worrying statistics are echoed by the Gallup engagement survey (2020) citing that only 36 per cent of employees define themselves as 'engaged' at work, with 14 per cent 'actively disengaged'. We have work to do!

We've talked about building congruity through your appearance, so think about all the ways you communicate your brand, which can be endless given that we communicate for some 80 per cent of our workday. Research from Noel Zandan at Quantified Communications (2020) suggests that the typical human is only aware of between 5 and 15 per cent of the communication signals they send, with up to a stellar 95 per cent of your communication unconscious. If you try to make all your habits conscious, you'll go mad, but start with five ways you communicate your brand:

1. The presentations you deliver.
2. The meetings you hold.
3. Your engagement with your team.
4. Your communication on social media.
5. How your team acts across the business.

How you align your values and your strengths with your behaviour is going to be distinctive to you, but here are some ideas to help you:

If you want your presence to be more *visible* (read more in Chapter 14):

- Ensure your presence at meetings is positive, not passive or dominant.
- Build on other people's contributions with questions, and affirmative actions.
- Network more broadly outside of your team and direct contacts. Build a strategic network of influencers.
- Contribute to efforts outside of your job, such as wellbeing committees or charitable concerns.

If you want to deliver *snappier* presentations (read more in Chapter 13):

- Write them from the audience perspective, *What do they really want to hear?*, and reduce your slides to fewer than five.
- Start with an energetic opening.

- Get people interacting with you.
- Go under, not over time (people will thank you!).

If you want your meetings to be more *successful* (see Chapter 14):

- Always ask why you need to be at this meeting: *What's the purpose? What value do you add? Why have you been invited?*
- If you're running it, set out an agenda beforehand and stick to time.
- Give everyone a voice, not allowing one person to dominate.
- Ask for actions: *What does this mean we do next? Who will take responsibility for this? How will we know this action has been achieved?*
- Have fewer meetings!

If you want to be more *engaged* with your team (read more in Chapter 5):

- Set out your vision and direction in an understandable way.
- Talk about your values, make them come alive, show how meaningful they are to you.
- Demonstrate the contribution your team makes.
- Celebrate achievements and help the team connect with each other, formally and informally.

When you're communicating on *social media*:

- Think about your purpose. Why are you communicating and what's your desired outcome?
- Think of what the readers really want to know. Make your posts meaningful.
- Keep it positive and short.
- Only engage on the platforms where you feel an affinity. One platform is enough!

Aligning your *team's actions* across the business:

- Ensure you have communicated your values and shared what is important.

- Be clear about the behaviour you expect.
- Build a team brand, so everyone is aligned, not just the interested few.
- Ask for feedback from other teams. How would they define your team's behaviour?

Ten top tips for building your brand

1. Your brand demonstrates what you stand *for*, and how you stand *out*.
2. Your brand consists of both reputation and reach.
   The more often someone thinks of you, and the higher their opinion of you, the stronger your reputation becomes.
3. Your brand needs to be distinctive.
   Your brand is not static, it is constantly developing. To stand out from the crowd, to be distinctive, people should remember who you are, what you do and what makes you different.
4. Your brand should be authentic and consistent.
   A powerful brand is always authentic, based on who you are and what your life and work are all about. You should aim to be the best you.
5. Your brand is valuable.
   A strong brand will make you stand out in the eyes of people who want to work with you. As a leader, people will want to follow you and clients will trust your team.
6. Your appearance is part of your brand.
   Your appearance is a key part of your brand identity, so it is worth devoting time and effort to it.
7. Your job title is not your brand.
   Your job title does not make you unique. At most, it indicates your position in a hierarchy, and perhaps the skills you possess.

8. Your brand should stand out like a tall building.
   Imagine your brand is a building under construction – you want it to be distinctive and clearly visible. However, before you build it, you must first prepare the ground... know your strengths.
9. Be consistent with your actions.
   Think about all the ways in which your behaviour radiates your values and dial up your positive actions.
10. Build a team brand.
    Ensure there is congruency and consistency with the actions of your team.

CHAPTER THIRTEEN

From inform to inspire

How to deliver a successful presentation and get the action you want

In a nutshell

Whether your presentations are small virtual meetings or large conference halls, shift your presentations from solely conveying information, to leaving your audience feeling inspired and wanting to take action. Understand the power of connection and have the audience at the heart of your planning and delivery. Use the six questions for focused content and practise the five ways to conquer your nerves. Altogether, this chapter helps you deliver your message with the engagement and the passion your audience deserves!

What's the problem?

Most business presentations are surprisingly dull. Surprising, because even though there's a wealth of material out there to help you spice up your presentations and deliver them with oomph and brilliance, business presentations continue to be stuffed full of interminable slides, protracted facts and endless information. Perhaps I exaggerate here, and your presentations hit the mark every time? I hope so, for when the magic happens and you listen to a presentation that combines startling facts with personal passion and an emotional call to action, it is joyful. Trust me, the audience is grateful!

The great Roman orator, Cicero, defined inspiration as the ability to *docere, delectare, et movere*. That is, to prove your proposal to the audience, to delight them, and to leave them emotionally moved. A great definition of inspiration. If we take a continuum with 'inform' at one end and 'inspire' at the other and consider your last presentation, where on the scale would you place it?

FIGURE 13.1   The inspiration continuum

Inform _____ Inspire
(Presenting the facts)   (Moved to action)

If your presentation sat towards the left-hand side of the scale, what prevented you from leaving your audience inspired, remembering you the next day, let alone the subsequent week?

Having coached leaders to present at small meetings through to stadiums, I reject the idea that this has anything to do with laziness or lack of ability. Most people care deeply about their communication, but are hampered by one major psychological barrier: *vulnerability*.

There are few roles in your business life that require you to stand up in front of people and be judged. It's probably the most exposing part of your role and taps into a deep fear of being 'found out' and sometimes a paralysing stage fright. Therefore, it's no wonder that you cover up this vulnerability in multiple ways:

- hide behind PowerPoint or SlideShare, ensuring the time you speak without slides is minimal;
- turn the lights down;
- stand behind a lectern;
- sit down and ensure the laptop covers most of your body;
- script your presentation and read it;
- put in so much information, hoping the right stuff sticks;
- talk about your organization and ALL your products and services;
- deliver the same presentation you always do, just change the client name;
- reveal nothing about yourself;
- stick to facts, no emotion, no storytelling;
- apologize as you start;
- and my pet hate, closing with the slide, 'Any Questions?'

I get it. I made my living in my early twenties singing and acting, accompanied by a crippling stage fright that made me leave the profession and move into sales. After I moved from Sales Director in London to General Manager in Sydney, I had to do large-scale presentations across the states of Australia and face my nerves. Coaching, hypnotherapy and a healthy dose of experience got me there, plus, to face my fears, I ran karaoke shows four nights a week!

Whatever your level of vulnerability, it's perfectly achievable to overcome your stage fright and nudge your presentations up the scale towards inspiration. That's my aim in this chapter, although it will take a desire from you to change habits, practise with an open mindset, and accept your vulnerability.

The big idea: The power of connection

What does an audience want from you? Less than you think as you prepare your lavish slide deck. What an audience is craving is connection. They are asking you to:

notice me
understand me
tell me what you can do for me
explain why you're better for me than someone else
help me make a decision

And you achieve connection in two main ways: through your planning and your delivery. Perhaps you sigh with frustration at the thought of planning being a big idea: 'You mean, that's it?' Yes, I do. Half of the art of inspiring through connection lies in the way you plan. The other half lies in your head and how you talk to yourself when you deliver a presentation. First things first.

The key point when planning for connection is to take an outwards focus. The vast majority of business presentations are prepared with one single question in mind: *What do I want to tell you?* You might ask the question more elegantly than this, but it boils down to this question.

So, let's reverse the focus with six questions that are all about placing the emphasis where it should be – on the audience.

Practical inspiration #1

Planning with an outwards focus

1. Who are you presenting to?
2. What is your single significant message?
3. What do they *really* want to hear?
4. What do you want them to feel?
5. What action do you want them to take?
6. Why do you care?

1. WHO ARE YOU PRESENTING TO?

Let's place the client at the front of your focus. If this is a small audience, think through the personalities you have in front of you and tailor your approach accordingly. Do they want a five-minute summary? All the analytics in a spreadsheet?

Multiple options, or a long chat before you get down to business?

What's the level of language or jargon you are safe with? What anecdotes or stories will work and resonate with the audience?

Ask yourself, *what will the audience have been doing before I speak?* This is a really important question. Are you going to be presenting at the end of a long pitch day (in which case, you'd better be very quick, and very energizing)? If you're presenting to 1,000 people, have they been sitting down for a long time (in which case, get them up)?

Question 1 gives you your LEVEL OF LANGUAGE.

2. WHAT IS YOUR SINGLE KEY MESSAGE?

Imagine this. You've delivered an important team presentation and I visit your team the next day and ask them the one big idea in the presentation. What do they remember? Will they give me the answer you want them to?

Question 2 gives you your FOCUS.

3. WHAT DO THEY (THE AUDIENCE, CLIENT OR TEAM) REALLY WANT TO KNOW?

This is the anchor point of your presentation. This is not what *you* want to tell them, but what do *they* genuinely want to know? Instead of the typical structure:

A reminder of who we are
Our background and history
The new idea
How it will work
Any questions?

you're designing your presentation around what they'll be thinking:

What's so great about this idea?
Will it be worth it?

Why should we bother?
What are our alternatives?
How much will it cost?
Why you?

Question 3 forms your DIRECTION OF CONTENT.

4. WHAT DO YOU WANT THEM TO FEEL?

This question is rarely asked in planning a presentation even though, behind your back, people will talk about you emotionally. You were surprising, fascinating, boring, pragmatic, easy-going, anxious, and so on. The audience will not be saying, 'Wow, slide 34, that was terrific. Great explanation of the budget…'

Look back at Chapter 12 on branding and think about the impact you want to leave people with. Consider what you want people to be saying about you behind your back. Do you want people to sense your confidence, to laugh, to be shocked into action or see your credibility?

Once you have thought this through and written it down, it will leak through into what you are saying and your impact.

Question 4 gives you your level of EMOTION.

5. WHAT ACTION DO YOU WANT YOUR AUDIENCE TO TAKE?

If you don't want your audience, however big or small, to take any action – you just want them to listen to your information – please don't waste everyone's time. Just send them an email with the material.

To shift your presentation from Inform to Inspire, there has to be a reason to take action. Inspiration is all about feeling moved, gaining a sense of connection, having a reason to act. This doesn't have to be vast; it might just be talking to you, giving you some feedback, engaging with you or your team in some way. But there is purpose to your presentation. And that purpose makes all the difference.

Question 5 gives your presentation momentum and purpose. It also gives you the CLOSE.

6. WHY DO YOU CARE?

An audience will forgive you many things if you are enthusiastic and passionate. They won't care that you went wrong in the middle, that you were nervous at the start, that the tech was a bit shaky at one point, because you care. And the fact you care was obvious and matters to the audience.

Question 6 gives you PASSION.

Try this out #1

As you look through the example here, think through a presentation you have coming up, and answer the six questions for your own situation:

Ali is a leader at a media agency. The subject of diversity and inclusion is important to the organization, one of their values and a personal passion for Ali. He believes that by recruiting a full-time Diversity Champion, discrimination will be reduced, and an inclusive working environment will become active and meaningful. Ali is presenting his proposal to the senior leadership team. His planning document looks like this:

1. Who are you presenting to?
   Eight people, mixed personalities but be brief. Talking at the end of SLT (senior leadership team) monthly meeting. Given 15 minutes but might be squeezed to 5. Some champions in the room, couple of sceptics. Most people think it should be everyone's role, not just one.
2. What is your single key message?
   *Good for us **and** good for business.*
3. What do they really want to know?
   Should we bother? Aren't we doing enough already?
   Why have a single person to do this? Isn't it everyone's job to do?
   What will they do?
   How do we get payback for this?

4 What do you want them to feel?
That I'm credible and convincing. Feel my passion.
5 What action do you want them to take?
Ideally sign off on the recruitment. If step too big at moment, look at case studies I've drawn up and what other companies have done in this space. Get involved. Be interested.
6 Why do you care?
I've faced discrimination and want D&I to be more than words. With someone at the helm, we can kickstart discussion, events and education.

Now Ali has answered these questions, he can start to design a presentation from the audience's perspective, with the right level of information and emotion.

FIGURE 13.2   The circle of inspiration

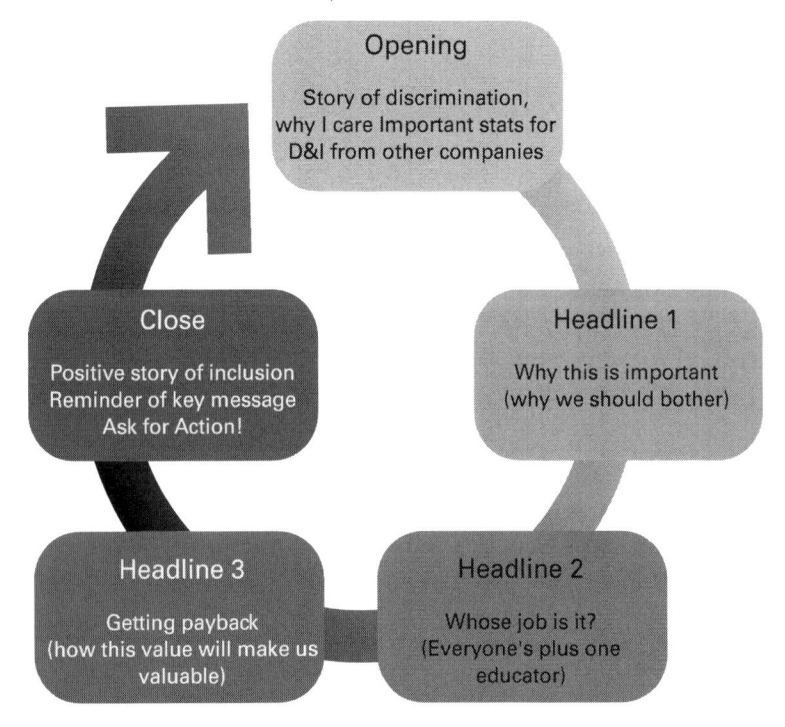

Opening
Story of discrimination, why I care Important stats for D&I from other companies

Headline 1
Why this is important (why we should bother)

Headline 2
Whose job is it? (Everyone's plus one educator)

Headline 3
Getting payback (how this value will make us valuable)

Close
Positive story of inclusion Reminder of key message Ask for Action!

What Ali is doing here is using the rhetorical questions he wrote down in answer to Question 3, 'What do they really want to know?', to form the foundation of his Circle of Inspiration.

Writing out your presentation in the form of the Circle has multiple benefits:

- You're telling us a story, with a beginning, a middle and an end.
- Keep to three headlines – the rule of three might be a cliché, but it works.
- Support each headline with interesting, relevant information – a visual, a story, a case study, evidential data.
- You feel confident, knowing you're answering what the audience wants to hear.
- You will stay on track, as the headlines and key words guide you through.
- If you've had your time shortened, you can easily decide where to concentrate your efforts.

Opening and closing

There is nothing more satisfying than a presentation with a good opening and a close. Even though you might think your subject is the driest business topic (and I've sat through presentations on catalytic converters, matchsticks and frozen peas), I can guarantee you there is no boring subject, only dull presenters! All business presentations are still stories, and deserve a beginning, a middle and an end. Or, like any good story, there is *a situation, a problem and a resolution*.

With your opening, bring your subject to life. Why do you care (look back at Question 6), why is this so important? Tell us and make us care about it too.

Ali will tell a story about the discrimination he has faced and the importance of the positive steps the organization has already taken. Then he is able to use his answers to the six questions to signpost the presentation:

In the next 15 minutes, I'll talk through why we should recruit a full-time diversity champion, what the role will involve, and importantly, how it will benefit the whole organization. My intention is for you to see that it's the right direction for us, and that it will ultimately be good for business too. By the end of the 15 minutes, I'd like to hear your questions and concerns so that we can take the next steps to looking for the right person.

With regards to closing, think about where you started and end the story. Remind your audience why it matters and what action you would like them to take. For example:

We're already making positive headway. When Glenda became the youngest director of our organization last month, her achievement was celebrated and she's already spearheading a 'young women into leadership' campaign. We can, and should, continue this journey and with your agreement today we can start recruitment.

Deliver for connection

I'm a big fan of scholar Brene Brown's work on vulnerability and imperfection. In her book, *The Gifts of Imperfection* (2010), she writes about 'letting go' in order to decrease vulnerability and increase connection.

To achieve this, there are two things you need to let go of:

Let go of being perfect.
Let go of everyone else's rules.

Perfectionism is not the same thing as striving to be your best. It is, as Brown says, 'A twenty-ton shield that we lug around thinking it will protect us'. You'll know you've caught the perfectionist habit if you spend hours tweaking your slides, memorizing your script for fear you might go wrong, practising moves that don't feel like you or just lying awake the entire night worrying.

I'm not saying you shouldn't practise. I am saying that at some point you have to let go of being perfect and know that you are OK. And if you go wrong, that's also OK. In fact, when you go wrong, it's often the first time the audience sees the real spontaneous human being behind the presenter. Embrace those opportunities to connect.

This means you have to work towards the mindset of confident uncertainty. I recommend this mindset for every presentation you deliver – confidence to know you've thought this through from the audience's perspective and that you've practised. And confident enough to know that you might not have the answer, but you do know where to find it.

Be your authentic self

What matters is that you understand the type of person you are as a presenter and work to your strengths. I was trained to present when I was 18 years old by an ex-policeman who blew a whistle every time I said 'umm' or moved my arms. As an expressive person, it hampered my movements for years!

- If you have a soft voice, increase your impact through stories, allow people to lean in and listen.
- If you have a monotone voice, place deliberate emphasis on your headlines.
- If you are animated, move with a purpose.
- If you are a still person, ensure your voice has enough light and shade to maintain interest.
- If you have a deep voice, keep impact at the end of your sentence.
- If you wave your arms around, use them for impact, not as a whirligig.

Above all, deliver your own material. Even if you have a corporate script and slides, rewrite elements so this presentation is yours, and yours alone.

Try this out #2

The circle of awareness

The first minute of your presentation matters and the desire to be perfect really kicks in. It's also when all the unconscious decisions are made about you by the client, and your body learns to fight or flight depending on the state of your mind. So, try out this simple technique:

At the start of your presentation, turn off your slides, put down your notes, shut your laptop. Accept your vulnerability and move to the front of the stage, the room or your virtual space. Look your audience in the eye. Ground yourself. Breathe deeply, once, twice, and smile. Pause. Allow the room to relax. Introduce yourself simply and say how good it is to meet them and to be here. That's it. Then continue.

Practical inspiration #2

Five ways to manage your 'stage fright'

Despite your planning and your desire for connection, sometimes that inner critic can get a fierce grip on your imagination. Nerves are good as they keep your guard up, prime you to perform and sustain the adrenaline. But when they feel out of control, here are five tried and tested ways to manage your mindset:

1 **Perspective.** Put this presentation into perspective by reminding yourself what else matters to you in the big scheme of life. For example, have a photo with you of your family or loved ones; a positive testimonial; a mantra; an object that connects you to something you love.
2 **Breathe.** Even better, yawn or sing (I know this might look strange, but it works!). You want to get your diaphragm

working and your breath coming from lower in your body, so that it isn't raging round your head.
3. **Take the spotlight off you.** At the start of your presentation get involvement and interaction, so that it's not all about you. Ask a question, hands up, hand out something, ask people to write something down, turn to their neighbour and tell them something. As soon as you've got the audience connected and working with you, your nerves will drop away.
4. **Visualize the future.** Imagine the positive things people will be saying after the presentation. Make this as vivid as possible. What adjectives will people be using? What single thing will they remember with interest? Why have they found this useful? Did you convey passion?
5. **Practise.** Practise. Practise. Say yes to every opportunity you are offered to present. You will never get better if you just think about presenting. You now have to take action. Video yourself. Ask for feedback from a trusted colleague.

This last point is a good place to end this chapter. Confidence comes from experience and experience comes from giving it a go – and not beating yourself up when it doesn't go exactly to plan. Learn from each experience and try again.

Ten top tips for delivering an inspiring presentation

1. Be interested in other people. How they react. How they feel. Be more interested in others than yourself and shift your focus to the audience.
2. Tell me a story. Having a strong narrative drive is what makes presentations sensational.
3. Prepare. Use the six questions. It's all about how you set it up, how you manage expectations and how you follow through afterwards.
4. Open and close well. The law of primacy and recency means the audience will remember the first and last things you said.

Grab the audience's attention, be outstanding and drive through the cacophony of sound.
5 Pare the heart of your presentation down to three points. The rule of three might be a cliché but it has stood the test of time and it works.
6 Don't be dull. Don't be complex.
7 Conviction is convincing. The passionate belief in the story you are telling can be enormously seductive.
8 Timing matters. Go under time, never over it. Know your time might be shortened so prepare to deliver your key message in 30 seconds and your three headlines in five minutes.
9 Don't let difficult behaviour derail you. If people yawn, walk away, switch off the zoom camera or look bored, focus on those who are interested.
10 Enjoy it!

CHAPTER FOURTEEN

How to extend your leadership influence, with integrity

In a nutshell

Influential leaders who act with integrity understand that success and positive outcomes can only be achieved through, with and by others. There are three ways to realize this and extend your influence: a) improve your engagement at meetings by ensuring your voice is heard; b) step out of your silo and be proactive with the scope and quality of your business network, and c) gain commitment to your ideas when influencing upwards and persuade wisely.

What's the problem?

The problem is very simple: as a leader you cannot but help have influence, and you have choices of how to use that power. If you look at the definition of influencing, 'The capacity (or power) of someone to be a compelling force on, or produce effects on, the actions, behaviours, opinions of others' (dictionary.com, 2021), that's a lot of responsibility for a leader! In essence it means that everything you do or don't do, say or don't say, be or choose not to be, has an effect, for good or ill.

As a leader you cast a shadow and this concept is a simple one: your team is a map of you and your shadow casts itself upon those under your authority. For example, your very presence at a meeting may influence people positively or negatively. The style or nature of your presence, what you say or how you say it and the attitude you project speaks volumes. The smarter you can get at knowing what you do, or what it is about you, that impacts on others, the more personally effective you can become.

This has to be more than using your authority though. You'll know from experience that the ability to influence others is synonymous with control. That is, once you have leadership status, it is not difficult to coerce, force or induce action on others. However, despite the considerable literature devoted to the perils of toxic leadership (e.g. Goldman, 2009), most leaders I encounter want to be a positive influencer, visible for the right reasons and to earn the trust of their followers.

So, influencing others is not just about getting others to always agree to your point of view – you may be able to influence them to cooperate with you AND they may not always agree with you. It is not about winning at all costs and having to get your own way all of the time. It is not about forcing or getting others to change – you cannot change others. Extending your influence IS about:

- being engaged and present at meetings;
- behaving in ways that offer others the invitation to change;
- stepping out of your silo and developing a broader wingspan across the organization;

- developing win/win relationships, based more on giving than taking;
- gaining commitment to your ideas;
- stepping back to step up, making time to reflect on the shadow you cast.

The big idea: Be present, be proactive, be persuasive

These three 'P's will help you extend your influence in the following ways:

Being present: more than visibility, this is about influencing through *engaged attention*, particularly at meetings.

Being proactive: deliberately expanding your influence by *mapping out your stakeholders* and making proactive steps forwards in your networking skills.

Being persuasive: understanding how to sell your ideas, gain commitment and influence the action you want.

Your presence is wanted: influencing at meetings

It is at meetings that your influence is most likely to be felt and noticed at work. Not only because it's a public show of your thoughts, your decision-making skills and relationship with the team. But also, because it's where you spend most of your time. Research suggests most leaders spend about 23 hours of their week in meetings (Perlow et al, 2017) and in my experience that figure errs on the low side, with many leaders I know spending up to 10 hours a day in back-to-back meetings, whether virtual or face to face. With such a demanding schedule, it's unsurprising that the call to be present, or fully engaged, at meetings wanes.

You can define your presence at meetings in three ways – being passive, dominant or engaged – and how you behave will depend on context, time of day and confidence. For example, if you're attending a meeting as a 'silent supporter' for one of your team, you might choose to take a more passive approach. If you've been in meetings all day, it's late, you're tired, people are talking for too long without getting anywhere, you might choose a more dominant approach for a quick decision. If you have the highest status in the room, people will often look to you for answers, adopting a more passive approach themselves. Alternatively, if you're the junior leader in the room, you might not speak up for fear of getting it wrong.

But if your choice is to be a positive influencer, you want to actively choose the state of engagement, because here is when the magic of influencing happens. As Patsy Rodenburg (2007) suggests, 'It is when fully present that we do our best work and make our deepest impression on others.'

The three gears of influencing

Think of these three states of presence as gears – a mechanism you can design or adjust to give you a different output. As you will see below, although the 'engaged' state is usually the most beneficial, there are benefits to being passive (you're there to support someone else), or dominant (calling the meeting to a point of decision). This means you can move between the gears, but the important point is to ensure the gear you choose comes from an *active and positive intention*.

Ensure the gear you choose comes from an active and positive intention.

Here's what you will experience with each of the three gears.

PASSIVE PRESENCE

FIGURE 14.1 The passive gear of influencing

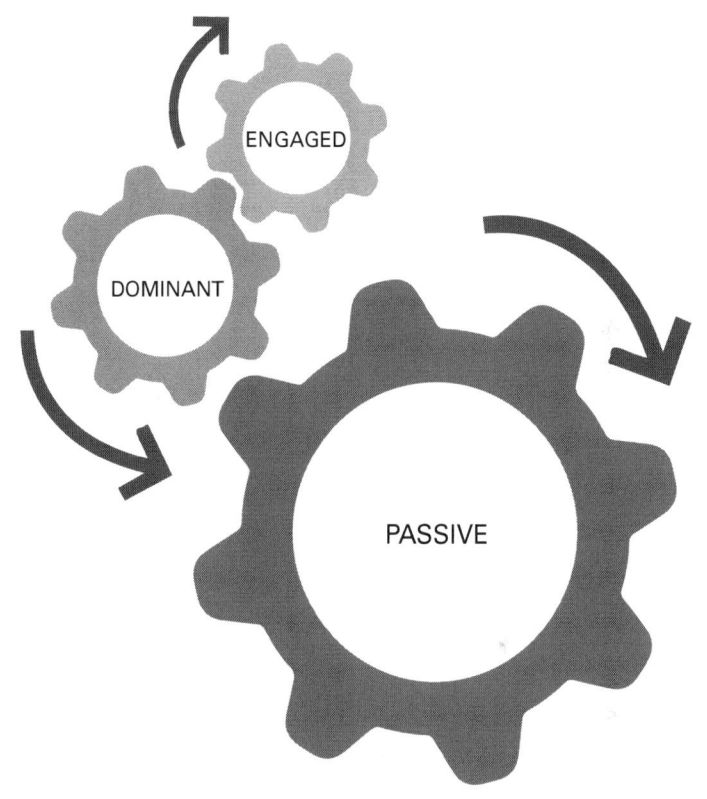

- You feel worried, thinking about how to interject but staying quiet.
- You are present, but quiet.
- You leave a meeting realizing you've barely talked.
- You often disengage from the discussion as you're not involved.
- You are there as an observer.
- You are content to let others shine.
- You feel frustrated at the dominant voices, in your view saying little, but loudly.
- People forget you were at the meeting.

DOMINANT PRESENCE

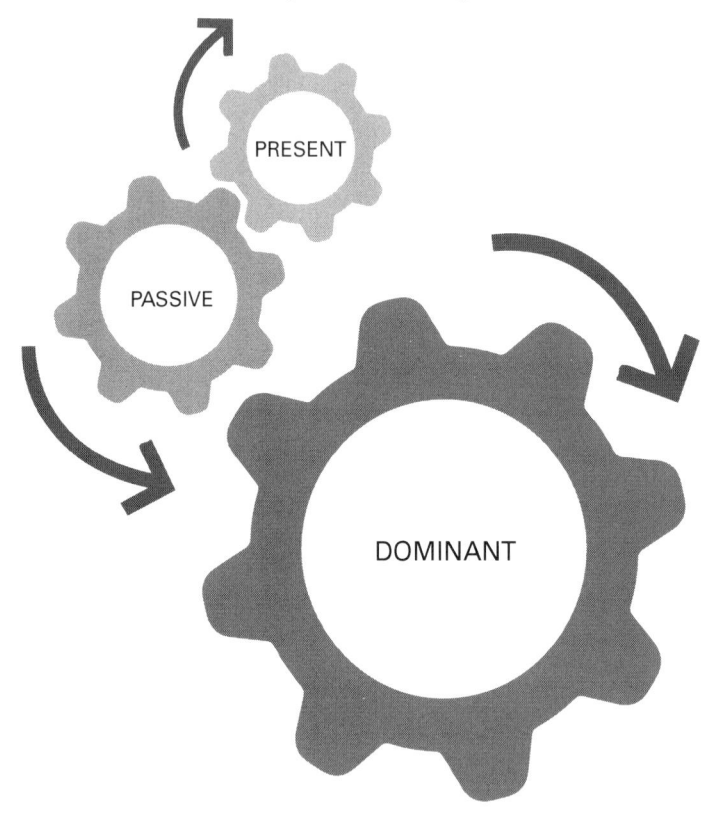

FIGURE 14.2   The dominant gear of influencing

- You feel frustrated at the lack of speedy decision making.
- You call people to a point of decision making.
- You interrupt people a lot.
- You feel impatient at others 'waffling'.
- You inject energy into the meeting.
- You take command of a discussion (sometimes too soon).
- You dismiss other people's ideas.

ENGAGED PRESENCE

FIGURE 14.3 The engaged gear of influence

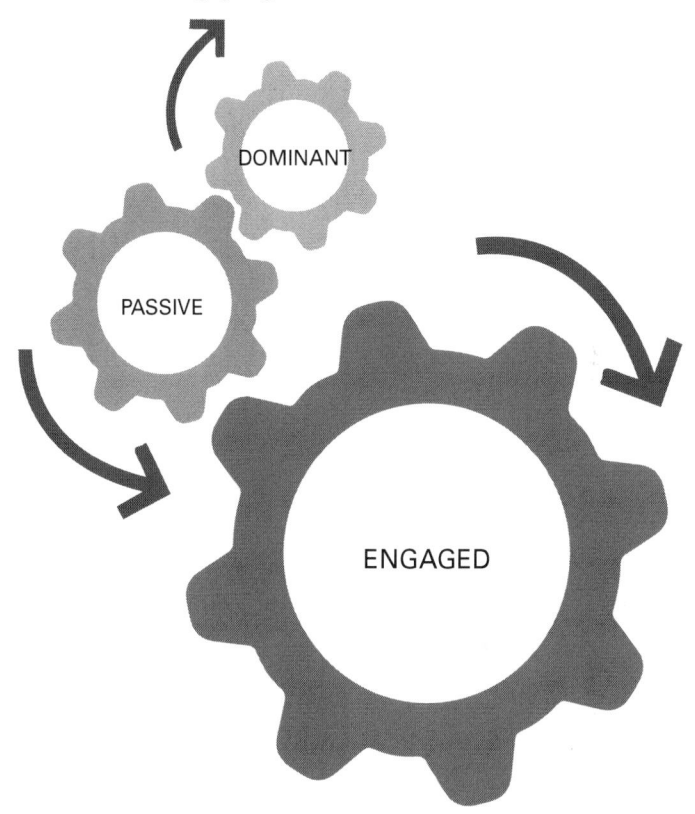

- You feel attentive and prepared.
- You learn and use other people's names.
- People listen to you when you talk.
- You ask a lot of questions.
- You share the 'air space', involving others and ensuring everyone gets to speak.
- You notice details in others – moods, body language, verbal language.
- You are curious about an idea – not judgemental.
- You acknowledge the feelings of others.

Time to reflect

Think about the meetings you've been in this week. Which gear prevailed in each of these meetings and why? Who or what shifted you into an unhelpful gear?

Stimulate your thinking further with these 10 questions, rating yourself from 1–10 (poor–consistent) for each of these influencing skills during your meetings:

1. I actively influence others to find a consensus solution. ☐
2. I am persuasive in meetings, without negating another person's contribution. ☐
3. I am assertive in meetings and will ensure that my voice is heard. ☐
4. I listen in equal measure to talking. ☐
5. I use questions in meetings to stimulate interest, gain information and encourage involvement. ☐
6. People would describe me as a good listener. ☐
7. I remain approachable when under stress. ☐
8. I encourage people to see the value of their contribution. ☐
9. I give credit for ideas and suggestions. ☐
10. I actively encourage disagreement, draw out contributions and facilitate the discussion. ☐

Practical inspiration #1

10 steps to engagement – getting your voice heard

If your score for the questions above is below 50, you're not alone. For many of the leaders I coach, they express frustration with their inability to get their voice heard or point across in a satisfying way. The more discouraged you get, the more passive or dominant your behaviour can become.

And so, as you reflect on your answers to the questions above, here are 10 practical ways to get your voice heard and extend your positive influencing skills:

1. **Stating your views**
   Use 'I' statements to distinguish your opinion from fact and to emphasize it is your view: *'As I see it, the problem is...'*, *'My experience is...'*
2. **Agreeing with other people's views and suggestions**
   It is helpful to others if you make your support explicit, rather than keeping quiet or nodding your head – actually say you agree. This helps to ensure useful suggestions are considered rather than ignored.
3. **Disagreeing and stating doubts**
   It is important to say where you stand, including when you do not agree or have significant doubts. However, these behaviours can stop a meeting progressing, so it's important to accept the responsibility that goes with the right. This means you need to be constructive:
   'I do have a doubt in that..., so how about...'
   'I agree with your overall approach, Val. However, the part I don't like is...'
   Give a reason for your doubt:
   'I see it differently.' *'My experience is different to that.'*
4. **Putting forward suggestions**
   Suggestions or proposals are statements of *action*. People are more likely to react positively if they perceive them as suggestions. Try starting with a phrase such as:
   'In my experience...'
   'How about...?'
   'Shall we...?'
   'I suggest/propose we...'
5. **Asking for clarification**
   Before you react to other people's views, you may need to check exactly what they meant. Don't put yourself down:

'Maybe it's just me, Bill, but I haven't understood...'
Be assertive:
'Farah, when you say the project, do you mean 'x' or 'y'?'
'Have I got this right; you want to...'
'What do you mean, Bill?'

6 **Interruptions**
Avoid interrupting others to make a point. To stave off interruptions from others:
'I'd just like to finish what I'm saying...'
'Let me just finish...'
'I will come back to you...'

7 **Asking for reactions from others**
People don't always make their position, views and ideas known. You can encourage them to do so by asking assertively:
'What do you think of my suggestion?'
'What's your view of...?'
'What ideas do you have for...?'

8 **Giving out win/win vibes: from can't to can**
For some people, turning 'can't' into 'can' is useful practice. Tell people what you **can** do, rather than what you **can't** do:
'I can do it, if I can get some help on the processing side.'
'I can do that for you, although we'd need to discuss the timescales you're suggesting.'
'I do want to help you with that project, so I can offer you one day a week.'

9 **Flag that you're aiming for a win/win**
'Can we find a way that'll work for both of us?'
'I'd like to agree an approach with you that we'll both feel happy about.'

10 **Sound and look positive!**
Voice should be steady and controlled.
Hand gestures open.
Facial expression is concerned, thoughtful and willing, rather than disbelieving.

Being proactive: stakeholder breadth and depth

Your next step to extend your influence is to examine your relationships with your stakeholders. You can get stuck in the role of being a great manager, a 'competency trap' (see Chapter 1), and so your job as a leader is to get out of your silo, broaden your connections internally and externally and deepen your relationships with those who matter. In this way, you solve systemic problems more effectively, while connecting your team to the broader organization.

Practical inspiration #2

The Influencing Map

In Chapter 1, I talked about networking. The Influencing Map is a simple and effective way to practically extend this idea and gain breadth and depth in your key relationships. It helps you to focus on the mutual benefits of the relationship, and to take small actions forwards. Small steps are important – anything too dramatic and it won't happen.

Draw a simple spidergram of your key relationships. Put yourself in the centre, and the name of each stakeholder (or organization, institute, association) in one of the squares. Go for a maximum of 10 people in this map.

For each connection, answer the following four questions:

a Out of 10, rate the state of the current relationship (yes, this is subjective but that's OK).
b WIFT: What's in it for *them* to increase the effectiveness of this relationship?
c WIFM: What's in it for *me* to increase the effectiveness of this relationship?
d What next? What one simple action can you take to nudge your score up a single point?

FIGURE 14.4 The Influencing Map

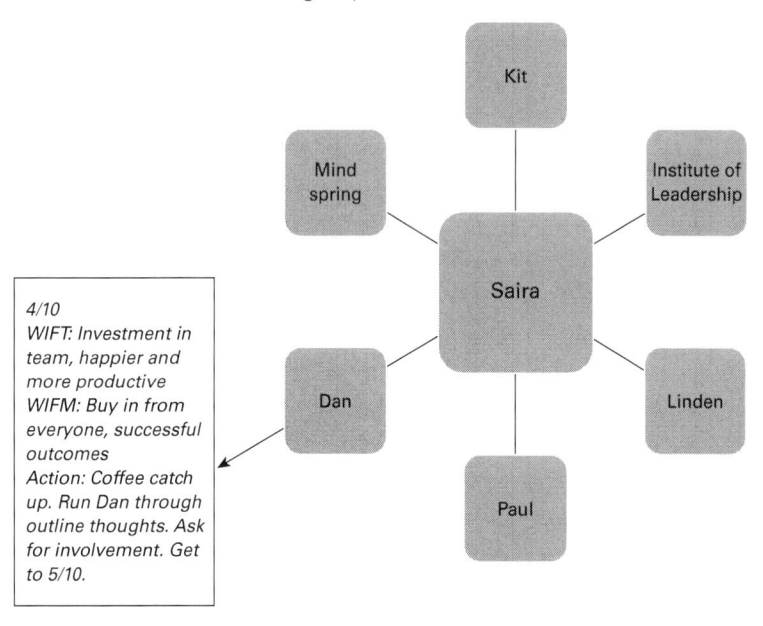

```
                    Kit
         Mind              Institute of
         spring            Leadership
                   Saira
         Dan               Linden
                   Paul
```

4/10
WIFT: Investment in team, happier and more productive
WIFM: Buy in from everyone, successful outcomes
Action: Coffee catch up. Run Dan through outline thoughts. Ask for involvement. Get to 5/10.

For example, here is the start of Saira's influencing map. Saira heads up the Learning and Development function and has been doing the role for six months. Kit is her boss, the Chief People Officer; Linden is her deputy; Paul and Dan are two peers she wants and needs to develop a closer relationship with. Saira has just started a new relationship with the Institute of Leadership to accredit their internal programmes, and Mindspring is her key external training supplier.

Taking just one of these stakeholders, Saira starts with Dan, Head of Commercial. She rates the relationship as a 4/10 as they have worked together on a few projects, but are yet to develop a trusting business partnership that delivers value. Saira knows that Dan is open and expressive, and protective of his team. She knows he has not felt involved in previous internal training programmes for his team, and her desire is to co-create outcomes that are relevant to his team, and productive. Her hope is for

Dan to become an L&D advocate and for a win/win relationship. To initially shift the relationship to a 5, Saira decides to start with an informal coffee and run through of her thinking for the commercial team.

Give and take

At the heart of the Influencing Map is the notion of give and take. It requires trust, credibility and positive intention to build great working relationships and reciprocity, the practice of exchanging things with others for mutual benefit, is core to your success. The concept has a rigorous evidence base for changing people's behaviour and fostering collaboration (Cialdini, 2007), and used well, comes from a position of integrity. It's about giving first. Instead of asking yourself what you can *get* from developing this potential stakeholder relationship, I'm asking you to question the value you can *give* that will enrich this person's way of working. That's because your stakeholders will quietly stop collaborating with you if they think developing this relationship is only about what you can get from it.

In Adam Grant's (2014) book, *Give and Take*, he stresses that givers, when they manage to give a lot without letting themselves get burned out or taken advantage of, create large networks of friends and allies and excellent reputations that work to their long-term advantage, whereas takers, even when they manage to create short-term giver reputations, end up with their selfish actions coming back later to ruin their reputations and destroy their networks and relationships. As Grant says, 'This is what I find most magnetic about successful givers: they get to the top without cutting others down, finding ways of expanding the pie that benefit themselves and the people around them.'

Try this out

Sketch out your influencing map. Think about:

- existing key stakeholders
- potential/desired key stakeholders
- external associations

and allocate a current score, mutual benefit and an action for each. Then, get started! Your influencing map is a dynamic tool, so revisit it in one month, adjust the scores and create new actions. Record the progress you are taking and the growth of each relationship.

Being persuasive: influencing upwards and gaining commitment

Many leaders are reluctant to embrace the skills of persuasion when influencing others and in my experience, this becomes particularly acute when you are influencing upwards. It's usually because you feel your status is lower, your confidence wanes and the nature of persuasion feels too close to manipulation and is therefore rejected. Here's the difference: manipulation is persuasion without trust, and I know you're a leader who wants to act with integrity and responsibility.

You'd be surprised how many boards and executive committees I've sat in with senior leaders expressing their frustration with the inability (or unwillingness) of a leader to convince others to act. Sell to us, they plea! Persuade us! Why should we do this? Make your recommendation!

Here are six ways to convert your good ideas into meaningful action:

1. BE PREPARED

How you prepare for a meeting with your seniors is vital. Most people prepare for the task and the meeting but not for the people. Find out who will be there and what they want from the meeting. If you need support for an initiative, find out your likely supportive stakeholders and talk to them prior to the meeting.

2. BE PERSUASIVE

They don't have to buy, you have to sell! Many leaders forget they have to persuade others to buy into their ideas and that's all about benefit selling. What's in it for them to buy? Relate to the larger needs of the organization, not just your function, and don't assume that your audience can automatically make the connection between the benefit to your function and the benefit to the larger organization. Put another way, 'The art of advocacy is to lead you to my conclusion on your terms' (Grant, 2014).

3. BE SUCCINCT

Know how to translate your extensive slide deck into five minutes. What really matters to this person or group of people? Start here. And don't assume that just because someone is senior to you, they will 'get' your idea. Turn your complex idea into a simple action that will make a positive difference.

4. BE REALISTIC

Present a realistic cost-benefit analysis of your idea. As Marshall Goldsmith (2004) suggests:

> Every organization has limited resources, time and energy. The acceptance of your idea may well mean the rejection of another idea that someone else believes is wonderful. Be prepared to have a realistic discussion of the costs of your idea. Acknowledge the fact that something else may have to be sacrificed in order to have your idea implemented.

5. BE AN EQUAL

When you meet someone you respect or who has significant power over you, you are likely to tend to change your behaviour dramatically. When you want to influence up, you need to believe that you are equals – there is nothing special about this situation. Those with influence don't patronize or look down on the people they are with. But they don't look up to them in awe or sycophancy. You understand that you both have strengths – neither superior to the other.

6. BE ASSERTIVE

What's your recommendation? While there might be options in your presentation, be assertive with the proposal you are recommending, together with your justification. Make a judgement call, stand by your idea and exude confidence!

Be a positive role model: a final word

Throughout this chapter, I've stressed that once you are a leader you have influence, and by your behaviour and actions, your language and attitude, you will be known. And it's contagious! The mood you are in will spread (like wildfire), your words will be reflected by others, and your performance copied. So here is a fourth 'P' – be a Positive role model by choosing how you show up in the organization each and every day. And I'd urge you to use this responsibility in a positive way, so that your followers get the leader they deserve.

To close this chapter, here is a quickfire way to get yourself in the right mood every morning, by being conscious and intentional. Use this two-minute daily reflection practice to review your choices and renew your leadership strengths. Just for starters, here are four daily questions:

1 How am I feeling?
2 How do I want to feel?
3 What do I need to do, think, feel, or hear to achieve this feeling?
4 What is my intention today?

Ten top tips for extending your influence

1. Be trustworthy, credible and intentional. Positive influencing is about the choices you make every day. Review and renew your choices every day through self-reflection.
2. If people don't trust you, they won't allow you to influence them. A smart, simple way to establish trust is to talk less and listen more.
3. Present a positive attitude. No one is saying that you aren't allowed to have a bad day, but if you can exhibit strength, calm and perseverance even during stressful times you will instil the same with your team.
4. A good guideline for influencing upwards is to remember you want to make a positive difference to the organization. Link your ideas with the bigger picture.
5. The small steps you take using your 'influencing map' will have the biggest impact on extending your network.
6. The more other people can 'win' with your idea, the more influence you will have.
7. Influence, don't manipulate. There's a simple difference. Manipulation is persuasion without trust.
8. Earn trust through integrity. Make decisions for the betterment of the business as a whole and give credit where it is due.
9. Give more than you take. Extend your influence by building a network of trusted colleagues.
10. Ensure your voice is heard through positive engagement. Be neither passive nor dominant, choosing active listening, asking, reflecting and suggesting.

PART FIVE

What next?

CHAPTER FIFTEEN

Enable your succession through progression planning

In a nutshell

Stepping up is not just about proving your own performance and potential. Great leadership is as much about enabling those in your team to succeed you and progress through the organization, as it is about your ability to let go. This chapter takes you through a progression coaching plan to develop individuals in your team, releasing you for your next career chapter.

What's the problem?

How do you answer the following question?

> *Have you, at least in your own mind, picked one or more potential successors?*

This is one of Robert Kaplan's (2011) critical business questions for leaders and he gets straight to the nub of succession. It's still surprising to me how few leaders are able to give an affirmative answer to this question, perhaps underestimating the problems lurking without a succession plan for you, or a progression plan for your team. Without one, the problems can be summed up in one word – 'stuck':

- You cannot move up without a successor (or an extensive and possibly unnecessary external search).
- Even if you're new into your role, without a succession plan you are unlikely to be delegating as extensively as you should be, stifling your own capability to act strategically.
- Your team are equally stuck, as without your succession plan they're unlikely to realize their potential. When I discuss career planning in coaching, it's a common response for junior leaders to feel stifled in their career by senior managers who have no progression plan in place, leaving their team adrift and unsure.
- Of course, anyone can leave your organization, but this means you lose precious talent and internal capability.

Why is there such a lack of succession planning? In my experience, here are the most common reasons:

a *'I've just got here!'* You've just been promoted to your leadership position because of your exceptional expertise, but now is the time to let that expertise go and develop critical thinking and leadership among your team – even if they're your former peers. This is hard work! When you have fought to achieve the leadership position that's been in your eye for some time, you're just getting your feet under the table and perhaps your self-assurance is still shaky, it feels anomalous to immediately turn your hand to developing others to get to the same point. Yet it's precisely what you have to do.

b '*It hurts to feel replaceable.*' Facing the fact that you're expendable and that the world will go on without you is painful. What if someone else is better? Your ego will remain intact if you just avoid thinking succession.
c '*I'll get round to it.*' Your team have personal development plans and objectives and that feels good enough for now.
d '*There's no obvious successor, so what's the point?*' You cannot see why you should expend effort here and will probably lean towards an external solution.
e '*I have no idea what I'm going to do myself yet.*' You don't have a plan yourself, or know your next step, so the last thing you're going to do is develop everyone else.
f '*I'm not about to retire you know!*' For too long, succession planning has sat firmly in the realm of future CEO preparation, letting other leaders across the business off the hook. Whatever leadership role you hold, you need a succession plan, that is, a plan for identifying and developing potential future leaders to fill business-critical roles. It doesn't have to be about your role, but you do have the responsibility to develop adaptable, capable talent who can take a number of routes and fill a variety of possible roles.
g '*I don't know how to do it.*' This last point is the easy one, and we'll get there in this chapter. Everything else is about your mindset towards development and that's what we will explore first, before turning our lens to your team.

Time to reflect

Are you an enabler or a blocker?

A good succession plan is built on strong foundations that start with you. There is little point developing a theoretical plan that looks great on paper, for your team to find that their progression is not taken as seriously in practice as it is in writing. As you read the statements above and consider your own position, reflect on these questions:

Reflection questions

1. What is my attitude to succession and how does this impact on my team?
2. In what ways am I acting as a 'blocker' to my team's potential to progress?
3. What do I need to do to release, and encourage, my team's potential?
4. In what ways am I acting as an 'enabler' to my team?
5. How can I strengthen this area and ensure the succession plan is strong?
6. What's my next step?

Practical inspiration

Developing a six-step progression plan

It's highly likely that your human resource team has a succession plan for your organization in place, talent mapping the performance and potential of future leaders. This doesn't let you off the hook! What we're exploring together in this chapter is how you enable other people to fulfil their potential through a progression plan, so that you, too, are able to step up.

From the get-go, let me emphasize that creating a progression plan is not just about finding one or two potential people to succeed you – now or in the future. That is one aspect of succession, but a narrow one. Great succession planning is also about developing a pool of agile leadership talent who can fulfil broad roles across your organization, possibly outside of their immediate area of expertise. These are people who will grow and develop as your organization shifts and changes and are invaluable to your business. Writing in *Personnel Today*, Miecha

Forbes (2020) calls this 'intentional pathway planning', that is, preparing your team for multiple possible positions.

Think of progression planning as building and leaving a legacy of learning. When you step away from your team, you don't just want to leave vague memories of what it was like being managed by you. What you want is to leave a legacy of great learning – you were the leader who guided, cajoled, challenged, nurtured and sponsored these individuals. This is your legacy as a leader. So, instead of thinking about your legacy as something you suddenly turn your mind to when you're about to retire – 'Help! What am I going to be remembered for?' – flip it on its head and think of building and leaving a learning legacy as an ongoing project, rather than the sum of all your knowledge and experience.

Think of progression planning as building and leaving a legacy of learning.

Figure 15.1 starts your progression planning with a simple matrix. But before you start using this, you have some basic work to do first.

Step 1: Reset

Setting expectations is fundamental to leadership. Imagine you've taken on a new team. You notice they have their own habits and behaviours built up over the years under different leadership, and you want to establish your way. Your first job is to reset expectations, set out what good looks like and establish the behavioural boundaries of the team.

TRY THIS OUT

You can do this by completing four statements together with your team:

The purpose of this team is…
This team adds value by…

We demonstrate trust and respect for each other in this team by…
Good looks like…

Step 2: Define

FIGURE 15.1   Progression planning matrix

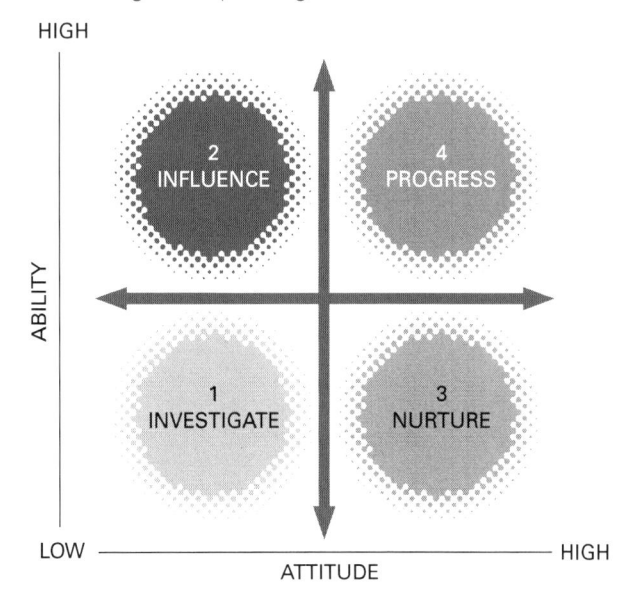

<image: Progression planning matrix with Ability (vertical) and Attitude (horizontal) axes. Quadrants: 1 INVESTIGATE (low ability, low attitude), 2 INFLUENCE (high ability, low attitude), 3 NURTURE (low ability, high attitude), 4 PROGRESS (high ability, high attitude).>

How are you currently assessing someone's ability to step up? You won't be alone if you're doing this subjectively. That is, your team member has been doing their job for a number of years and their performance is good, they've been on a number of courses and had on-the-job training. They're well respected across the organization and appear ready.

I recommend adding a layer here that is more transparently objective, assessing 'hard and soft' skill competencies. The hard skills (Ability axis) will be functional and depend on your business and departmental needs. Soft skills (Attitude axis) are often harder to pin down, but I'll give you some ideas for this.

ABILITY

Firstly, let's define the Ability axis. Over the last decade, I've led several research projects to define the skills of great leadership. I've whittled these down to the top 20.

ASSESSING LEADERSHIP SKILLS

Demonstrate insight

Self-awareness   Have a clear and realistic understanding of own emotions, strengths and weaknesses.
Self-confidence   Communicate in an honest and open way and are comfortable with not knowing the answer or being wrong.
Integrity   Have meaningful values which people can identify with and believe.
Learner   Take personal responsibility for development needs, regularly learning.

Practise resilience

Optimistic   Through adopting an optimistic outlook, have the mental strength to keep moving forwards, even in the face of setbacks.
Self-regulate   Understand personal triggers and be able to control your moods and emotional impulses.
Perspective   Provide perspective and be able to act cool and calm in a crisis.
Energy   Look after yourself physically and manage own stress levels.

Inspire others

Clarity   Communicate with clarity, making the complex simple.
Passion   Show a sincere and genuine excitement for your business.
Inclusive   Drive collaboration by expressing own views in an honest and independent way, listening to others and accepting different points of view.

Trust Build a climate of trust and openness in which people are valued for saying what they really think, feel and believe and can do so without fear of criticism or judgement.

Drive for action

Achiever Driven to achieve and display an unflagging energy to do things better.

Focus Work with the team to develop a set of priorities that focus energy and resources.

Pace Provide pace, momentum and a drive to action for the business.

Uncertainty Able to cope with uncertainty and make decisions in the light of ambiguous and complex data.

Empower the team

Coach Help others grow professionally through a development plan, coaching and mentoring.

Delegate Allow others to shine and take the lead, to operate autonomously and make mistakes.

Feedback Make difficult decisions when they are called for without allowing tricky situations to remain unheeded.

Compassion Be genuinely interested in other people and demonstrate care and compassion to others.

TRY THIS OUT

Before you start to work with your team, I recommend you explore your own skills first. Look at each of these 20 leadership factors and score yourself from 1–4 on each skill:

1 = You rarely exhibit this behaviour and consider it a development need.
2 = You sometimes do this, but not in a consistent way.
3 = You consistently demonstrate this behaviour to a high level.
4 = This is an exceptional strength and you're considered a role model to others.

Score interpretation:

Between 20–39
You still need to work hard on your leadership skills. The good news is that this score is not fixed, and you can increase these skills through learning. Use more of these skills at work, at home and in the community and you'll be a real asset to the people around you. You can do it, and now is a great time to start!

Between 40–59
You're doing OK as a leader, and you have the potential to do much better. While you've built the foundation of effective leadership, this is your opportunity to improve your skills and become the best you can be. Examine the areas where you lost points and determine what you can do to develop skills in these areas.

Between 60–80
Excellent! You're well on your way to becoming a great leader. However, there is always room for improvement and learning in leadership as you can never be too experienced, so look at the areas where you didn't give yourself maximum points and figure out what you can do to improve your leadership.

Increase your reflection with the following questions:

a What are your strengths?
b What are your weaknesses?
c If you were prioritizing your areas for development, how would you rank them?
d What simple steps can you take to strengthen your skills?

As you familiarize yourself with the skills, start to assess the ability of your team. This is much better achieved as a mutual conversation, and you can use these same four questions to guide your coaching conversation.

ATTITUDE

So, you've now placed some objectivity to the Ability axis of the model. Now let's turn to the Attitude axis. Assessing 'attitude' is subjective. You're looking at motivation, mindset and willingness to develop. Here's how to spot great attitude in your team member:

- The language used. Language is such a powerful indicator of attitude. Listen to how this person talks about their role. Do they use words such as 'have to', 'made to', 'got to do this'? Or do they choose language such as 'want to' or 'love to'? This gives you a signal as to whether the person is extrinsically or intrinsically motivated (and you can read more about this in Chapter 5, using the Motivation Scale).
- The tasks they choose to undertake, moving beyond the strict boundaries of their job function.
- The help they give others.
- The willingness to go 'above and beyond' when needed, demonstrating commitment.
- Their response to getting it wrong, holding a growth mindset towards failure.

Step 3: Understand

QUADRANT 1: INVESTIGATE

Low ability
Low attitude

Whenever a leader draws up their progression planning matrix, I'm often concerned that the individuals placed in Quadrant 1 are written off as 'poor recruitment'. My first question is, 'did you bring the person into this team in this state?' This is unlikely, so what happened? Your first stage here is to **investigate**. What has caused this person to be in Quadrant 1? Look at the coaching questions in Step 4 for a way forwards with this individual. Seek to understand before you make a decision.

QUADRANT 2: INFLUENCE

High ability
Low attitude

In a previous career incarnation as Training Director of Europe's largest sales training organization, I was responsible for developing about 50 graduates each month for their new sales positions. Inevitably, every month, there would be one or two graduates who needed my so-called 'influencing chat'. These were bright graduates, high ability, with the potential to be future sales stars for their organization. Their ability was marred by their attitude, either 'playing the clown', coming in late, apathetic about learning and always dragging others into their games. The 'influencing chat' always followed a pretty simple formula, like this:

You have great ability, and with ability comes power.
You have choices.
You can choose to influence others negatively, or positively.
At the moment you're choosing the former, which has a detrimental impact on others.
What are the reasons for this?
What will it take for you to choose to influence others positively?
You have the potential to be a superstar if you choose this path...

Usually it worked a dream, with people recognizing their influencing power at an early stage of their career and choosing to use that muscle for good!

There are so many reasons for people in your team to end up in Quadrant 2. Perhaps they wanted your job? Or a different leader? Maybe they've fallen out of love with your company or function, or they're just plain bored?

Your first stage here is to investigate *and* **influence**. Alongside the coaching questions I've suggested below, you also need to give an individual in Quadrant 2 strong feedback. If their negative influence takes a grip on the team, they can be a damaging force for the direction of change.

QUADRANT 3: NURTURE

Low ability
High attitude

Typically, individuals in Quadrant 3 are new to their roles, with a current inability to perform well in their job. But their attitude is great, which is invaluable for future potential.

Your first stage here is to **nurture**. Train for ability and nurture their attitude.

QUADRANT 4: PROGRESS

High ability
High attitude

Individuals in Quadrant 4 are ready to **progress** and it's your job to make this happen. When you have nurtured someone to the point of high performance coupled with a committed attitude, help them step up – guide, challenge, delegate and encourage their progression. Above all, do not stand in this person's way!

TRY THIS OUT
Where is your team?

- Place your team in the quadrants – where do you think your team sits in the plan?
- Importantly, have a mutual conversation with each member of the team and use the coaching questions below to guide this conversation. Be clear with your expectations.
- Sometimes you need to prepare for a difficult conversation if your assessments differ. Structure this conversation well (see Chapter 10 for help with this).
- Together create a progression plan. Start with the coaching questions in Step 4.

Step 4: Develop

Here is a bank of coaching questions to help you develop your progression plan:

QUADRANT 1: INVESTIGATE

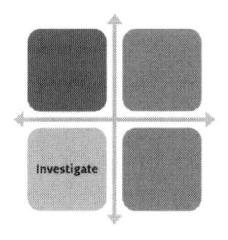

Coaching questions:

1. Why do you identify with this quadrant?
2. What's happened in your career to be here?
3. Why has your motivation decreased?
4. What would you like to be doing instead?
5. What support do you need to make a change?

QUADRANT 2: INFLUENCE

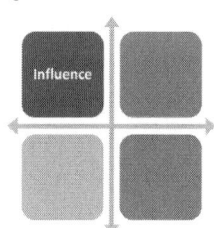

Coaching questions:

1. What kind of influencer do you want to be?
2. What impact do you think you have on the team?
3. What impact would you like to have on the team?
4. What would motivate you to learn next?
5. What would you like responsibility for?

QUADRANT 3: NURTURE

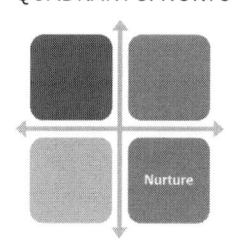

Coaching questions:

1. What training do you need to increase your capability in this role?
2. How do you learn best?
3. What support would you like from me?
4. How often do you want coaching?
5. How can the team support you best?

QUADRANT 4: PROGRESS

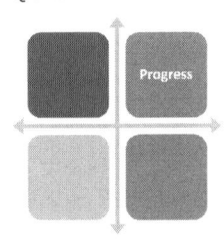

Coaching questions:

1. What's your ideal next step?
2. What help do you need from me to get there?
3. What thoughts do you have about a sponsor/mentor or coach?
4. What else would you like to do that would challenge you now?
5. What will stretch you enough to help you meet this new challenge?

Step 5: Build

Coaching is just one element of your progression coaching plan. If you're serious about succession, then it's also worth building a legacy of learning, by making it central and natural to the everyday functioning of your team:

i At meetings, demonstrate curiosity and be open to new ways of doing familiar tasks.
ii Ask team members to choose new topics for learning each month and encourage breadth of thinking.
iii Make learning self-directed. Give team members autonomy in choosing learning programmes for themselves.
iv Encourage cross-functional role-swapping to develop depth of organizational knowledge.
v Enable learning to be broader than the job function at hand.
vi Ensure your senior team members have sponsorship and mentorship from the executive level of your organization.
vii Role-model learning behaviours and bring new ideas to the team.

And in your meetings, ask broader and more challenging questions. Jon Hagel (2021) insists that great leadership is all about asking better questions, suggesting, for example:

- What is a game-changing opportunity that could create much more value than we have delivered in the past?
- What are emerging unmet needs of our customers that could provide the foundation for an entirely new business?

Step 6: Let go!

My ardent hope is that your team aren't desperate for you to go! However, I do hope they are ready for your departure. You've developed an autonomously learning team, they've had the benefit of your leadership, they're stepping up themselves to new and exciting pastures, and someone is ready to succeed you. Now you have to let go. How do you know it's time to let go?

If you're honest with yourself, there's little challenge left in your role.
You're not learning anything new.
People are asking you about your next step.
Your motivation is dipping, and your curiosity is piquing!
You find yourself scanning jobsites or talking to head-hunters.
There is someone waiting in the wings to step up to your role.
You're not going because you're scared.

These are all signs that it's time to be courageous and take your next step seriously. Be the enabler within your organization, not the blocker, and know that you're building, and leaving, a learning legacy that will be much prized by your followers. And if you're questioning your future purpose, read the next chapter to help you reflect on happiness, meaning and what makes life worth living for you!

Ten top tips for progression planning

1. Start progression planning from day one in your leadership role.
2. Make progression planning a transparent and mutual process. Have conversations with your team to understand how best you can support them to succeed.
3. Role-model behaviours that drive a culture of learning in your team, generating insight.
4. Drive autonomy in learning, encouraging self-directed breadth and depth.
5. Every individual in your team will need a different approach from you. Be flexible and supportive in your progression planning.
6. Start with great questions and inspire people to ask for help when they need it.
7. Seed your talent, from a desert to an oasis. Succession planning matters.
8. Empower your team to come up with solutions and champion their efforts. The more they shine, the more you shine.
9. If you find you're having a number of 'difficult' conversations with team members, this is the result of poor progression planning, lacking clarity in expectations.
10. Know when it's time for you to let go. Be the leader who enabled others and is remembered for the right reasons!

CHAPTER SIXTEEN

Time out

Reflections on happiness and leadership

In a nutshell

Your happiness matters. And alongside the science linking fulfilled leaders with high-performing teams, it is as important to reflect on your life evaluation and where you choose to invest your time. Happiness is about purpose, engagement, people, making progress and feeling good, and this chapter considers how to achieve a vital balance between these elements and make yourself lastingly happier.

What's the problem?

There's an interesting conundrum with the two words, happiness and leadership, which is that they're rarely mentioned in the same breath unless we're talking philosophy or self-help. If you scan the content of some of the more familiar books on leadership, the subject of happiness barely gets a look-in.

I've come to the conclusion there are two reasons for this. The first is that happiness is considered by many to be a flimsy topic that doesn't stack up against the sturdier leadership subjects such as, let's say, strategy and innovation. You're not going to find a leader being scoffed at when they say that they're off to study 'strategic leadership'. But try doing the same with happiness. As someone who gave up a couple of years to study for a Master's in Positive Psychology, I can vouch for the rise of the sceptics – *'Happiness?... haven't you something better to do with your time?... two years? I'll give you a couple of books and you'll do it in an evening'*, etc! Granted this was a decade ago and there are changes afoot with the reception towards the science of positive psychology, but the word 'happiness' can still come adrift when coupled with 'leadership'.

Strange really. Because if you ask any parent what they want for their child, the first sentence is usually, 'I just want them to be happy.' So, it's considered vital for our children but not for ourselves or when we're in the position of leading others.

The second reason is that for many leaders the study of happiness feels selfish or irrelevant to their role. It's probably been a recurring theme in your career that a great leader enables others to fulfil their potential and earns their followership through servant leadership, *not* to pursue their individual path in the name of happiness. And given that time is one of your most precious commodities, you're unlikely to spend it here. And so, you're left with the question:

Does happiness actually matter to leaders?

Yes, but you might not realize it until you've lost it. Perhaps you feel adrift in your career, out of balance, or at a transition point. And in that moment of reflection, you ask yourself the question, 'Am I happy?' and recognize that you're not sure of the answer. In fact, you're not even sure you understand what it means.

Let's start with the meaning. Given that the concept of happiness has a culturally and philosophically diverse history, there is unlikely to be a single definition that applies to all people at all times. However, Sonja Lyubomirsky (2008), in her book *The How of Happiness*, states that happiness is 'the experience of joy, contentment, or positive well-being, combined with a sense that one's life is good, meaningful, and worthwhile'. Or, as Martin Seligman (2003), pioneer of the field of positive psychology, suggests, a happy life is one with a balance of pleasure, engagement and meaning.

So, does it matter? Well, there's considerable science (e.g. Chan, 2009) that links happy, satisfied and fulfilled people with stronger immune systems, creativity, financial success, positive relationships and resilience, while positive leadership is correlated with high-performing teams (you can read more about this in Chapter 6). But at its heart, happiness is how you evaluate your life – and a positive evaluation is worthy of your attention.

Time to reflect #1

How happy are you?

Ed Diener (1996) is a leading happiness scientist and one of his greatest contributions to the field of wellbeing concerns the measurement of happiness itself, or what Diener calls subjective wellbeing. Diener contends that in general people are happy if they think they are happy. Or at least, each person is the best judge of whether they are in fact happy or not. He poses pretty simple questions including these four, which you can answer now:

On a scale of 1–10 (1 being very low and 10 being very high):

a I would rate my happiness as…
b As I reflect on my life, I would rate my satisfaction levels towards my life as…

c So far, I've achieved the important things I want in life.
d If I could live my life over, I'd change almost nothing.

His work from around the world suggests that most people are happy, not unhappy. A minority of respondents are basically unhappy and a smaller percentage depressed, and it's rare for people to remain elated or extremely happy for long. The average person is slightly to moderately happy (a score averaging 6–7). In conversation with Michaela Chan (2009), Ed Diener concluded that humans are basically predisposed to mild happiness.

The score you've given yourself to these questions can be summed up as your happiness 'set point'. This is a psychological term to describe your general level of happiness. Each of us has a different one based on our genetics and our conditioning. Some scientists (Diener and Diener, 1996) are firm that, while you may have emotional ups and downs throughout your life, these are temporary. No matter what life throws at you, over time, your happiness bounces back to the same point. While others believe that there is flex in this set point (Haidt, 2006), I'm always on the side of science that views life's skills, talents and traits as moveable, as opposed to being fixed. So, think of your happiness capability as having a range, rather than a fixed point, that you have agency to change and lastingly expand. How you can do this is the subject of the next section.

The big idea: Rebalancing happiness

Happiness can be elusive and many of the routes you naturally pursue to increase it won't work. Chase happiness via increased money, status or material goods and you'll get a diminishing rate of return – we get used to what we have and then want more (it's called the *hedonic treadmill*). Compare yourself to others and feel your sense of happiness deteriorate – it's a notorious killer of joy and nothing good comes from it. There will always be someone with more, better, faster or bigger (and that's *social comparison theory*).

What is useful is to explore happiness through the lens of five factors: positive emotions, passion, people, purpose and progress. You're human and unlikely to be consistently happy across all five dimensions, so in this section we're going to explore understanding and *rebalancing* your happiness. Once you know why and how your happiness might have gone asunder, you can take charge and do something about it. Read and reflect on the meaning of each of the five factors in the next section along with the coaching questions, so you can start to judge where your happiness is now, and where you want it to be in the future.

Time to reflect #2

Five factors of happiness

POSITIVE EMOTIONS

Positive emotion is about feeling good and the most direct route to feeling happy. It's not just about a momentary delight (though that helps!); it also involves positive reflection about your past, or at least acceptance of it, and a positive anticipation of the future:

How frequently do you experience a sense of unbridled joy?
Generally, do you experience more positive emotions, such as kindness, forgiveness, hope, gratitude and optimism, than negative emotions?

PASSION

Passion is all about getting immersed or engaged in particular activities that play to your strengths and you experience a state called 'flow' (Csikszentmihalyi, 1990). Time flies, you feel at your peak, you don't want any interruptions – you're in the zone!

What are your greatest talents, and how are you using (or wasting) them?
When were you last so engrossed in an activity that nothing else mattered?
And what were you doing?

PEOPLE
Having positive relationships with people where you experience a depth of understanding, emotional support and respect has a high correlation with happiness. We are hard-wired to not just want, but need, love, appreciation, affection and connection. It's common for leaders to prioritize their positive attention at work, offering a frazzled self at home. So:

Who gets your time when you're at your best?
How can you live your work life in a way that leaves room for those you love in your life?

PROGRESS
Happiness comes more from making progress towards goals (Haidt, 2006) than the achieving of them (when you often feel a sense of let-down, or 'what next?'). And the autonomy, perseverance and challenge you experience through goal-setting, with every step moving you forwards, is all part of your positive, productive journey:

How are you marking the progress you're making towards your goals?
How can you celebrate the journey towards achievement, rather than making a list of goals?

PURPOSE
A sense of purpose is guided by your personal values and what's *really* important to you in life. It's usually described as serving something greater than yourself and can be found in your profession, a social or political cause, your family and way of life or

spiritual beliefs. Having purpose gives you a focus and a sense of direction towards what matters to you:

What are your central values, and how are they reflected in your work?
How aligned is the life you're leading with the values that are important to you?

Try this out

Where are you now?

Grab a piece of paper and draw five circles on it, considering each of the five dimensions and the coaching questions above. The size of each circle should reflect how you feel your life is at the moment with each dimension and the time you are giving it. There is no right or wrong size, shape or distance between the circles, just go with your instincts. Below are two examples to guide you, but your experience will be unique:

Example 1: Nathan inherited the family business of Italian restaurants eight years ago. His purpose was writ large by the family legacy of passing on an independent, successful business from generation to generation, which links with Nathan's values of independence, family and financial security. The business is going well, and they have opened up two further restaurants and are making firm progress towards over-achieving on their financial targets for the year. Nathan is also passionate about cooking, a love that's been passed down from his grandmother and something he does for sheer joy. However, instead of cooking, Nathan is a leader with 83 staff. In fact, he cannot remember the last time he cooked a dinner for friends just for fun. Instead of spending time with his growing family, he is night and day between the restaurants, which he justifies to himself and his partner by stating 'he is doing it for them and their future'. He is tired and frazzled, arguments are more frequent at home, but he continues marching forwards, making progress towards his purpose. When I ask Nathan if he's happy with his life, he says 'probably not but then it's not about me is it?'

FIGURE 16.1   Rebalancing happiness, example 1

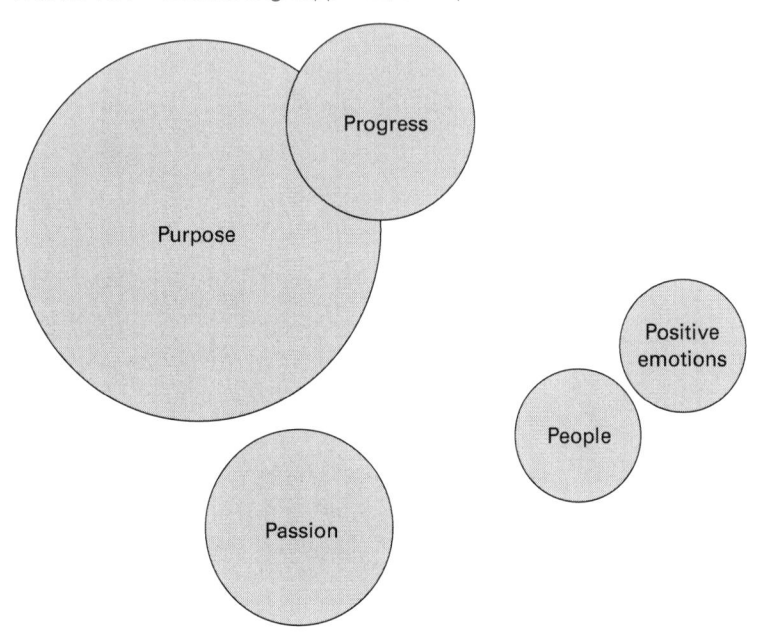

Example 2: Dominique (Dom) describes herself as a 'people pleaser'. She likes this term as her values of kindness, love and service are strongly linked with the actions she takes every day in the service of her family, her team and her friends. Working for a non-profit organization, ever short of resources, is both energizing and draining in equal measure, but she feels a sense of purpose through helping other people, whether at home or at work. Dom cannot give me an example of the last time she did something for herself, or set herself goals for her own life, rather than for other people. Her love of nature, gardening, hillwalking and swimming have taken a back seat in her life as she sorts out everybody else's lives. When I ask her if she's happy with her life,

she's silent for a while, then shakes her head and then says, 'I've lost a sense of me along the way but that's a pretty selfish attitude isn't it?'

FIGURE 16.2   Rebalancing happiness, example 2

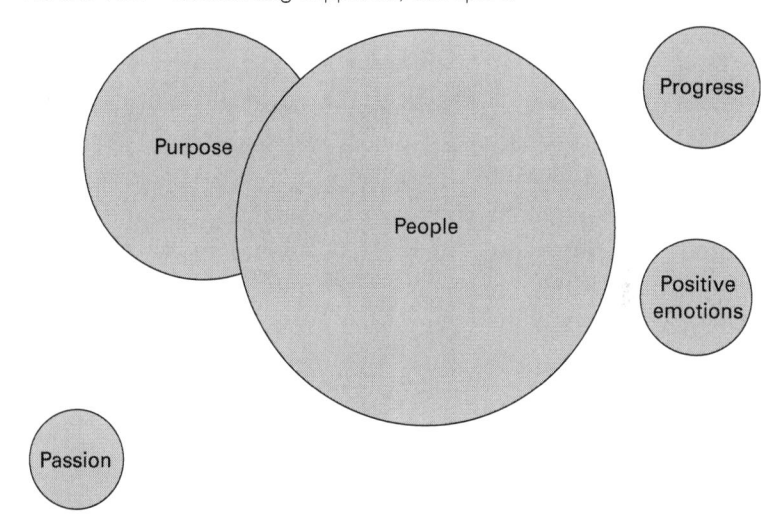

Time to reflect #3

What do you want instead?

As you reflect on the diagram you've drawn, the question to ask is:

> *How satisfied are you with this present state and what changes do you want or need to make to provide a better basis for the future?*

Now redraw the diagram as you'd like your future to be.

Nathan redrew his diagram with a greater focus on people and positive emotions. He sat down with his partner for a thoughtful discussion on their future happiness. Nathan loves his family business, and is proud of the purpose it gives him, and together they decided on three actions: to develop two directors and prioritize the workload; boundary time together as a family that was practical and consistent, as well as prioritizing fun through cooking for friends every week. Nathan feels a sense of delight with his natural passions taking root again and is learning to enjoy his lifestyle that the business affords him.

In redrawing her diagram, Dom had a moment of recognition. She didn't have to sacrifice her desire for helping other people in the service of her own happiness. She could blend the two. Her single action was simple but had a profound impact on her life. Dom joined a women's hillwalking group and every Saturday afternoon, once the kids' tasks, clubs and lunches were sorted, she went walking for two hours. With just two hours and consistent action, Dom's friendship group expanded, and her enjoyment increased, positively impacting her evaluation of her happy life.

Practical inspiration

7 ways to become lastingly happier

As you look at the two diagrams you've drawn, you'll notice that the circles are interdependent. Writing in *Forbes* magazine about finding happiness and balance in life, Chris Myers (2018) suggests, 'It's all too easy to fall victim to siloed thinking, that our job, family, passions, and desires are all separate and unrelated aspects of our lives. It is possible to be true to your passions, live a life of consequence, and still use business as a medium of expression.'

Here are seven exercises for you to consider that will increase the joy and fulfilment you experience in your life, at work, home and play. Some are quick and simple; others take a little longer. Naturally, as a pragmatic psychologist, the exercises have scientific validation, but more importantly, positive feedback and results from happier clients.

1. CREATE A COMPELLING FUTURE

Visualize how you want your life to look 10 years from now. How are you spending your days? Where are you living? What people are you spending time with? If you know where you're going, it's easier to know what to focus on and why doing it matters. To achieve this, blend writing with meditation. Simply ask yourself, 'How does my ideal life look 10 years from now?', allow your mind space to create and then write down what comes to mind.

Fiona Parashar (2021), CEO of Leadership Coaching and author of *A Beautiful Way to Coach*, often stretches this visualization out to reverse-engineer back from your 80th birthday, imagining all you have in your life then and how you got there.

2. UNLEASH YOUR PASSION

In Chapter 12, there's a list of 24 strengths from the field of positive psychology to help you build your brand. Look at this list or take an online questionnaire such as the Values in Action Inventory or the Clifton Strengths Assessment to discover your strengths and where your passion lies:

a Consider your top strengths and ask yourself how often you are using them and how you can broaden their efficacy in your life. How can you use them differently and in varied ways?
b Now take a good look at those strengths you've forgotten. Ones you used to love but have slipped lower down the list and out of your life. For me, it was *Creativity* and *Humour*. My top strengths of *Love of Learning* and *Curiosity* had overwhelmed my working life, but at some point, the joy had gone. I was working and studying hard, earning great money with terrific clients. But it was a training treadmill that was taking a toll on me. Reconnecting with creativity and humour was delightful. I'd forgotten just how passionate I was about creativity in many forms and how playful it could be given

airtime. What strengths do you need to unleash or rekindle to tap into your real passions in life?

3. RECHARGE YOUR PURPOSE

In Chapter 2, there is a Resilience Healthcheck exploring your mental, physical, social, emotional and purposeful energies. I promised to revisit the purpose questions in this chapter as we further explore the link to happiness. These are the questions I suggested you reflected on:

1 I understand my strengths, and have time at work to be the best leader I can be.
2 I know where I'm heading and am passionate about my direction.
3 I can articulate my values, and what is important to me.
4 My values are aligned with how I live my life in actuality.
5 Every day, I take time to reflect on what is important to the way I lead others.

You've taken steps to answer the first two questions above, so let's continue the quest for meaning and living a life of positive consequence. This isn't onerous – the meaning you give to life is joyful, subjective and just as valid as anyone else's – but it is important. Having a purpose in life predicts health, longevity and is one of strongest mechanisms underlying resilience (Frankl, 1946; George and Park, 2016). A sense of purpose guides life decisions, influences behaviour, shapes your goals, offers a sense of direction and creates meaning.

Figure 16.3 is a short list of values you can use for this exercise, but if you go online, you'll find plentiful examples of values lists that you can use to add to this one:

- Make a rough list of the jobs you've held over your career: what are the themes that have mattered to you? Where have you found purpose in your career?
- Using the list in Figure 16.3, or from your own personal knowledge, rank on a sheet of paper your personal values (I suggest fewer than five).

- Ask three people you trust to select values you demonstrate. How aligned is their list with yours?
- Ask yourself 'why?' Why are these values important to you? How do they matter to you?
- Consider how aligned your chosen values are with the life you are leading. What needs to change to recharge your purpose?
- Finally, link your values with your leadership purpose. In 25 words or fewer, describe your purpose as a leader.

FIGURE 16.3 List of core values

Achievement	Contribution	Health	Recognition
Acknowledgement	Control	Honesty	Relaxation
Action	Coping	Honour	Reward
Adventure	Creativity	Independence	Roots
Affection	Directness	Inspiration	Security
Ambition	Ease	Integrity	Self-reliance
Authenticity	Enjoyment	Intimacy	Service
Balance	Environment	Joy	Spirituality
Being me	Excitement	Learning	Stability
Belonging	Exploration	Love	Strength
Challenge	Faithfulness	Nature	Success
Choice	Family	Opportunity	Trust
Clarity	Financial security	Peace of mind	Usefulness
Closeness	Freedom	Performance	Vitality
Competitiveness	Friendship	Power	Warmth
Confidence	Fun	Progress	Wealth
Connection	Generosity	Quality of life	Wellbeing

4. DIARIZE YOUR GRATITUDE

This might be a familiar exercise to many of you, and if you have done it, you'll know that its simplicity belies its worth (Emmons and McCullough, 2003). I love it and find it to be a moving and grounding exercise which I do each time I feel my anchor is drifting away from what's important in my life. It's easy to do. Each night, jot down three things you are grateful for, from tiny observations to profound realizations – anything goes. Do this for two weeks (I find it becomes less fun, and more of a chore after this) and notice the patterns of what matters to you in life. Think of this exercise as a toothbrush for your mind.

5. PRIORITIZE BALANCE AND LEARN TO SAY NO

If your five circles are unbalanced, inevitably you will have said yes to many people at the expense of your own happiness. What would it look like to prioritize balance and your own happiness more? What would you have to say no to? How can you do this without compromising your values?

6. OPEN YOURSELF UP TO EXPLORATION, NEW EXPERIENCES AND LEARN TO SAY YES

Once you've learned to say no to other people's demands, you have to learn to say yes to opening yourself up to a personal expansion of your passion and positive emotions. As Martin Seligman says in his book *Flourish* (2011), 'You have the power within you to figure what inspires you, what makes you laugh, or what gives you hope, and to cultivate those emotions.'

What do you want to say yes to that will fuel your spirit and bring you joy? What does your inner critic prevent you from saying yes to (telling you that you're selfish and don't deserve to do this)? How can you do this too without compromising your values?

7. FOCUS OUTWARDS AND APPRECIATE OTHERS

While this chapter is all about you and your future happiness, I want to end it with perhaps the simplest, yet most profound leadership practice. I've repeated throughout this book people's need for appreciation, but perhaps I haven't laboured the point that the act of appreciating others will fuel your own happiness as a leader. Their joy will become your delight.

When I interviewed Dee Ford for the preface of this book, she described this exercise as 'disproportionately important' to the success of a leader and the happiness of their team and practises it every day.

All you have to do is, every day, send someone an email acknowledging their help, teamwork, progress, strength or achievement, and copy in everyone who knows them. Allow them to shine and see how appreciated they are by you.

Ten top tips for happiness and leadership

1. Recognize that happiness and leadership are interdependent, creating virtuous circles. The happier you are, the more positive and productive your team, fuelling your positivity.
2. There is no single key to happiness. Think of it as a recipe with multiple ingredients put together in the right way. Balance the five 'P's to find your recipe.
3. Your happiness level is not fixed, and it is in your power to change through your mindset and actions. Use your agency wisely.
4. Chasing leadership wealth and status might make you happy in the short term, but alone, their pursuit will have a diminishing impact on your wellbeing. Balance is the key.
5. Prioritize your investment in good friends and family. People who care about you and whom you care about deeply. This is your most important route to a satisfied life.

6 Involve yourself in activities that you value as much as those activities that interest you and offer enjoyment.
7 When you can define your purpose in life, it will feel as if your life makes sense and matters. Invest time in defining your leadership purpose.
8 Making progress towards accomplishments will boost you in many ways by the feeling of being productive and a sense of moving forwards.
9 Decide your values and walk your talk. Show they matter to your team and that you're prepared to make serious decisions based on acting in an authentic way.
10 Control how you look at the world. Train yourself not to make a big deal of trivial little hassles; focus on the process of working towards your goals and make a habit of noticing the good things in your life.

References

Chapter 1

Bridges, W and Bridges, S (2017) *Managing Transitions: Making the most of change*, Revised 4th Edition, Nicholas Brealey Publishing, London

Heifetz, R A, Linsky, M and Grashow, A (2009) *The Practice of Adapative Leadership: Tools and tactics for changing your organization and the world*, Harvard Business Review Press, USA

Ibarra, H (2015) *Act like a Leader, Think like a Leader*, Harvard Business Review Press, USA

Wichert, I (2018) *Accelerated Leadership Development: How to turn your top talent into leaders*, Kogan Page, London

Chapter 2

Achor, S (2011) *The Happiness Advantage: The seven principles of positive psychology that fuel success and performance at work*, Virgin Books, USA

Boniwell, I and Ryan, L (2012) SPARK: A Resilience Curriculum, www.mindspring.uk.com (archived at https://perma.cc/W4LN-GR9W)

Hartling L M, (2008) Strengthening resilience in a risky world: It's all about relationships, *Women and Therapy*, **31** (2–4), pp 51–70

Hurley, K (2020) What is Resilience? Your guide to facing life's challenges, adversities, and crises, *Everyday Health*, https://www.everydayhealth.com/wellness/resilience/ (archived at https://perma.cc/CY5P-FNDM)

Lieberman, M D (2013) *Social: Why our brains are hard wired to connect*, Crown, USA

Loehr, J and Schwartz, T (2003) *The Power of Full Engagement*, The Free Press, New York

Mental Health Foundation (2018) Mental health statistics: stress, www.mentalhealth.org.uk (archived at https://perma.cc/HJ6P-7Z4V)

Moss, J (2021) Beyond burned out, *Harvard Business Review*, February

Quinn, R E, Fessell, D P and Porges, S W (2021) How to keep your cool in high stress situations, *Harvard Business Review*, January

Reivich, K and Shatté, A (2002) *The Resilience Factor: 7 essential skills for overcoming life's inevitable obstacles*, Broadway Books

Sapolsky, R M (2004) *Why Zebra's Don't Get Ulcers*, Henry Holt and Co, New York

Seligman, M E P (2011) Building Resilience, *Harvard Business Review*, April

Southwick, S M and Charney, D S (2018) *Resilience: The science of mastering life's greatest challenges*, Cambridge University Press, USA

Thomas, M (2020) It's time to face facts: burnout is rampant, *Forbes*, https://www.forbes.com/sites/maurathomas/2020/08/28/its-time-to-face-facts-burnout-is-rampant/?sh=777b7f063861 (archived at https://perma.cc/VSC9-EB3A)

Walker, M (2017) *Why We Sleep*, Allen Lane, London, UK

Chapter 3

Barsade, S G (2002) The Ripple Effect: Emotional contagion and its influence on group behavior, *Administrative Science Quarterly*, **47** (4), pp 644–75

Cameron, K (2012) *Positive Leadership: Strategies for extraordinary performance*, Berrett-Koehler, San Francisco, USA

CIPD (2020) *Health and Well-being at Work*, Chartered Institute of Professional Development, London

Cooperrider, D L and Whitney, D (2005) *Appreciative Inquiry: A positive revolution in change*, Berrett-Koehler, San Francisco, USA

Derler, A (2019) Growth Mindset Culture, IDEA report for the NeuroLeadership Institute, NY

Dutton, J E and Spreitzer, G M (2014) *How to be a positive leader: insights from leading thinkers on positive organizations*, Berrett-Koehler, San Francisco, USA

Dweck, C (2008) *Mindset: Changing the way you think to fulfil your potential*, Little Brown, USA

Fredrickson, B L (2001) The role of positive emotions in positive psychology: The broaden-and-build theory of positive emotions, *American Psychologist*, **56**, pp 218–26

Fredrickson, B L (2003) Positive emotions and upwards spirals in organizations, in Cameron, K, Dutton, J E and Quinn, R E (Eds) *Positive Organizational Scholarship*, Berrett-Koehler, San Francisco, USA

Gable, S L, Reis, H T, Impett, E A and Asher, E R (2004) What do you do when things go right? The intrapersonal and interpersonal benefits of sharing positive event, *Journal of Personality and Social Psychology*, 87, 228–45

Harter, J (2020) 4 Factors Driving Record-High Employee Engagement in U.S., https://www.gallup.com/workplace/284180/factors-driving-record-high-employee-engagement.aspx (archived at https://perma.cc/W6C2-W6RE)

HSE Labour Force Survey (2020) Work-related stress, anxiety or depression statistics in Great Britain, https://www.hse.gov.uk/statistics/causdis/stress.pdf (archived at https://perma.cc/3P6T-CVXQ)

Keating, L A and Heslin, P A (2015) The potential role of mindsets in unleashing employee engagement, *Human Resource Management Review*, 25, pp 329–41

Perkbox (2020) The 2020 UK workplace stress survey, www.perkbox.com/uk/resources/library/2020-workplace-stress-survey (archived at https://perma.cc/CE6S-UF92)

Roberts, G L (2019) Workplace stress is costing European businesses billions, https://www.entrepreneur.com/article/336011 (archived at https://perma.cc/3H8N-UBQ8)

Chapter 4

Bandura, A (1977) Self-efficacy: Toward a unifying theory of behavioral change, *Psychological Review*, 84 (2), pp 191–215

Brown, B (2010) *The Gifts of Imperfection: Let go of who you think you're supposed to be and embrace who you are*, Hazelden, Center City, Minnesota, USA

Catalyst Report (2020) Women 'take care', men 'take charge', https://www.catalyst.org/research/women-take-care-men-take-charge-stereotyping-of-u-s-business-leaders-exposed (archived at https://perma.cc/S8BP-HCY6)

Dao, F (2018) Without confidence, there is no leadership, *Inc magazine*, https://www.inc.com/resources/leadership/articles/20080301/dao.html (archived at https://perma.cc/W6LW-XEKH)

Hadfield, C (2015) *An Astronaut's Guide to Life on Earth*, Pan Publishing, USA

Morse, G (2020) Confidence doesn't always boost performance, *Harvard Business Review*, November–December

Moss Kanter, R (2006) *Confidence: How winning streaks and losing streaks begin and end*, Crown Business Publishing

Peters, S (2012) *The Chimp Paradox: The mind management programme to help you achieve success, confidence and happiness*, Vermilion Press, London

Soll, J B, Milkman, K L and Payne, J W (2015) Outsmart Your Own Biases: How to broaden your thinking and make better decisions, *Harvard Business Review*, May

Chapter 5

Csikszentmihalyi, M (1990) *Flow: The psychology of optimal experience*, Harper and Row, New York, NY

Deci, E L, and Ryan, R M (2012) Self-determination theory, in P A M Van Lange, A W Kruglanski and E T Higgins (Eds) *Handbook of Theories of Social Psychology* pp 416–36, Sage Publications Ltd. https://doi.org/10.4135/9781446249215.n21 (archived at https://perma.cc/WKP4-ZK9A)

Fiorina, C (2003) Moving Mountains, *Harvard Business Review*, January

Herzberg, F (2003) One more time: how do you motivate employees? *Harvard Business Review*, January

Pink, D H (2011) *Drive: The surprising truth about what motivates us*, Canongate books, USA

Chapter 6

Chamorro-Premuzic, T (2016) Strengths-based coaching can actually weaken you, *Harvard Business Review*, January

Jackson, P Z and McKergow, M (2006) *The Solutions Focus: A simple way to positive change*, Nicholas Brealey, London, UK

Linley, P A (2008) *Average to A+: Realising strengths in yourself and others*, CAPP Press, UK

Rath, T and Conchie, B (2019) *Summary of Strengths Based Leadership: Great leaders, teams, and why people follow*, Abbey Beathen Publishing, USA

Seligman, M E P (2011) *Flourish*, Nicholas Brealey, London, UK

van Hool, J (2021) *The Listening Shift*, Practical Inspiration Publishing, London, UK

Chapter 7

Brooke, D (2017) Diversity makes us more creative, *Campaign*, April

Ely, R J and Thomas, D A (2020) Getting serious about diversity, *Harvard Business Review*, November

Ibarra, H (2015) *Act like a Leader, Think like a Leader*, Harvard Business Review Press, USA

Jacob, K, Unerman, S and Edwards, M (2020) *Belonging*, Bloomsbury Press, London, UK

Raval, A and Amphlett, J (2021) How business can tackle race inequality in the workplace, https://www.peoplemanagement.co.uk/experts/legal/how-businesses-can-tackle-race-inequality-in-the-workplace#gref (archived at https://perma.cc/GKW9-42W6)

Syed, M (2020) *Rebel Ideas: The power of diverse thinking*, John Murray publishing

Chapter 8

Drucker, P (1954) *The Practice of Management*, Harper Business

Harris, M and Tayler, B (2019) Don't let metrics undermine your business, *Harvard Business Review*, September/October

Massey, P (2018) A simple technique to improve your call centre strategy, https://www.callcentrehelper.com/technique-improve-contact-centre-strategy-41186.htm (archived at https://perma.cc/B9UZ-942W)

Rawson, A, Duncan, E and Jones, C (2013) The truth about customer experience, *Harvard Business Review*, September

Shaw, C and Ivens, J (2005) *Building Great Customer Experiences*, Palgrave Macmillan, Hampshire, UK

Shaw, C (2013) 15 statistics that should change the business world – but haven't, https://beyondphilosophy.com/15-statistics-that-should-change-the-business-world-but-havent/ (archived at https://perma.cc/7CB8-AV6D)

Chapter 9

Boaz, N and Fox, E A (2014) Change leader: change thyself, *McKinsey Quarterly*, March

Bridges, W and Bridges, S (2017) *Managing Transitions: Making the most of change*, Revised 4th Edition, Nicholas Brealey Publishing, London

Heath, C and Heath, D (2011) *Switch: How to change things when change is hard*, Random House Publishing, USA

Kubler-Ross, E (1969) *On Death and Dying*, Simon and Schuster, New York, USA

Meinert, E (2018) How to avoid common mistakes in change management, *Society for Human Resource Management*, https://www.shrm.org/hr-today/news/hr-magazine/0218/pages/how-to-avoid-common-mistakes-in-change-management.aspx (archived at https://perma.cc/BV8Q-WAHE)

Tolstoy, L (1900) Three Methods of Reform, in *Pamphlets*: Translated from the Russian by Aylmer Maude, p 29

Whitney, D and Trosten-Bloom, A (2003) *The Power of Appreciative Inquiry*, Berrett-Koehler, San Francisco, USA

Chapter 10

Goldsmith, M (2015) *Triggers: Creating behavior that lasts*, Penguin Random House, USA

Ibarra, H (2015) *Act Like a Leader, Think like a Leader*, Harvard Business Review Press, USA

Patterson, K, Grenny, J, McMillan, R and Switzler, A (2011) *Crucial Conversations: Tools for talking when stakes are high*, 2nd Ed, McGraw Hill, USA

Scott, K (2019) *Radical Candor: How to get what you want by saying what you mean*, Revised Edition, Pan, USA

Valcour, M (2017) 8 ways to get a difficult conversation back on track, *Harvard Business Review*, May

Weeks, H (2010) *Failure to Communicate: Why conversations go wrong and what you can do to right them*, Harvard Business Review Press, USA

Chapter 11

Bregman, R (2020) *Humankind*, Bloomsbury Publishing, London, UK

Brown, B (2015) *Daring Greatly: How the courage to be vulnerable transforms the way we live, love, parent*, Penguin Life, USA

Covey, S (2008) *The Speed of Trust: The one thing that changes everything*, Free Press, USA

Dallocchio, M (2017) *The Desert Warrior*, Latte Books, USA

Dawkins, R (2016) *The Selfish Gene*, 40th anniversary edition, OUP Oxford, UK

Deal, T and Kennedy, A (2000) *Corporate Cultures: The rites and rituals of corporate life*, Perseus, New York

Duhigg, C (2016) What google learned from its quest to build the perfect team, *New York Times*, https://www.nytimes.com/2016/02/28/magazine/what-google-learned-from-its-quest-to-build-the-perfect-team.html (archived at https://perma.cc/J6KZ-ZTND)

Grant, R (2018) Do trees talk to each other? *Smithsonian Magazine*, https://www.smithsonianmag.com/science-nature/the-whispering-trees-180968084/ (archived at https://perma.cc/ZYM2-ZP3R)

Lencioni, P M (2002) *The Five Dysfunctions of a Team: A leadership fable*, John Wiley and Sons, USA

Loehr, J and Schwartz, T (2003) *The Power of Full Engagement*, The Free Press, New York

Moss, J (2021) Beyond burned out, *Harvard Business Review*, February

Reeves, M and Whitaker, K (2020) A guide to building a more resilient business, *Harvard Business Review*, July

Rogelberg, S G (2019) *The Surprising Science of Meetings: How to lead your teams to peak performance*, OUP, USA

Seligman, M E P (2011) Building Resilience, *Harvard Business Review*, April

Suarez, F F and Montes, J S (2020) Building Organizational Resilience, *Harvard Business Review*, November–December

Wohlleben, P (2018) *The Hidden Life of Trees: What they feel, how they communicate*, Williams Collins, USA

Wooten, L P and James, E H (2014) Create opportunity from crisis, in Dutton, J E and Spreitzer, G M, *How to be a Positive Leader: Insights from leading thinkers on positive organizations*, Berrett-Koehler, San Francisco, USA

Chapter 12

Baumeister, R F, Bratslavsky, E, Finkenauer, C and Vohs, K D (2001) Bad is stronger than good, *Review of General Psychology*, 5, pp 323–70

Edelman Trust Barometer (2020) https://www.edelman.com/trust/2020-trust-barometer (archived at https://perma.cc/QD2H-R42N)

Galloni, A (2007) Interview, 'Fashion is how you present yourself to the world', *Wall Street Journal*, http://online.wsj.com/article/SB116907065754279376.html (archived at https://perma.cc/WY5N-3MPY)

Gallup Engagement Survey (2020) https://www.gallup.com/topic/employee_engagement.aspx (archived at https://perma.cc/CCQ8-RKRH)

Goffee, R and Jones, G (2006) *Why Should Anyone be Led by You? What it takes to be an authentic leader*, Harvard Business School Press, Boston, Mass

Longfellow, H W (1847) *Evangeline: A tale of Acadie*, www.deadtreepublishing.com (archived at https://perma.cc/D939-4VSG)

Peterson, C and Seligman, M E P (2004) *Character Strengths and Virtues: A handbook and classification*, APA and Oxford University Press, New York, NY

Zandan, N (2020) The most important leadership development skills in 2020, https://www.quantified.ai/blog/the-most-important-leadership-development-skills-2020 (archived at https://perma.cc/T66G-RFDD)

Chapter 13

Brown, B (2010) *The Gifts of Imperfection: Let go of who you think you're supposed to be and embrace who you are*, Hazelden, Center City, Minnesota, USA

Chapter 14

Cialdini, R B (2007) *Influence: The psychology of persuasion*, First Collins Business Essentials, New York, NY

Goldman, A (2009) *Transforming Toxic Leaders*, Stanford University Press, CA, USA

Goldsmith, M (2004) Effectively influencing up: Ensuring that your knowledge makes a difference, in M Goldsmith, H Morgan and A Ogg (Eds), *Leading Organizational Learning*, Jossey-Bass, New York

Grant, G (2014) *Give and Take: Why helping others drives our success*, Penguin Books, London, UK

Hagel, J (2021) Good leadership is about asking good questions, *Harvard Business Review*, January

Perlow, L A, Hadley, C N and Eun, E (2017) Stop the meeting madness: How to free up time for meaningful work, *Harvard Business Review*, July–August

Rodenburg, P (2007) *Presence: How to use positive energy for success in every situation*, Penguin books, London, UK

Chapter 15

Chan, M (2009) *FAQ Ed Diener: A primer for reporters and newcomers*, http://labs.psychology.illinois.edu/~ediener/faq.html (archived at https://perma.cc/8TK6-E9V2)

Csikszentmihalyi, M (1990) *Flow: The psychology of optimal experience*, Harper and Row, New York, NY

Diener, E and Diener, C (1996) Most people are happy, *Psychological Science*, 7, pp 181–85

REFERENCES

Emmons, R S and McCullough, M E (2003) Counting blessings versus burdens: an experimental investigation of gratitude and subjective well-being in daily life, *Journal of Personality and Social Psychology*, **84** (2), pp 377–89

Forbes, M (2020) Is succession planning an outdated concept? *Personnel Today*, https://www.personneltoday.com/hr/is-succession-planning-an-outdated-concept/ (archived at https://perma.cc/53N7-S84M)

Frankl, V (1959) *Man's Search for Meaning*, Washington Square Press (Original work published 1946)

George, L S and Park, C L (2016) Meaning in life as comprehension, purpose, and mattering: Toward integration and new research questions, *Review of General Psychology*, **20** (3), pp 205–20

Hagel, J (2021) Good leadership is about asking good questions, *Harvard Business Review*, January

Haidt, J (2006) *The Happiness Hypothesis*, William Heineman, London, UK

Kaplan, R S (2011) *What to Ask the Person in the Mirror*, Harvard Business Review Press, New York, NY

Lyubomirsky, S (2008) *The How of Happiness*, Penguin Press, New York, NY

Myers, C (2018) How to find your ikagai and transform your outlook on life and business, *Forbes* magazine, February edition

Parashar, F (2021) *A Beautiful Way to Coach*, Routledge, London, UK

Seligman, M E P (2003) *Authentic Happiness*, Nicolas Brealey, London, UK

Seligman, M E P (2011) *Flourish*, Nicholas Brealey, London, UK

Index

NB: page numbers in *italic* indicate figures or tables

ACE (acknowledge, clarify, explain) 118
achievements, celebrating 84
Achor, Shawn 40
Active Constructive Responding 53
Act Like a Leader, Think Like a Leader 20, 162
adrenaline 36
agile, remaining 23
'always on', being 26
apologizing 171
appreciation for others, showing 84, 89–90, 273
Appreciative Inquiry 50, 150
Astronaut's Guide to Life on Earth, An 69
authentic, being 197–98, 219
autonomy, fostering 83, 88
avoidance, of difficult issues 160

Bandura, Albert 70
Barsade, Sigal 54
Baumeister, Roy 199
Beautiful Way to Coach, A 269
Belonging 108, 117
belonging *see* diversity, fostering
Blackett, Karen 115–16
blame, avoiding 119, 124, 161
blocker, being a 246
board, engaging the 133–34
Boaz, N and Fox, E 145
Boniwell, Ilona 34
brand, your 195–208
  actions, your 204–07
    engagement, building 206
    meetings, better 206
    on social media 206
    presentations, better 205–06
    team, your 206–07
    visibility, building 205

authentic, being 197–98
image, your 201–04
strengths, finding your 199–200
'stuck', getting 196–97
ten top tips 207–08
Bregman, Rutger 188
Bridges, William 18, 145–46, 152
Brooke, Dan 109, 110
Brown, Brene 188, 218
Building Great Customer Experiences 127
bullying 45, 115
burnout 26–27, 176
BusinessBalls 90

Cameron, Kim 45–46
challenging teams 83, 88–89
Chamorro-Premuzic, T 93
change, leading 141–58
  assumptions around change 142
  change management vs change leadership 142–43
  'how?' *155*, 155–57
    action, taking 155–56
    consistency 156
    letting go, facilitating 156–57
    realistic, staying 157
    successes, celebrating 157
  mindset, your 143–45, *144*
  people, understanding 145–48
    change curve, the 146
    personalities, different 146–48
  road map *148*
  ten top tips 158
  'what?' *153*, 153–54
  'why?' *149*, 149–52
    change advocates, finding 151
    communication, importance of 151–52

INDEX

What already Works (WoWs) 150–51
Chan, Michael 262
Chimp Paradox, The 63
Cicero 210
circle of awareness 220
circle of inspiration *216*, 217
CliftonStrengths Talent Assessment 98, 269
compassion 161–62
'competency trap' 20, 233
Confidence 58
confidence, building your 56–72
    confidence as an expectation 58–59
    confidence, defining 57
    gender, impact of 57–58
    'gremlins', your 63
    'imposter syndrome' 56, 57
    'matrix' of confidence *64*, 64–66
    overconfidence 70–71
    steps to confidence
        acting 'as if' 69–70
        action, taking 70
        control 69
        state, changing your 68–69
        thinking, challenging your 69
    ten top tips 72
    thinking, impact on feelings / actions 59, 59–63, *60*
Confidence Continuum, the *163*, 163
connective resilience 28
contributions, recognizing 81, 87
CORE (compassion, openness, resourcefulness, expectations) 188–89
cortisol 36
Covey, Stephen 179
    and change 142
    and resilience 174, 178
    and stress 26, 44
Covid-19 pandemic 5
crises, reframing 184–85
Crucial Conversations 165
curiosity, developing 49–51
customer focus, developing 121–37
    five principles of 124–35, *125*
        board, engaging the 133–34
        listening and learning 124–26
        looking inside 131–33
        measuring what matters 134–35
        showing you care 126–31, *128*, *129*, *130*
    ten top tips 137

Dallocchio, Michelle 188
Dao, Francisco 57
Dawkins, Richard 188
Deal, Terrence and Kennedy, Allan 174
Desert Warrior, The 188
dialling up/dialling down 98–99
'diamond' feedback 54
Diener, Ed 261, 262
difficult conversations 155, 159–73
    compassion 161–62
    Confidence Continuum, the *163*, 163
    derailers 163–64
    mindset questions 165
    POEMS model 159, 162, 166–72, *167*
        explore 169
        make it safe to talk 169–71
        opening 168–69
        prepare 166, 168
        summarize 171–72
    ten top tips 172–73
    'what if' thinking 160
diversity, fostering 107–20
    action plan for *111*, 111–16
        action, taking 117–19
        awareness 111–12
        empathizing 115–17
        energizing 112–15
        connection, forming a meaningful 110
        fear 109
    ten top tips 119–20
    who owns diversity 108–09
Do/Think/Feel model 88
'drains and energizers' 32–34, *33*, 186
Drucker, Peter 123
Dweck, Carol 47

Edwards, Mark 108
emotional contagion 54–55

INDEX

emotional resilience 28
enabler, being an 246
energy, managing your 25–42
  burnout 26–27
  'drains and energizers' 32–34, *33*
  'five batteries' 27–28
    body 29, 31–32
    connections 30, 39–40
    heart 29–30, 36
    mind 29, 34
    purpose 30
  'friendship circles' *40*, 40–41
  'from name to neutralize' *37*, 37–39, *38*
  Resilience Healthcheck 28–31
  'Sticky Path' 34–36
  ten top tips 42
Evangeline 197
extrinsic motivation 77

failure, accepting 119
Failure to Communicate 160
feedback, giving 83, 88
'fight or flight' response 36
'five batteries' 27–28
  body 29, 31–32
  connections 30, 39–40
  heart 29–30, 36
  mind 29, 34
  purpose 30
fixed mindset 47
Flourish 93, 272
'flow' 79, 89, 263
Forbes, Inc 120
Forbes, Miecha 246–47
Ford, Dee 273
'friendship circles' *40*, 40–41

Gable, S *et al* 53
gender, impact of 57–58
Gifts of Imperfection, The 218
Give and Take 235
Goffee, R and Jones, G 201
Goldsmith, Marshall 164, 237
Google 181
Grant, Adam 235
gratitude diary, keeping a 272
Greater Good Science Centre 120
'gremlins', your 63

Grove, Andy 187
growth mindset 46, 47–48, *48*
  encouraging a 49

Hadfield, Chris 69
Hagel, Jon 257
Haines, Julie-Ann 136
Hale, Jo 121
happiness 5–6, 259–74
  appreciation for others, showing 273
  defining 261
  five factors of
    passion 263–64
    people 264
    positive emotions 263
    progress 264
    purpose 264
  gratitude diary, keeping a 272
  hedonic treadmill, the 262
  ideal future, your 269
  importance of 260–61
  'no', saying 272
  rebalancing 265–68, *266*, *267*
  'set point', your 262
  social comparison theory 263
  strengths, finding your 269–70
  ten top tips 273–74
  values, your 270–71, *271*
  'yes', saying 272
harassment 115
Harvard Business Review 120
Heath, Chip and Dan 155, 157
hedonic treadmill, the 262
Heifetz, R *et al* 14
Herzberg, Frederick 77
Hidden Life of Trees, The 176
Hines, Julie Ann 21
HIPPO thinking 118
hormones 36
How of Happiness, The 261
Humankind 188

Ibarra, Herminia 20, 109, 162
icebreakers, using 90
ideal future, your 269
ill-health at work 44–45
image, your 201–04
'imposter syndrome' 56, 57

inclusion *see* diversity, fostering
Inclusion Works 120
influential, becoming more 223–39
    influence, defining 224
    'influencing upwards' 236–38
    at meetings 225–32
        dominant presence *228*, 228
        engaged presence *229*, 229
        passive presence *227*, 227
    role model, being a 238
    stakeholders, your 233–36
        give and take, idea of 235
        influencing map 19, 233–35, *234*
    ten top tips 239
'inspiration continuum', the 210, *210*
'intentional pathway planning' 247
intrinsic motivation 77
Ivens, John 127

Jackson, P and McKergow, M 102
Jacob, Kathryn 108

Kaplan, Robert 244
Kübler Ross, Elisabeth 146

leader, defining 3
leadership balance, your 11–24
    agile, remaining 23
    asking vs telling 13
    coaching imbalances 16, *17*
    leadership imbalances 16, *16*
    leadership vs managing vs coaching 13, *13*
    letting go 18–19
    management imbalances 15, *15*
    networking for the future 20
    new vision, crafting a 19–20
    space to reflect, creating 21–23
        on others 23
        on yourself 22
    ten top tips 23–24
leadership skills 249–50
'leaveism' 44
Lencioni, P 179
letting go, facilitating 156–57
Listening Shift, The 95
Lyubomirsky, Sonja 261

Managing Transitions 145, 152
Massey, Peter 133
meditation 269
meetings
    better 186–87, 206
    excessive 186
    influential, becoming more 225–32
        dominant presence *228*, 228
        engaged presence *229*, 229
        passive presence *227*, 227
mental resilience 28
mentoring 117–18
milestones, project 87–88
mind maps 153
Moss Kanter, Rosabeth 58
motivating your team 75–91
    20 ideas for change 86–90
    desire, will and drive 76–77
    extrinsic motivation 77
    intrinsic motivation 77
    Motivation Scale, the 77–79, *78*, 252
    Motivation Wheel, the 81–84, *82*
        connections 81, 84
        direction 81, 83
        progression 81, 83
    ten top tips 90–91
Myers, Chris 268

Narcissistic Principle 162
National Star College 177–78
negative leadership 45
negativity bias 93, 95
net promoter score (NPS) 127, 134, 136, 137
networking 20
'neutral zone' 18
'no', saying 272

objectives, setting 83
O'Neill, Mary Beth 161
'Outsight' 20
overconfidence 70–71

Parashar, Fiona 269
peer coaching 189–90
perfectionism, overcoming 218–19
pessimism 182–83, *184*

Peters, Steve 63
physical resilience 28
play, in a team 84, 90
POEMS model 159, 162, 166–72, *167*
   explore 169
   make it safe to talk 169–71
   opening 168–69
   prepare 166, 168
   summarize 171–72
positive leadership 43–55
   actions 52–53
   bullying 45
   curiosity, developing 49–51
   emotional contagion 54–55
   fixed mindset 47
   growth mindset 46, 47–48, *48*
      encouraging 49
   'positive climate', fostering a 52
   positive responding 53–54
   practices of 46
   stress in the workplace 44–45
   ten top tips 55
Positive Leadership 45
Positive Psychology 93, 261
PowerPoint 211
Practice of Adaptive Leadership, The 14
Prada, Miuccia 201
presentations, better 205–06, 209–22
   authenticity 219
   circle of awareness 220
   circle of inspiration *216*, 217
   close, the 214, 218
   content, direction of 213–14
   emotion, level of 214
   focus, your 213
   'inspiration continuum', the 210, *210*
   language, level of 212–13
   opening 217–18
   passion 215
   perfectionism, overcoming 218–19
   stage fright 210–11, 220–21
   ten top tips 221–22
'presenteeism' 44
progression planning 243–58, *248*
   blocker, being a 246
   building 256–57
   defining 248–52
      ability 249–51
      attitude 252
   developing 255–56
      influence quadrant 255
      investigate quadrant 255
      nurture quadrant 255
      progress quadrant 256
   enabler, being an 246
   'intentional pathway planning' 247
   letting go 257
   reasons not to 244–45
   resetting 247–48
   'stuck', getting 244
   ten top tips 258
   understanding 252–54
      influence quadrant 253
      investigate quadrant 252
      nurture quadrant 254
      progress quadrant 254
'Project Aristotle' 181
psychological safety 117–18, 181
purpose, team 81, 87
purposeful resilience 28

questions, common 2

Radical Candor 162
Raval, A and Amphlett, J 114
'realistic optimism' 35
realistic, staying 157
Rebel Ideas 116
resilience, building your 25–42
   burnout 26–27
   'drains and energizers' 32–34, *33*
   'five batteries' 27–28
      body 29, 31–32
      connections 30, 39–40
      heart 29–30, 36
      mind 29, 34
      purpose 30
   'friendship circles' 40, 40–41
   'from name to neutralize' 37, 37–39, *38*
   Resilience Healthcheck 28–31
   'Sticky Path' 34–36
   ten top tips 42

Resilience Healthcheck 28–31, 270
resilience, organizational 174–91
    burnout 176
    and Covid-19 174
    crises, reframing 184–85
    defining 175
    flexibility 181–84
        optimism 182–83, *184*
    peer coaching 189–90
    roots, establishing firm 177–78, *179*
    space, allowing 185–87
        meetings, better 186–87
    support, within teams 188–89
    ten top tips 190–91
    trust, importance of 176–77, 179–81, *180*
roadbumps, hitting 4–5
    see also difficult conversations; resilience, organizational
Rodenburg, Patsy 226
Rogelberg, Stephen 186

SABAT coaching model *100*, 100–05
    action, taking 103
    affirming 102
    asking and agreeing 101
    building and broadening 101–02
    in practice 103, *103–05*
    setting up 101
Scott, Kim 162
Selfish Gene, The 188
Seligman, Martin 93, 261, 272
Shaw, Colin 127, 128
silos, removing 132–33
SlideShare 211
social comparison theory 263
social media 206
Solutions Focus, The 102
Southwick, Stephen 26
SPARK 34
Speed of Trust, The 179
stage fright 210–11, 220–21
'Sticky Path' 34–36
'stop for 60' 37, 39
strengths
    finding your 199–200, 269–70
    recognizing employee 83

strengths-based coaching 92–106
    dialling up/dialling down 98–99
    listening for strengths 95–96
        distractions 95
        problems, focus on 96
        'tug of tell', the 96
    mindset, your 94–95
    Positive Psychology 93
    practise, willingness to 96
    SABAT coaching model *100*, 100–05
        action, taking 103
        affirming 102
        asking and agreeing 101
        building and broadening 101–02
        in practice 103, *103–05*
        setting up 101
    strengths, discovering 97–98
    ten top tips 102
    timeline exercise 96–97, *97*
Strengthscope tool 98
stress 44–45
    leadership styles under 164
'stuck', getting 196–97, 244
successes, celebrating 157
succession planning *see* progression planning
Switch 155
SWOT analysis 19
Syed, Matthew 116

team spirit, fostering 84, 90
TED talks 120
ten top tips
    brand, your 207–08
    change, leading 158
    confidence, building your 72
    customer focus, developing 137
    difficult conversations 172–73
    diversity, fostering 119–20
    energy, managing your 42
    happiness 273–74
    influential, becoming more 239
    leadership balance, your 23–24
    motivating your team 90–91
    positive leadership 55
    presentations, better 221–22

progression planning 258
resilience
    organizational 190–91
    personal 42
    strengths-based coaching 102
Thomas, M 27
Tolstoy, Leo 144
toxic leadership 70–71
Triggers 164
trust, importance of 176–77, 179–81, *180*
'tug of tell', the 5, 96, 169

Unerman, Sue 108–09

Valcour, Monique 169
values
    organizational 87
    personal 270–71, *271*

Values in Action (VIA) Character Strengths Survey 98, 269
van Hool, Janie 95
vision, team 81, 87
vulnerability 5

Walker, Matthew 32
Weeks, Holly 160
Welch, Simon 178
What already Works (WoWs) 150–51
'what if' thinking 160
Why We Sleep 32
Wichert, Ines 21
Will to Change, The 120
'winging it' 161
Wohlleben, Peter 176

'yes', saying 272

Zandan, Noel 205